D1823865

DEMOCRATIC COMMUNICATIONS
IN THE INFORMATION AGE

Janet Wasko and Vincent Mosco, Editors

Garamond Press, Toronto
Ablex Publishing, New Jersey

First published in Canada in 1992 by
GARAMOND PRESS
77 Mowat Ave., Suite 403
Toronto, Ont. M6K 3E3

First published in the U.S. in 1992 by
ABLEX PUBLISHING CORPORATION
355 Chestnut St.
Norwood, N.J. 07648

Publisher: Peter Saunders
Editor: Robert Clarke
Typesetting and Design: Robin Brass Studio

Printed and bound in Canada

Canadian Cataloguing in Publication Data

Main entry under title:

Democratic communications in the information age

Includes bibliographical references and index.
ISBN 0-920059-83-X

1. Communication. 2. Information science.
I. Wasko, Janet II. Mosco, Vincent.

P91.D45 1992   302.2   C92-093875-2

Library of Congress Cataloguing in Publication
Data Available

Ablex ISBN 0-89391-907-1

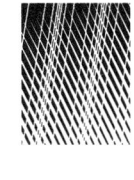

Contents

Acknowledgements

The editors would like to thank Carlos R. Calderon for advice during the preparation of the introduction to this volume, Mashoed Bailie for assistance in proofing the final manuscript, and Peter Saunders and Robert Clarke for editorial advice and assistance.

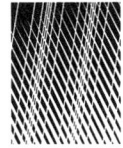

Introduction:
Go Tell It to the Spartans

Janet Wasko

IN 490 B.C. PHILIPPIDES, a young messenger in the Athenian army, ran a gruelling twenty-six miles from Athens to Sparta to deliver a message for help from the besieged Greeks facing the brunt of an invading Persian army at Marathon. Philippides, according to legend, delivered his general's message and then, exhausted and dehydrated, collapsed.

Since Philippides' marathon run over two millennia ago, communications technology has advanced by quantum leaps and bounds – today messengers do not have to run for a full day or more across difficult terrain to deliver their communiqués, and information can be transmitted and received almost instantaneously. Communications satellites, computers, radio, television, phone systems, and telex and facsimile machines have replaced the human messengers of pre-electronic times. News and information, cultural events and entertainment, good or bad, can reach all corners of the globe within minutes or even seconds.

The Instantaneous War
On January 17, 1991, some 150 Tomahawk Cruise missiles launched from U.S. naval warships ringing the Persian Gulf streaked across the nocturnal desert sky and knocked out radar installations, missile sites, and other key targets in Iraq and Kuwait. Minutes later some 2,235 combat aircraft followed the air corridors cleared by the Tomahawks and pounded Iraq in the most highly co-ordinated aerial bombardment in history. The dawn of "high tech warfare" had arrived with terrifying suddenness, especially for Iraq, and the news of the outbreak of war was immediately flashed across the United States and around the world.

Some heard the news by word of mouth in grocery stores or at work, others caught it on their car radios, many more were informed shortly after turning on their television sets to watch their favourite shows. For some twelve thousand cheering Duke University basketball fans, the news came when the public-address announcer read a press release announcing "the liberation of Kuwait" minutes into a game between the Blue Devils and a league rival. But whatever the initial source, for the next six hours much of North America sat transfixed in front of television sets watching with a mixture of awe, fascination, and disbelief as the major networks and CNN preempted their regular programming with a night of special broadcasts on the war.

What ensued was unprecedented in the annals of both warfare and its coverage by the media. In thirty-nine days, seventeen different types of warplanes from nine different countries, with pilots speaking four different languages, pounded Iraqi targets with 88,500 tons of bombs, rockets, and missiles – or the equivalent of five and a half Hiroshima bombs. Bridges, communications centres, hardened aircraft bunkers, runways, nuclear and chemical plants, warehouses, and missile and radar sites as well as troop and tank emplacements were attacked. Some were taken out in the first strike and others had to be bombed repeatedly. High on the target list was Iraq's electrical power-generating system and its electrical grid, as well as its petroleum refineries – for without electrical power and petrol any modern country comes to a grinding halt, especially its communications. Hydro-electric plants were bombed with "smart" laser-guided bombs and the transformers were doused with tons of small metallic filaments, which had the effect of short-circuiting the system.

To co-ordinate the various disparate units into a cohesive fighting force, the U.S. Central Command used several banks of computers to produce a daily six-hundred-page printout. The document, called the Air Tasking Order, was the blueprint for co-ordinating the air campaign and was distributed to every allied air base. "A lot of computers bring together the tens of thousands of minute details – radio frequencies, altitudes, tanker rendezvous, bomb configurations, who supports whom, who's flying escort," said U.S. Air Force General Charles Horner, the Central Command's air commander.

The results were inevitable. A modern Arab country, whose communications, industrial, engineering, and technical infrastructure had taken almost four decades to build, was flattened in less than forty days and forty nights of bombing. It was not only the precision of the new weapons systems but also the ability to capture the war on film or video that captivated the world's imagination and attention, as television aired daily footage of the eerie saga unfolding in a land almost forgotten by the sands of time. By virtue of broadcasting technology, reinforced by the print media, even the most militarily illiterate armchair generals became experts in the techno-phraseology of warfare in the late 20th century. Phrases and acronyms once the exclusive domain of the military became catchwords at social gatherings and after-hours taverns. Laser-guided "smart" bombs, infra-red and thermal imaging systems, Tomahawk and Patriot missiles, F-14 Tomcats, and Bradley fighting vehicles entered the popular vocabulary.

For two weeks immediately after the outbreak of hostilities, television held the public hostage as more and more viewers became addicts of war coverage. Retail sales of all types dropped dramatically, and restaurants reported a signifi- cant loss of customers. North Americans who would normally go out shopping or dining were instead glued to their television sets at home. Video stores were among the hardest hit, some of them reporting that rentals dropped off as much as 80 per cent immediately after news of the attack.

"It was like a morgue in here," said Bill Acheson, owner of Bill's Video Stores in Winnipeg. "When war in the gulf broke out, CNN had a field day. Now [two weeks later] I'm getting the impression that people are coming back in droves. They need some fantasy to take home."

In the end the war turned out to be one of the shortest of humanity's conflicts – though also one of the most dramatic, both for the high-tech wonder weapons and by sheer virtue of its coverage. Some three thousand journalists had con- verged on Riyadh, Saudi Arabia, to report on the war, inundating the Pentagon's public-relations department. And in the end it became another example of the use of the new technologies of information and of war, and of the speed that infor- mation travels in the information age.

Yet another case occurred in 1986 when the space shuttle Challenger exploded in midflight seventy-three seconds after takeoff, killing all seven astronauts aboard. Many watchers saw the explosion live, recorded on television cameras by CNN. Within minutes the news of the disaster spread via the airwaves, telephone, and word of mouth to a stunned nation. For the next ten hours, millions of Ameri- cans sat watching their television sets in disbelief as all three major networks dropped their regular programming to broadcast video replays of the incident and to attempt an instant analysis into its causes.

One of the ironies of the Challenger explosion was that the spacecraft carried, among other things, communications satellites, thus making the seven astronauts the modern-day equivalent of Philippides.

The "Information Revolution"
The evolution and revolution of communications – from messenger, to signal flags, to the printing press, to telegraph, to the wireless, to television, and into the realm of space, lasers, and computers – have been among the most overchronicled developments of the past decade. Corporate advertisers plus a host of popular writers and communications researchers have extolled the virtues of instant com- munications, of the role miniaturization has played in the computer revolution, and of the development of the "information age" and the coming of the "infor- mation society." They have, in essence, traced the annals of communications de- velopments and described what communications do and will be able to do in the future – but they have either forgotten or ignored the very essence of communi- cations systems. Who owns them? Who controls them? And for what purposes?

Just as a researcher of ancient communications might ask, "Who ordered Philippides to run to his death?" a researcher of current systems might want to know, "Who ordered the bombing of Iraq? Who ordered the mission that sent the seven Challenger astronauts to their deaths, and who pressed the button?" These are valid and important questions. But of equal importance is: "Who benefited from the military and communications technology employed and the coverage by the media?" In the case of the Challenger, "Who owns the buttons that were pressed that sent the astronauts to their deaths? Who owns the rockets? Who built them? Who owns the satellites the astronauts were sent to launch into orbit? Who built them and for what purposes? In short, who owns the information the satellites produce and process?"

Such probing questions are not asked for mere academic debate or to challenge established ideas merely for the sake of being obstreperous, but for valid reasons.

The Declaration of Independence, for example, states "that all men are created equal and are entitled to life, liberty and the pursuit of happiness." This may be true, and it certainly ranks as one of the most noble political statements in all of human history. However, the Declaration of Independence no longer seems applicable when it comes to access to computers, to editorial space in *The New York Times*, and to time on the airwaves. A conservative interest group or a conservative writer or political analyst, for example, has access to all the state-of-the-art technology of the "information age" to help deliver messages to the inhabitants of North America. But what chance does a migrant farmworker, who simply wants the benefits of a union, have to air his grievances?

Journalists such as William Safire and George Wills have the print media and the electronic media to argue for support for right-wing dictatorships in Latin America – but what chance does a poor peasant who is fighting for social justice have to get his point across? What chances do the migrant farm worker and the peasant in Latin America have to speak their piece? Consider the forces arrayed against them. A migrant farm worker must overcome an immensely powerful agribusiness, an antagonistic governor, powerful lobbies in a state and a national Congress, the police and the courts, and, lastly, an often hostile local press. A Latin American peasant must overcome local death squads, the military, the local political power structure, the local media, a U.S. president, powerful lobbies in the U.S. Congress, and a score of right-wing columnists in the nation's most prestigious newspapers.

True, both the migrant farmworker and the Latin American peasant have their allies – but the forces arrayed against them are immensely powerful and neither of them has access to the media in the way that, say, Patrick Buchanan or William Buckley do. Imagine what would happen if a representative of the farm workers or a representative of the peasants in Latin America had the same access to *The New York Times*, the *Washington Post, Time* magazine, CBS, ABC, NBC, CNN, the AP wire service, and several radio networks every time a crucial vote came before the Congress on an issue vital to their interests?

The issue, for critical communications researchers, is not just technology and its ability to process information – but who owns the technology, who controls it, and who has access to it. In short, who presses the buttons? And therein lies the crux of democratic communications.

Information Age Technologies: Hope or Hype?

We continue to hear claims about the democratic potential of the information age. On the one hand, there are corporate and technocratic promises of *Computopia* – societies based on the full potential of human creativity, participatory democracies. Consider the following statements:

> We foresee a time when the promise of the Information Age will be realized. People will participate in a world-wide Telecommunity through a vast, global network of networks, the merging of communication and computers. They'll be able to handle information in any form – conversation, data, images, text – as easily as they make a phone call today. (AT&T advertisement, *Editor & Publisher*, July 18, 1987)

> Intelligence amplification in the service of a democratic society – this is the goal of a strategy of the information age. It is a goal squarely within our national mythos.... The objective, after all, is the construction of a national (and eventually global) interactive information grid, capable of connecting everyone on earth with everyone else and with a wide array of information resources. (Dizard,1982:10)

On the other hand, groups or movements devoted to social change provide radically different visions of alternative communications networks, of inexpensive, user-friendly technology that would challenge the dominant ideology. An example:

> New possibilities of intercommunications and of consciousness may in turn lead to significant new forms of working-class organization. It is now possible to envision a social order based on information in which current class and economic relations would no longer exist. In such a case, as well, there would be new cultural and political possibilities. (Goldhaber, 1983:257)

From a critical perspective, it may be easy to discount the first accounts as simply corporate and technocratic hype. In light of the dominant forces in control of information technology – primarily, the business sector and the military – universal access becomes merely an illusion.

But how much hope can we place in the alternative version? Do we discount progressive visions of the emancipatory potential of information technologies as mostly idealist and unrealistic? What *is* the outlook for democratic communications in an information age?

Exploiting the Problems and the Potential

In our previous collection of articles, *The Political Economy of Information* (Mosco and Wasko, 1988), contributors analyzed information as a commodity and documented the historical and contemporary development of information production, distribution, and consumption in an evolving capitalist system. The focus was on information technologies as a form of social control and economic advantage. For the most part, contributors found that current developments provided reinforcement for existing social relations rather than a social revolution resulting in a new social formation. In other words, the current so-called information society is a misnomer: It is hardly more democratic than the previous industrial society.

Yet, as Vincent Mosco points out in the introduction to that book, there may still be some cause for hope due to the problems confronting the information age controllers and the potential of some information technologies. The enormous problems of developing information as a commodity are documented by the contributors to *The Political Economy of Information*. But there is also resistance to – and, sometimes, outright rejection of – these developments. The elimination of jobs by computerized and automated systems and the increased use of resources for military defence may actually fertilize "green shoots" on an otherwise bleak landscape. In addition, there are now people actively developing other potentials of the technology or, in other words, working for emancipation rather than social control and profit. Consider, for instance, the role of computer networks linking peace groups or the possibilities of desktop publishing or public-access cable channels.

The contributors to *Democratic Communications in the Information Age* explore some of these forms of resistance and alternative development, critically assessing the potential for information and communication resources to challenge and transform this dominant political economy. The collection, therefore, provides critical assessment of "democratic communications" in an "information age." We approach these dual mythologies, as Mark Schulman notes, from the "liberated zone" of critical scholarship and practice within "contested terrain," and we ask the following questions:

- What is democratic communications and its role in a democratic society?
- How are new information technologies enhancing (or inhibiting) democratic communications?
- How are communications resources enhancing (or inhibiting) democratic progressive movements devoted to social change?
- Can social movements rely on mainstream media to convey their messages to the public?
- What is the prognosis for democratized communication, as well as for democratization through media or information systems?

This analysis begins with a discussion of theoretical issues involved in democratic, participatory, alternative, and community communications. In light of these concepts, the authors explore various alternative developments in new communications and information technologies, as well as the media and information strategies of various social movements in local, national, and international settings.

Theoretical Issues

The last decade has focused a good deal of attention on the issue of democratic communications, in part due to the debate over the new international information order and the UNESCO study of communications (MacBride Report, 1980). But despite serving as an ideal in communications research and policy areas, the notion of democratic communications is seldom carefully defined or explored in any depth.

In the first chapter, Ingunn Hagen argues that the concept of democracy must be considered more carefully before we can examine democratic communications. She traces the development of participatory, elitist, and discourse theories of democracy, arguing that participation is a key element in a truly democratic process. She contends that the role of communications in democracy involves the entire communications *process*. Participation in media decision-making is only one part of this process, which also involves the public's right and access to information, as well as the representation of various social groups and movements in the media.

Thus the concept of democratic communications is two-fold, involving participation in media as well as in society. In other words, the process involves democratization *of* the media as well as democratization *through* the media.

This distinction provides a framework for the rest of the volume, as contributors assess:

1. *democratization of* media and information technologies, or participatory and alternative media forms and democratic uses of information technologies; and
2. *democratization through* media and information technologies, or media strategies of various social movements and groups devoted to progressive issues and social change.

The discussion of democratic communications leads to another emerging academic field: community communications. Mark Schulman presents an overview of the study of community communications, which involves identifying patterns of information sharing in neighbourhoods or commonages. He explains that the goals of such work are to encourage distribution and discourage inhibition of information, and to increase possibilities and decrease obstacles for media access and participation.

Obviously, these questions are those subsumed within democratic communications, which, Schulman points out, have shared boundaries with community communications. In addition, he observes that issues of information equity and lateral communication are prevalent themes in the community as well as at the international level in the New World Information Order debate.

One of the models for community communications that Schulman discusses was developed by Kusum Singh. In her chapter, Singh says that the manipulation of images can undermine democracy and thus represents a threat to democratic communications. She also differentiates between elitist and democratic styles of image-making, using Ronald Reagan and Mohandas Gandhi as examples. She identifies Reagan's major images as strength, freedom, individualism, patriotism, and sincerity. While the images of Gandhi feature similar themes, his communication style emphasized "reality-based imagery and examples of personal bravery." Singh calls for more action-oriented research to challenge false images, such as Reagan's, and encourage progressive imagery, such as Gandhi's, which promotes participation and genuine democracy.

New Technologies: New Promises and Old Problems

Although the emerging new information technologies have been accompanied by promises of more information and the prospects for a more democratic society, as many of our authors point out these new technologies don't necessarily solve existing societal problems.

Dwayne Winseck examines the Cable News Network (CNN), which has been touted as the gem of the information age in its provision of twenty-four-hour news to many parts of the world. However, his analysis of CNN's ties to other U.S. media sources reinforces the dilemma of the continuing concentrated power in the production of knowledge and information. While CNN received a good deal of attention for its coverage of the Gulf War, Winseck argues that the network's compliance with government restrictions (especially the press pool) and the sharing of news coverage limited its ability to offer any real alternative to the "old" news sources, the major television networks.

Old problems also surfaced during the Gulf War, as Mashoed Bailie and David Frank illustrate in their chapter describing the orientalist perspective prevalent in the major U.S. media's war coverage. After dissecting some examples of this orientation, the authors point out that the development of new information technologies and weapons of mass destruction brings the Occident and the Orient closer together. While these new media sources (such as CNN, for instance) may be able to bring "news" of the world more quickly and efficiently, Bailie and Frank argue that the mythic notions of Orientalism still prevail and must be revealed and critiqued before true understanding of the Orient is possible.

Giovanni Cesareo also observes that there are many "black holes" – misunderstandings and contradictions – that must be faced to find the real path to democratic development of information systems. He examines this problem by looking at the issues of social control and privacy and by relating the continuing debates over privacy to the concept of secrecy. He argues that privacy is defended because of "abuses from the top" but that secrecy "at the top" must also be attacked to encourage intervention and decision-making "from the bottom."

Along with other authors in this book, Cesareo examines the rights of the public to protect information and to be informed. He also discusses the problems of competence and skill in information systems, introducing the concept of social or public utility information networks. Finally, in accessing the prospects for communications democracy via information systems, Cesareo adds an important addendum to the common assertion that "information is power." Information does not give power in itself. He points out that those who have authority may better exert power if well-informed, yet those who are only well-informed may not necessarily become empowered because of the information they possess.

New Technologies and Oppositional Cultural Practice

In Part III, looking more closely at some of the new technologies that are part of the so-called "information society," we consider their democratic and progressive potentials as well as some of the problems faced by those trying to pursue this "emancipatory potential" of the new technologies.

Computers have been at the forefront of the "information revolution," and personal computers especially are often lauded as truly revolutionary technologies, offering individuals the potential to gain access to more information and to communicate more efficiently. There is a common vision of the average citizen empowered by computer technology, able to communicate honestly and directly, challenging established power and planning political actions that advance democracy. But how are computers actually being used to enhance democratic impulses and activities?

Indeed, social movements and democratization projects are increasingly putting alternative forms of communications resources into use for local, national, and global communication and solidarity. Much mention has been made of the Community Memory Project – public computers for public use. Other examples might include projects that have developed over the last ten years in Latin America, where "computers have settled – despite uncertainties and incomplete knowledge – in development research centres, trade unions, church organizations, institutions devoted to women's development, and popular documentation centres," such as IBASE in Brazil, DESCO in Peru, and the Alternative Communication Resources Network in Bolivia (Matta, 1987: 4).

This use of new technologies has prompted a wide array of international and regional projects. These include international networks such as INTERDOC, established in Rome, 1984; GEOMET, initially a network for environmental groups, currently uniting several social development organizations; and TIPS, an experimental technology information project. Regional projects include IRED, Innovations and Networks for Development, and experiments at ILET, a network of non-governmental development institutions joined through microcomputers (Matta, 1987: 5).

Besides computer networks there are other new communications technologies that may provide access for progressive ideas. Communication satellites have been used to beam progressive programs around the country and the globe. New video and film technologies make it possible for independent and alternative filmmakers to produce and distribute their work more efficiently and cheaply. Radio and low-power television stations have also been discussed as potential community-oriented, participatory communication resources.

Cable television is another area where media activists have concentrated efforts in recent years. Douglas Kellner makes a strong case for public-access television's potential for alternative political debate. Kellner discusses examples of community-based programming, focusing especially on "Alternative Views," the oldest continuous public-access show in the United States. Kellner argues that "progressive use of television will thus help progressive movements and struggles gain legitimacy and force in the shifting and contradictory field of U.S. politics."

It is said that existing forms of popular culture have become more accessible to people in an "information age," as well as providing the potential for oppositional cultural practice. In "Of the People? The Case of Popular Music," Deanna Robinson argues that local music production, as opposed to popular music produced by major corporations, is very much alive, not only in North America but also throughout the world. She describes the production and distribution of popular music, especially noting the increased concentration in the "core" music industry. But because of these changes and because of population shifts and advances in recording technology, she concludes, "Musicians and audiences can set themselves apart or bring themselves together through musical exchange on a global scale."

Photographic art has served as another form of oppositional cultural practice, as described by Fred Lonidier in "Working with Unions II." He explains his photo/text documentaries dealing with labour issues, and he discusses their role in the art world and in trade unions. While Lonidier's photos are intended for display in union meeting halls or workplaces, we have included samples of his work to supplement his text.

Lonidier refers to recent media interest by U.S. trade unions, through projects such as the Labor Institute of Public Affairs, labour cable shows and art programs, as well as other left media/art projects. Yet he also notes that "radical art is a small-shop home industry ... taking on the multinational conglomerate for the allegiance of the masses. The outcome of this marginalization is that most oppositional cultural practice is largely invisible even to those of us who are obsessed with it." Another problem is the lack of connection between "cultural contenders" and left intellectuals steeped in critical theory. Lonidier observes that the left intellectuals "are preoccupied with the postmodern" and "have remained aloof from contemporary art-in-struggle."

As for the role of oppositional art in the "information age," Lonidier argues that *place* is still an important consideration. He points to millions of people who are still rooted somewhere, attached to locality and provincial outlooks, as well as many socially committed artists who continue to work in non-electronic media – "painting and drawing and sculpting and writing poems and songs, by hand even."

Social Movements and Information Strategies

Another aspect of democratic communications is the media's representation of social groups and movements, as well ideas relating to social change and democratic transformation. In other words, the process of democratization *through* the media. Many communications researchers have addressed the question of how the mainstream media represent opposition to a dominant ideology. While several authors refer to this work, the focus here is on the media strategies of social movements and groups, on assessing the extent of democratization possible through the traditional media and new information technologies. If the media represent contradictions, what are those contradictions? Can social movements use them, or will the movements inevitably be co-opted in the process?

Peter Bruck argues that the media production process – especially news production – should be thought of as "constrained rather than controlled or determined." The system should not be considered closed but should be thought of as "contradictory operations." In other words, all social dissent is not recuperated or co-opted, and social movements may indeed find open space for their messages. An understanding of the various discourses represented in news production may be a necessary step in exploiting such open spaces. To exemplify his arguments, Bruck examines the peace movement and its representation in the Canadian press, focusing especially on the controversy surrounding Cruise missile testing in Canada in the early 1980s.

Sean Cassidy also examines social movements and media strategies, as he investigates various tactics employed by the environmental movement. He describes a specific campaign by Friends of the Earth, who worked within the legal system to gain access to the media. Cassidy finds, however, that the group was ultimately at the mercy of shifts in the state, in general, and broadcasting deregulation, in particular. Another strategy has been employed by Greenpeace, through their direct-action protests to attract media coverage. Cassidy assesses the extent to which these actions successfully challenge the dominant hegemony.

In the next chapter, Marc Raboy looks at popular uses of media in Quebec, where communications issues have been at the forefront of social struggle over the last twenty-five years. Raboy notes that Quebec's experiences provide important insights into the limits and possibilities of democratic media; those experiences include the entire process of communication, as described in the introductory chapters of this book. Popular movements in Quebec have been critical of the mainstream press. Media workers have challenged the media from within these institutions. Autonomous media alternatives have been created. State media policies have been confronted. And popular movements have used direct action aimed at appropriating mainstream media space as well as formulating strategies to gain access to media.

Third World Struggles for Democracy
Social movements struggling for democracy in various Third World countries have employed a wide range of media and information strategies aimed at national and international audiences. While a complete exploration of the strategies used in various struggles would be the subject of yet another book, the authors in this section look at examples that focus on somewhat different strategies in three

different contexts: a national political movement's efforts to influence public opinion in another country, a social movement's use of media to promote democratic reform, and the national transmission and reception of information about international labour issues.

In the first example, David Frank looks at *The New York Times* coverage of the overthrow of the Marcos regime in the Philippines. He examines the strategies used, especially by Corazon Aquino and her followers, and by Ferdinand Marcos, to influence public opinion in the United States. Frank says that social movements, especially in the Third World, have become increasingly aware that they must address a global as well as a local audience.

Through an analysis of *The New York Times* reports of the Philippine revolution, Frank argues that Aquino received media attention because she was able to confront Marcos in a manner consistent with media expectations. He explores this "movement-media dance" in some detail, including the involvement of U.S. public-relations firms, the personalization of the campaign, and a "palatable" presentation of the Communist insurgency for a U.S. audience.

Stephen and Sara Douglas present the story of Aliran, a social movement in Malaysia that has relied heavily on media for its campaign of social consciousness. Aliran (which means "national consciousness trend") has been the most active and visible progressive group in Malaysia, challenging the government and demanding democratic reforms, especially in the area of freedom of expression. Its struggle has ignited the debate in Malaysia over the Official Secrets Act and the limitations of the mass media. Aliran has used a wide range of media, including print, audio, and video-cassettes, and its visibility in a wide range of societal issues has been notable and influential with other groups.

Official and legal attempts in Malaysia to discourage dissent, in fact, have had the opposite effect – at least, until October 1987. At that time, as the authors report, the Malaysian police closed down a number of newspapers and arrested over a hundred political activists, among them the leaders of Aliran. But although Aliran's progress has been halted, at least for the near future, the authors argue that attempts to silence dissent are "superficial" and that Aliran's efforts will yet serve to inspire democratic opposition, not only in Malaysia but in neighbouring countries as well.

The international distribution of information is the subject of the last chapter, by Peter Waterman. His research examines the transmission and reception of international labour information in Peru but is concerned more generally with the role of communications as "the nervous system of internationalism and solidarity." Through interviews with labour leaders, media specialists, workers, and trade unionists and an examination of left and socialist products, Waterman assesses the exchange of labour information internationally. By looking in depth at workers and union leaders in one country, he is able to draw conclusions about the need for a new model of international labour communication and a new understanding of internationalism.

Waterman concludes with the hope that by increasing communication and solidarity action, "We may yet see a new labour internationalism making its long-missing and much-needed addition to the internationalism of the women's, human-rights, peace, environmental, and other such movements."

Dialectics of the Information Age: Pessimistic Mind, Optimistic Spirit

This book's goal is to look at the prognosis for democracy and democratic communications in a changing information environment. While some of the authors have pointed to hopeful signs that the new information age technologies are contributing to democratic movements, we have also attempted to realistically confront the obstacles these activities face. It seems clear that these efforts have provided no simple answers. Indeed, various authors may even appear to be somewhat contradictory in their analyses. It is hoped, however, that discussions such as these may at least generate more understanding and debate, especially among those people who are dedicated to building truly democratic, participatory societies.

In the 1970s, Hans Magnus Enzensberger wrote a well-known essay on the emancipatory potential of media. In addition to his rich insights on media manipulation, he recalls a quote by Antonio Gramsci that seems a fitting conclusion to this survey of democratic communications in the information age: "Pessimism of the intelligence, optimism of the will."

While an honest assessment of the forces to be resisted and opposed in an "age of information" may result in a certain pessimism, there are also problems and contradictions to be exploited. The will to struggle for alternative, democratic solutions will remain essential, and *Democratic Communications in the Information Age* is an attempt to engage in such struggle.

References

Dizard, Jr., Wilson P. (1982). *The Coming Information Age: An Overview of Technology, Economics and Politics.* New York: Longman.

Dordick, Herbert S. (1986). *Understanding Modern Telecommunications.* New York: McGraw-Hill Book Co.

Enzensberger, Hans Magnus (1976). "Constituents of a Theory of the Media." In *Raids and Reconstructions: Essays on Politics, Crime and Culture.* London: Pluto Press.

Goldhaber, Michael (1983). "Microelectronic Networks: A New Workers' Culture in Formation?" In Vincent Mosco and Janet Wasko, eds., *The Critical Communications Review*, Vol.I, *Labor, the Working Class, and the Media.* Norwood, N.J.: Ablex Publishing, 1983.

MacBride Report (1980). *Many Voices, One World: Communication and Society, Today and Tomorrow: Towards a More Just and More Efficient World Information and Communication Order.* "Report by the International Commission for the Study of Communication Problems." London: K. Page.

Matta, Fernando Reyes (1987). "Networks and Journalism: New Avenues for Change." Paper prepared for the International Communication Forum, on the occasion of the 25th Anniversary of the newspaper *El Dia*, June, Mexico.

Mosco, Vincent and Janet Wasko, eds. (1988). *The Political Economy of Information.* Madison, Wis.: University of Wisconsin Press.

Part I

Theoretical Issues

Democratic Communication: Media and Social Participation

Ingunn Hagen

DEMOCRATIC COMMUNICATION is like a "God-word" – a concept that many people agree is an ideal. The concept of democratization is often used to legitimize a state's media policy, as in Scandinavia, for example, but there is no agreement on the definition of democratic communication or on what the term implies. In this chapter I will make some clarifications of the distinctions and conflicts and argue that democratization must further participatory democracy – and that an evaluation of democratization attempts must incorporate all the different stages in the communication process.

Democracy: An Ambiguous Term

In contemporary usage, "The more 'democracy' has come to be a universally accepted honorific term, the more it has undergone verbal stretching and has become the loosest label of its kind" (Sartori, 1968:112). The term literally means rule by the people. The original meaning of democracy stems from the Greek *demos*, "the people," and *kratos*, "rule."

A standard encyclopedia presents the term in a number of different usages. First, *direct democracy* refers to a procedure of majority rule. A radical variant of this usage is rule or government by the common people. Second, *representative* or *parliamentarian democracy* refers to citizens exercising their right to make decisions through chosen representatives. Third, *constitutional* or *liberal democracy* refers to the powers of the majority being bound by a framework of constitutional restraints designed to guarantee certain individual and collective rights, such as freedom of speech, religion, opinion, and association (*Encyclopaedia Britannica* [EB], *Micropaedia*, 1974:458). These are concepts used in Western liberal democracies, and they emphasize the exercise of political privileges.

A fourth meaning of the term democracy is any political or social system that attempts to minimize social or economic differences, especially those arising out of the unequal distribution of wealth, resources, or private property. This is known as *social* or *economic democracy*, even when the political system is not democratic in any of the first three senses mentioned (EB, *Micropaedia*, 1974:458). Social democracy emphasizes the elimination or the absence of hereditary or class distinctions or privileges. The significance of this usage is that it extends the egalitarian ethic beyond political arenas. In the liberal pluralist tradition, this is sometimes called a secondary meaning of democracy (see, for instance, Sartori, 1968:113). But in Scandinavia, for example, "democracy" denotes more than a political machinery; it also denotes a way of living, a "social democracy." The concept democracy can thus be used both to describe a form of government and a kind of society.

There are at least two other historical cases in which the notion of democracy goes beyond the political sense. These other forms have been identified as the Soviet/communist and the Third World versions (Macpherson, 1966). Other theorists have referred to them as the communist and the socialist variants of democracy (von Beyme, 1973). These cases in particular illustrate that the West does not have a monopoly on the concept of democracy and that the term is also used as a norm for quite different kinds of societies. Democracy as a kind of government is, then, a narrow interpretation of the concept, while democracy in a broader sense refers to a kind of society (Macpherson, 1966:18). Democracy as a kind of society must imply that people have already obtained certain basic political privileges.

The Role of Participation: Contemporary Theories of Democracy

Essential to the concept of democracy as a kind of society is the role of participation, which is in itself a controversial concept within democratic theory. Social scientists provide different classifications for this idea and practice of participation. Ragnvald Kalleberg's distinctions of *competitive* democrats, *participatory* democrats, and *dialogue* democrats can provide a fruitful starting point (1984:372). The theorists of competitive or elite democracy (for example, Dahl, 1956) are concerned with political governing, such as citizens voting for competing political parties. As stated by Dahl, "Democratic theory is concerned with processes by which ordinary citizens exert a relatively high degree of control over leaders" (1956:3). This approach can be connected with bourgeois liberalism and is most concerned with democracy in the political sense. The main emphasis is on indirect, representative democracy rather than on more direct and participatory forms.

Participatory democrats are concerned with studying and facilitating political systems where the members not only choose their leaders but also participate themselves in the decision-making processes. This approach deals with democracy in the broader sense, as a kind of society. Kalleberg calls this approach populist (1984:372). The primary spokesperson for the notion of participatory democracy is Carole Pateman. Her concern with the role of participation in the modern theory of democracy is based on the work of earlier writers on democracy (the so-called "classical theorists") who shared the idea of maximum participation of all the people.

The starting point for the participatory democratic theorists is a criticism of the elite theorists for seeing dangers in the classical approach to democracy, for fearing that mass participation would upset the stability of the democratic system based on "scientific and empirical facts" (Pateman, 1970:3). For example, Dahl (1956) sees the possible dangers inherent in an increase in participation on the part of ordinary people because lower socioeconomic groups are expected to have more "authoritarian" personalities. Thus an increase in the existing amount of participation could be dangerous to the stability of the democratic system. Pateman (1970:11) also argues that all of Sartori's arguments are coloured by the fear that active participation in the political process leads straight to totalitarianism. In the elite theories, "participation," at least for the majority of citizens, signifies participation in the choice of decision-makers. The democratic method is justified by the achievement of this protective aim.

The critics of elite democratic theory argue that its advocates have misunderstood the classical theory, which they say was not a descriptive but rather a prescriptive, normative theory. The classical theorists of participatory democracy, such as Jean-Jacques Rousseau, John Stuart Mill, and G.D.H. Cole, argue that the attainment of democracy is only possible through participation in the many spheres of society. The theory assumes that an individual "learns democracy" through participation at the local level (Pateman, 1970:29).

Further, participatory democrats argue that the existence of representative institutions at a national level is not enough to establish democracy, but that democracy must take place in other spheres as well, so the necessary individual attitudes and psychological qualities can be developed (through socialization or social training). While it can be argued that representative institutions are necessary, they are not sufficient.

For a democratic polity to exist it is thus necessary for a participatory society to exist – that is, a society in which all political systems have been democratized and socialization through participation can take place in all areas. For Pateman the most important arena of democratization is industry, which implies a form of workplace or industrial democracy. She argues that the educative effect of participation in local government and industry could be generalized to cover the effect of participation in all "lower level" authority structures or political systems (Pateman, 1970:35).

This argument is also valid for mass communications. Through participation in mass communication citizens can be expected to learn and have their consciousness raised, a condition that will then increase the possibility of their participation in other social and political spheres. To sum up, the theory of participatory democracy – in contrast to the elitist theory – places a basic stress on participation in decision-making at all levels.

But participatory democratic theory can also be criticized. Jon Elster, for instance, harshly attacks "self-realization democracy," the label he gives to Pateman's approach. According to Elster, self-realization cannot be the main goal of political participation; it cannot be anything but a byproduct (1983:8). Participation in politics must thus have a goal going beyond itself. However, Elster's interpretation of Pateman and the participatory democratic theory seems too limited. The concept of participation as education is, rather, a first step towards participation for instrumental purposes.

William M. Lafferty (1983) expresses a totally different understanding of Pateman and the participatory democratic theory. He argues that the theory does not see self-respect or self-actualization as an isolated value; it is seen as a necessary element in the learning process, an element that is supposed to give a feeling of improved political abilities. Self-respect thus represents an interaction between politics as instrumental and expressive activity. Self-respect is seen in relation to the goal of politics, which is to establish a political system in which everybody has the same ability (power) to influence the content of decisions (1983:9).

The third category, dialogue democrats, includes authors such as Jürgen Habermas and John Stuart Mill. Theorists who take this position concentrate on opinion and opinion formation in the political system: Dialogue democrats are concerned with studying and facilitating decision-making processes built on interactive and rational persuasion between the members. Kalleberg labels this approach socialist (1984:372); others call it critical. The same approach is also suggested by Elster (who calls it "discourse democracy" based on Habermas, 1982) as an alternative to participatory democratic theory. This approach has an instrumental view of politics and puts emphasis on the public characteristics of politics. Elster argues that the advantage of "discourse democracy" is the possibility of changing preferences through public and rational debate (1983:17).

From a critical (in many cases Marxist) perspective the concept of participation is not without its problems. The "critical model" is based on the idea that the mass media reflect the existing power structure or ideological hegemony operating in society's various institutions (Lindblad, 1983:190). Within this perspective public access and participation can be seen as an aspect of the repressive tolerance of a democratic bourgeois society (Lindblad, 1983:117). It should be recognized that the Marxist theories are mainly developed as critiques of why capitalism does not work.

The critical model's view of participation is conflicting, since the opportunity for participation is also seen as a way of raising critical consciousness and further social change. This fits with the idea of participatory democratic theory. But when Anders Lindblad (1983:193) argues that there is no equivalent of the participation concept in the critical model, he must have in mind only what has been called discourse or dialogue democratic theory. A dominant line of thought in this is the so-called "public sphere theory" (Habermas, 1971). Thus, Lindblad compares participation with what within this critical model is labelled the "proletarian public sphere." In contrast, Elster labels the discourse approach a "theory of participatory democracy" because it emphasizes that the political process must build on active participation and discussion (1983:13).

The Concept of Participation

The distinction between the three described democratic approaches – elite, participatory, and dialogue – can be clarified by the double meaning built into the concept of participation. Lafferty (1983) has done a semantic analysis of participation. According to him, participation means both "to take part" and "to share." The first meaning connotes an individual connection, while the second connotes common action; co-operation. Thus, participation is a concept connecting one part's interests to a collective action directed towards a common interest. Participation can be expressed as a personal involvement and responsibility directed towards – and dependent on – the common good.

Lafferty also identifies three views of the function of participation in democratic norms (1983:34). First, an *instrumental* perspective sees participation as power and influence, which is in line with the liberalist view. Second, an *expressive* perspective views participation as externalizing and dialogue. Third, a *learning* perspective implies participation as learning and consciousness-raising. However, participation should be viewed as a dialectic concept with both instrumental and expressive elements. Participation as learning means more than democratic education, it means raising consciousness, which implies that the results are unpredictable.

Participation then, is the fundamental democratic principle – a viewpoint shared by Raymond Williams, who argues that general participation in common decision-making is the deepest principle in democracy itself (1983:102). M.I. Finley (1985) makes a similar point, arguing that public participation in political activity plays an essential role in public "education."

Democracy in the broader sense as a kind of society is most relevant to the discussion of democratic communication, implying participation in all spheres of society. But the three democratic theories differ in their views of participation: the elitist theory is sceptical about popular participation; the participatory democratic theory views participation as important and positive; and discourse theory sees the concept as problematic. The concept of participation is most adequately discussed by participatory democrats, but the conflict of participation indicated by the critical model should also be kept in mind.

Participatory democracy emphasizes that people must play an important part in public affairs. However, citizens must be informed before such participation can be a realistic possibility. It is then important that different interest groups are able to provide their own perspectives, rather than there being an ideological hegemony as described in the critical model. Indeed, the power to control information is of major importance in controlling society (Bagdikian, 1983).

An active participation in politics and in society requires a high level of knowledge among citizens. Good political decisions are dependent on the best possible "delivery of premises" (agenda-setting) on the part of the citizen. A participatory democracy implies that people should be able to influence the institutions that play a major role in their lives. The mass media do indeed play such a role. The people themselves are the only ones who can articulate their needs. They must thus have access to receive, produce, and exchange information. Consequently, communication systems in a society must be democratized.

Democratization of Communication

The term communication derives from the latin word *communicare*, which means to make common, to have in common, or to tie together. Communication is most often used to describe the process, method, or activity whereby messages are exchanged. Real communication thus implies a two-way flow. The concept of communication is sometimes used interchangeably with that of information, which comes from the latin term *informare* (meaning knowledge, education, research) and tends to be used to describe the content or product of communication. But information usually implies a one-way flow of messages.

For its part, *mass* communication is characterized by a one-way flow of messages/information with few or no possibilities for feedback. Mass communication – as opposed to interpersonal communication – is public, simultaneous, and impersonal (Hedebro, 1980; Høyer, 1982; MacBride Report, 1980; and McQuail, 1983). However, it is possible to alter the one-way flow of messages in mass communication by means of increased popular participation.

If a society's aim is to democratize communication structures, all the stages in the communication process need to be considered (Østbye 1985:158), including the transmitter, the message, and the receiver stages. The concept of representation is of importance at all stages.

At the transmitter stage, the fundamental concept is freedom of expression. Democratization at this stage takes place when groups who were not previously able to transmit their message are secured access. This applies especially to large groups, but it is important that smaller groups, such as ethnic and cultural minorities, are also secured access.

A major issue is whether a general policy of extended access can achieve these aims, or whether a selective policy by which underprivileged groups are given privileged access is necessary. This is a distinction between the "freedom" and the "equality" aspects of democratization (Syvertsen, 1986a:79). In any case, the aim is to increase participation – a concept that is quite controversial in democratic theory. Even so, Helge Østbye's model implies that increased participation or an extension of access to production is not enough or may not even be the best approach.

Concerning content or message, the fundamental concept of a democratic policy is greater pluralism in the mass media output. This goal can be reached by having many channels transmitting messages with limited perspectives or by having each broadcasting institution (for example, a public-service monopoly) providing diverse output. This result *can* be achieved by increased participation, *if* new groups are provided access, but it is not a necessary consequence, as indicated by the experiences of independent local broadcasting in several countries. For example, increased possibility for participation in local independent radio in Norway has often resulted in "music-radio." In addition the broadcasting should reflect the perspectives of different subcultures, not just the "mainstream" ideology.

Concerning audience, the fundamental concept is the right to information. Democratization at this stage can be achieved by providing access for groups who were earlier underprivileged as receivers, by reducing information or knowledge gaps. It is important to note as well the possible contradictions in the results of democratization at the different stages in the communication process. Increased access and participation could, for instance, result in very similar content. Sometimes a public-service monopoly can provide the most adequate information about certain issues. However, such a monopoly will often anticipate and reflect consensus in a certain society rather than reflect a conflict of interests (between social classes or genders, for example).

The democratization of communication, then, must imply more than just access to production. However, the possibility for participating in media production is important because it gives people increased insight into how the media functions and thus promotes a demystification of the media. But the result of this participation can also be the formation of a new media elite – people who become fascinated with the medium itself and in many cases most concerned with furthering their own (professional) media careers. Part of the problem is also that in many countries state funds are necessary to secure proper popular access. To ensure independence from the state it may be necessary to have revenue provided by several sources. Education and training are also needed to ensure the participation of underprivileged groups. Finally, democratization is just as relevant to media content and to receivers' right to information.

Østbye's attempt to concretize the concept of democratization of communication is a valuable one. This schema can, for example, be used as goals for policy suggestions or to evaluate whether democratization is really taking place or not. However, Østbye's model does not account for the learning aspect of participation (as suggested by Pateman). Besides, the model could have focused more on the role of democratization of communication structures in democratizing society.

However, democratization of the media is not only about policy-making. It is also a matter of how various groups and social movements demand access to the media as part of their strategies for social change (Syvertsen 1986a:123). This demand for democratic media at grassroots levels has been especially voiced in UNESCO, which has been the most significant forum for the debate about the democratization of communication that began in the 1970s.

In fact, the demand for democratic communication can be argued to be the essence of a "New World Communication and Information Order," for which UNESCO has been the main proponent (for example, Hagen, 1986; Thorud, 1985).

In this context, democratization is defined as the process whereby the individual becomes an active partner and not just an object of communication, whereby the variety of messages exchanged increases, and whereby the extent and quality of social representation or participation in communication are increased (MacBride Report, 1980:166).

Participation is central to this demand for democratization. The awakening and moulding of consciousness are seen as a crucial aspect of democratization in the communication process. In line with the participatory democratic theory, participation is key to achieving this consciousness (through learning and socialization). Also, increased participation by readers, viewers, and listeners in the decision-making and programming activities of the media is seen as a prerequisite for democratic communication (MacBride Report, 1980:174). This participation implies participation in program planning and decision-making and not just in program production. Participation in this broad sense also implies that different social groups own and have financial control over their own media.

Two-fold Participation

To democratize communication the role of participation has to be two-fold: participation in the media and participation in society. The question, then, is whether the aim is to democratize the media structure or whether the democratization of communication is just an instrument to achieve a more democratic society. Lindblad has called this a distinction between democratization *of* the media and a democratization *through* the media (1983:13). Democratization *of* the media implies that people get the chance to participate in the media in different ways. In many cases, the concept of "public access" fits into the democratization *of* the media category. Democratization *through* the media, however, refers to the long-term effects on the democratic processes that can be expected in general in a society, for example, the effects on the overall allocation of resources.

The broader concept, democratization *through* the media, thus relates the democratization of communication to the process of social change (White 1982:1). The broad processes of societal democratization and democratization of communication are interconnected. For example, access to information is essential for a person to satisfy her/his basic human needs, for education, for political participation, and also as a basis for decision-making and allocation of resources in society (Syvertsen, 1986a:69). Underlying these aspects is a view of information as a social good rather than as a commodity.

Fernando Reyes Matta provides a similar distinction in his outline of a model for democratic communication. The purpose of democratic communication as stated in the model is to raise the educational levels for a better understanding of the communication process and to create "true participation" based upon "adequate social awareness" (Matta, 1981:79). A positive aspect of this proposed model is that the participation process is defined as a mechanism that permits the access of organized audiences to decision-making and internal planning structures, as well as to organizations to deliver education for communication. But the model can be criticized for its vague and abstract concepts – it is nice in theory but it is difficult in practice to realize what the concepts imply.

Some Attempts to Democratize Communication

Experiments with local independent broadcasting in Norway is defined by policy-makers as a strategy for democratization of communication. This is a policy of democratization *of* the media, rather than democratization in a broader sense. In Norway, democratization is thus used to legitimize deregulation. Democratization in this context is defined as granting formal access to broadcasting production on a local level (Syvertsen, 1986a:121). But, as it has been argued, granting formal access to production is not sufficient to democratize the communication structure.

In Scandinavia it is now common to equate decentralization trends with democratization. As stated by Lindblad, "Common to all official statements behind the emergence of various local media [in Sweden] is the theme of the potential that all have for strengthening democracy" (1983:189). Syvertsen too argues that in Norway (as in Europe and the United States) the ideology behind most of the attempts at independent local broadcasting has perceived decentralization as equal to democratization (1986b:110).

However, studies of these phenomena do not provide support for this equalization. For example, Lindblad has found that in Swedish local independent media, it is people in mainly high status groups who are recruited to program production. This unequal recruitment of participants makes it doubtful whether new groups, values, topics, and perspectives emerge in the broadcast output (Lindblad, 1983:94). Similarly, Ole Prehn's study of local TV in Denmark and Great Britain indicates that local media had reinforced the existing social distinctions in the community (Prehn, 1981:229).

Similar results have been found in Norway. Reviews of licences achieved for independent local radio and TV have indicated a strengthening of monopoly tendencies. The licensees were mostly well-established organizations and institutions (Syvertsen, 1985:49). However, more positive tendencies did appear: Some new groups were involved as transmitters, and some small minorities had increased their possibilities for communication through the local media reform. Besides, there was increased pluralism at a national level. But there was hardly better representation of underprivileged groups in the media system. Trine Syvertsen (1986b:166) considers it doubtful that there has been increased participation in the planning and decision-making.

Decentralization does not necessarily result in democratization. General access to local broadcasting cannot be expected to make up for the social differences resulting in differences to access to communication channels. To increase participation it may be necessary to introduce selective policies, for example, to set up workshops in which underprivileged groups can improve their skills.

Based on his experiences with "public-access television" in Austin, Texas,

Douglas Kellner provides an example of the potential for democratization of the media as a way to influence society. Compared to the results from the Scandinavian context, Kellner's viewpoints are hopeful. He argues that public-access television provides quite another possibility for the left to use the broadcast media to transmit alternative information, to make progressive struggles and social movements legitimate, and to shape public opinion and use the media as instruments of political intervention (1985:79).

Public-access television is a valuable supplement to North American commercial TV. It can provide increased participation and help to air alternative viewpoints. But to have an impact on the audience the programs must indeed be watched. These experiments also need to be evaluated to see whether democratization really takes place at the different stages of the communication process.

Conclusion

The concept of democratic communication should imply direct and participatory democracy rather than other democratic variants. Even if we look on democracy as a kind of society rather than a kind of government, certain political privileges, such as freedom of speech, must be a prerequisite for democratization of communication. Participatory democracy implies that people participate in many spheres of society. The claim of participatory democratic theory is that the necessary condition for the establishment of a democratic polity is a participatory society. Through participation the individual will "learn democracy" and develop skills to participate in other political arenas. Empirical research is ambivalent as to whether this really happens.

For people to play an active part in public affairs, they must inform themselves using the mass media as well as other alternatives. Democracy requires that each individual is aware of the society in which he or she lives. This necessitates a diverse content, which has to be relevant to people's needs. Participatory democracy relies on the ability of citizens to make informed decisions rather than to choose between elites to make decisions for them.

Also, the question of whether the communication structures really are democratized as a result of a policy needs to be explored empirically. We then need to consider the different stages in the communication process. At the transmitter stage, access to broadcasting needs to be provided to all socioeconomic and racial groups living in a society (Hagen, 1986:119). In addition to access to production, participation in planning and decision-making should be secured. It may be necessary with a selective policy to secure access to groups that are underprivileged in communication. Education can be needed to improve their skills. Indicators of democratization are also increased pluralism in the media output and reduced knowledge-gaps in society.

Democratic communication should imply a two-fold concept of participation: participation in the media and participation in society. These concepts are interrelated, so democratization *of* the media should only be a part of democratization *through* the media. People need to have access to the media to exchange messages. The media should also serve as an instrument for increasing people's knowledge or consciousness about public issues so they have the possibility to take part in decision-making in society. This process could prevent control of information being used as a means to concentrate power and authority by an institutionalized political elite. Democratic communication, then, has the potential for furthering participatory democracy or democratization of society.

The question we're left with is: How is the potential to be realized? New media technology is mostly developed with military or profit-making intentions in mind. However, new technology provides new media forms that sometimes do have the potential for societal democratization. But democratization has to come about as a result of media policies or of the demands of social movements or "alternative" groups for "access." As a concept democratic communication has little value unless the implicit distinctions and conflicts are made explicit. The concept of democratic communication is not without its problems. But it is still valuable as an ideal – and especially as a tool that will help us achieve a more participatory, democratic society.

References

Bagdikian, Ben H. (1983). *The Media Monopoly*. Boston: Beacon Press.
Bergh, Trond, ed. (1983). *Deltakerdemokratiet – teori og praksis* (participatory democracy – theory and practice). Oslo: Universitetsforlaget.
Bergh, Trond (1983). "Forord" (Introduction). In Bergh (1983).
Dahl, Robert A. (1956). *A Preface to Democratic Theory*. London: University of Chicago Press.
Elster, Jon (1983). "Offentlighet og deltakelse – to teorier om deltakerdemokratiet" (public sphere and participation – two theories about participatory democracy). In Bergh (1983).
Encyclopaedia Britannica (EB), Micropaedia (1974). Vol.III. London: Encyclopaedia Britannica Inc.
Finley, M.I. (1985). *Democracy Ancient and Modern*. Revised Edition. New Jersey: Rutgers University Press.
Habermas, J. (1971). *Borgerlig offentlighet* (bourgeois public sphere). Oslo: Gyldendal.
Habermas, J. (1982). "Diskursethik – Notizen zu einem Begrundungsprogram." In D. Bøhlman and W. Kuhlman, eds., *Kommunikation und Reflexion*. Frankfurt: Suhrkamp.
Hagen, Ingunn (1986). "A Theoretical Discussion of the Concept Democratic/ Participatory Communication in Light of the Demands for a 'New World Information and Communication Order.'" M.A. thesis, University of California, Santa Barbara.
Hedebro, Göran (1982). *Communication and Social Change in Developing Nations: A Critical View*. Ames: The Iowa State University Press.
Høyer, Svennik (1982). "Om makt og medier" (about power and media). In Svennik Høyer, Kjell O. Mathisen, Anita Werner, and Helge Østbye, eds., *Maktutredningen – Rapporten om massemedier* (report on power in the mass media). NOU 1982:30, Oslo: Universitetsforlaget.*
Kalleberg, Ragnvald (1984). "Demokratisering av foretak" (democratization of institutions). In Bernt Hagtvet and William M. Lafferty, eds., *Demokrati og demokratisering* (democracy and democratization). Oslo: Aschehoug.

Kellner, Douglas (1985). "Public Access Television: Alternative Views." In Radical Science Collective, eds., *Making Waves: The Politics of Communications*. London: Free Association Books.

Lafferty, William M. (1983). "Deltakelse og demokrati – momenter i en uendelig dialog" (participation and democracy – aspects in an endless dialogue). In Bergh (1983).

Lindblad, Anders (1983). "Lokal radio og TV – en analys av publikstruktur och deltagande" (local radio and TV – an analysis of audience structure and participation). Department of Sociology, University of Umeå.

MacBride Report (1980). *Many Voices, One World: Communication and Society, Today and Tomorrow: Towards a More Just and More Efficient World Information and Communication Order*. "Report by the International Commission for the Study of Communication Problems." London: K. Page.

Macpherson, C.B. (1966). *The Real World of Democracy*. Oxford: Clarendon Press.

Matta, Fernando Reyes (1981). "A Model for Democratic Communication," *Development Dialogue*, 2.

McQuail, Denis (1983). *Mass Communication Theory – An Introduction*. London: Sage Publications.

Pateman, Carole (1970). *Participation and Democratic Theory*. London: Cambridge University Press.

Prehn, Ole (1981). *Lokal TV, 1970ernes erfaringer i England og Danmark* (local TV in the 1970s in England and Denmark). Aalborg: Aalborg Universitetsforlag.

Sartori, Giovanni (1968). "Democracy." In David L. Sills, ed., *International Yearbook of the Social Sciences*. Vol.4. New York: The Macmillan Company & The Free Press.

Syvertsen, Trine (1985). "Forsøk med lokal radio og fjernsyn i Norge – en oversiktsrapport" (attempts with local radio and television in Norway – an overview). Workpaper. Bergen: Senter for mediefag.

Syvertsen, Trine (1986a). "Broadcasting in Norway in the 1980s: Internationalization, Decentralization, Deregulation and Democratisation." M.A. thesis, Centre for Mass Communication Research, University of Leicester.

Syvertsen, Trine (1986b). "Ny teknikk, ny politikk og 'nye' medier" (new technique, new policy and 'new' media). Hovedoppgave (Norwegian M.A. thesis), Institutt for massekommunikasjon, Samfunnsvitenskapelig seksjon, Universitetet i Bergen.

Thorud, Johan (1985). "Et forsok på dialog" (an attempt for dialogue). In Knut Sogstad og Liv Mellum, eds., *Nyheter fra sør til nord – om u-landsnyheter i norske medier* (news from south to north – about news from underdeveloped countries in Norwegian media). Fredrikstad: Institutt for Journalistikk.

von Beyme, Klaus (1973). "Democracy." In C.D. Kernig, ed., *Marxism, Communism, and the Western Society*. Vol.III. New York: Herder & Herder.

White, R.A. (1982). *Contradictions in Contemporary Policies for Democratic Communication*. London: Centre for the Study of Communication and Culture.

Williams, Raymond (1983). *Towards 2000*. Middlesex: Penguin.

Østbye, Helge (1985). "Lokal-TV: aktivisering eller passivisering – økt eller redusert demokrati?" (local TV: activization or passivization – increased or reduced democracy?). *TV2*. NOU 1985:11, Oslo: Universitetsforlaget.*

* Publications marked * are Norwegian Official Publications. "NOU" indicates reports written by government commissions.

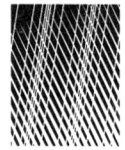

Communications in the Community: Critical Scholarship in an Emerging Field

Mark Schulman

THIS IS A REPORT from a contested terrain.

Over the last decade I have engaged in action-research aimed at aiding the effort to produce a theoretical framework for the emerging field of community communication as an element of critical scholarship in the communications discipline.

From that decade of effort emerges this report. The terrain in contention, from which I am filing it, is the primary discursive dispute (I was tempted to write "battlefield," but that seemed too militaristic) within the communication studies discipline. That dispute, as reflected both here and in other chapters of this book, reflects the attempt to carve out a "liberated zone" for critical scholarship within the domain of mainstream communications thought. It is the essence, I think, of the dialectic embedded in the title of this book. "Democratic Communications," the liberating antithesis, must be for critical scholars an intellectual tool to contest the bourgeois thesis assumed by, and subsumed within, the phrase "The Information Age."

What I hope to demonstrate in the following pages is the development of critical scholarship in community communication as a synthesis. The dialectical consciousness that progressive, democratic communicators focus on their efforts in this realm will be one aspect (of course, by no means the only one – and probably it is among many significant foci that will grow as the intellectual struggles continue) of an oppositional presence in the communications discipline.

The questions themselves are straightforward. In the development of community communication, where are we now? And, in what direction are we headed?

The answers, more complex than I can hope to present in my allotted space, are surveyed in the fragmentary sections that follow.

Community Communication Present: Where Are We Now?

According to Terry Eagleton in *Literary Theory: An Introduction* (1983), the work of developing criticism in the discipline of "literature" needs broadening to include the concerns of a critical communication theory. Though Eagleton does not use that phrase, his approach to the subject indicates a similar state of mind, and his call for the radical critic to be eclectic "about questions of theory and method" echoes the critical perspective.

The critical-theorist-as-pluralist recognizes theory and its methodological accoutrements as tools used to *accomplish* certain tasks. These tools are strategic because, according to Eagleton, "What you choose and reject theoretically, then, depends on what you are practically trying to do."

For me, Eagleton's statement of how to proceed serves as a guideline for articulating a sharply defined community communication statement:

> No theory or method, in any case, will have merely one strategic use. They can be mobilized in a variety of different strategies for a variety of ends. But not all methods will be equally amenable to particular ends. It is a matter of finding out, not of assuming from the start that a single method or theory will do.... It is not a matter of starting from certain theoretical or methodological problems: it is a matter of starting from what we want to do, and then seeing which methods and theories will best help us to achieve these ends. (Eagleton, 1983)

The chance to develop a new field – or, more accurately, to take up a position on a level playing field – creates a unique opportunity for critical communication scholars. Following Eagleton's model, we can say that community communication is both a social theory and a methodological tool, which together evolve from a starting point of *what we want to do*. We must also keep in mind, as Kusum Singh puts it, that "community communication at the level of neighborhoods or other relatively small geographical units" is "a relatively new subject of study" aimed at controversial, significant hypotheses (Singh, 1981).

Or, as put another way, by Frances Berrigan:

> The importance of research in the area of community communications cannot be underestimated. This is a new area and, as such, it demands not only research into ways of making its efforts more effective, but new ways of carrying out research. Most communications research, as we have seen, is summative in that it sets out to tell what has happened. Such research is valuable, for it can be used to inform future projects. But what is lacking is research which can inform projects while they are under way, which can reshape and redirect projects which are in existence and which have meaning for the people involved in those projects, not just for academics. (1981)

At its present stage of development as an area of study, community communication consists of the following construct:

- *Community communication* identifies the patterns of information sharing in a neighbourhood or a commonage. A neighbourhood is a small physical space with recognized boundaries in a metropolitan area. A commonage is a geographically identifiable unit, physically larger than a neighbourhood, with recognized "boundary regions": a space defined partially by proximity but also by the common cultural interests of its members. (Many towns, for example, and some rural areas with commonalities could be labelled commonages.)

- *Community communication research* focuses on the way of life of a people in a neighbourhood or commonage. Things separated from their meanings to these people or events outside the collective experience are *not* part of community communications research. This does not mean we ignore issues of national and international dimension; we aim to avoid both ungroundedness and parochialism in this research. The *goals* of community communication research are:
    1) to encourage distribution and discourage inhibition of information; and
    2) to increase possibilities and decrease obstacles for media access and participation.
- *Community communication studies* are a form of cultural analysis. Within a neighbourhood or commonage this analysis considers three main elements.
    - *Face-to face communication*: deals with leadership/fellowship styles and lifestyles of the community members.
    - *Information flow*: includes internal (wholly within) community and the external (from and to) community connections, through individuals and institutions, which determine the level of public awareness.
    - *Local communications policy*: examines the structure of mainstream and alternative media as those media restrict or permit access and participation for community members.

Community communication studies involve six phases. Although these phases are not always discrete and not necessarily sequential, they generally follow this pattern:

1) *Social Exploration* of the local history and human ecology;
2) *Participatory Analysis* to define categories and appropriate methods, and to test those categories and methods with community help;
3) *Needs Assessment* to uncover what the community perceives as strengths and problems;
4) *Communication Audit* to dissect what exists and what improvements the community desires;
5) *Self-reflexive Reporting* to engage in a dialogue about results and generalize what others may learn;
6) *Social Animation* to educate cultural workers who continue the processes and themselves teach others.

The three main aspects and six phases form a matrix, which the community communication researcher uses as a formative guideline.

Over the last decade, two critical communication scholars – Kusum Singh and Frances Berrigan – have presented relatively complete versions of community communications as I have delineated it here. The models they have developed provide a slightly different spin on the contemporary theoretical framework I have outlined.

The Berrigan Model

Frances Berrigan's main theoretical statement is *Community Communications: The Role of Community Media in Development*, which UNESCO published in 1981 as one of its "Reports and Papers in Mass Communication Series." In this short treatise, Berrigan is clearly more concerned with *processes* than *technologies*. UNESCO makes clear, in its institutional voice in the Preface, that this is conceptual groundbreaking for communications scholarship:

> This study reviews progress so far and analyzes the difficulties which underlie the transfer and adaptation of community communications. It has deliberately been written at a time when we have seen some tentative experiences in this new field, are in the process of evaluating some more, and are to consider the most opportune thrusts for our next effort. (Berrigan, 1981)

Of Berrigan's four chapters – "Community Communications in Development," "The Practice of Community Communications," "The Community Media Methodology," and "An Appropriate Methodology for Development" – three are descriptive. The projects and activities described are worldwide and fascinating, mostly drawn from rural areas and all from developing countries. Berrigan's definitions tie into the critical perspective on development as connected to "relatively new uses of media." She states, "Uses of communication media which include two-way communication have been called 'community communications' or 'community media.'" These forms of communications "are adaptations of media for use by the community, for whatever purposes the community decides" (Berrigan, 1981).

Since the idea of community communications "embodies the notions of access and participation through media," it reflects "concerns about the part the individual might play in shaping his own socio-political, cultural and economic environment" (Berrigan, 1981). In clarifying the distinctions between access and participation, and in her chapters that demonstrate the application of community communications to events and processes, Berrigan makes a major theoretical contribution. She clarifies "the horizontally-layered process, in which community groups consider and decide priorities for development," as the key to the operation of community communication (Berrigan, 1981). This clarification of forms of community involvement in turn grew out of the deliberations of a 1977 international conference in Belgrade on "Self-Management, Access and Participation." The definitions of terms that the conference adopted have become crucial to the participatory model of community communication. Berrigan's understated summary of the argument embedded in the terms is accurate: "A reading of these definitions gives a clear picture of a demand for radical reforms in the management of communications systems" (Berrigan, 1977).

A major strength of Berrigan's model is her emphasis on the practice of community communication, which she says "will depend upon how far the notions of access and participation are accepted within particular socio-political contexts" (Berrigan, 1981). Berrigan's stress on media, however, limits her model. In addition, a strong reliance on the development communications framework, while not a limiting factor, shifts her conception to a geographically larger, more rural, and diffusion-dominated orientation in place of an overall generic community communications approach. But her perspective does move beyond media into a new construct. According to Berrigan, community communications are an *approach* or a *technique*; they are not limited to particular types of media, to particular types of communication, to particular uses. The type of involvement, whether it is feedback, self-management, participation in production, planning, or performance, can vary according to circumstances and resources.

The Singh Model

The other researcher who has contributed greatly to this new construct is Kusum Singh, who has extended the humanistic and behavioural science antecedents and consciously worked from the mainstream community and communication studies roots of the emerging field.

Singh states that such a "relatively new subject of study" goes beyond traditional community studies in sociology or anthropology by describing "from the viewpoint of the many given people in any given community" the interrelationships of information transfer via mass media, small media, and non-media. She says that research in the field "brings together three aspects of communication that are usually pursued separately: mass media, organizational communication, and human or interpersonal communication." The community communications researcher must pay attention "to the flows of information within the community, from the community to so-called 'higher' levels of authority or control" and between the community members and other groups or people in larger social organizations, such as the city. An important component of the empirical data-gathering is the effort "to assess the conflicting tendencies toward democratic or authoritarian approaches to communication" (Singh, 1981).

In her work "Some Guidelines for Research and Action on Community Communication" (1982), Singh draws attention to the "premises which guide our work and which we try to state as explicitly as possible. They are not hypotheses to be tested. Nor are they fixed axioms, since we try to improve them as we go along." Her first two sections define "communication" and "community." In her terminology she uses "big media" and "small media" roughly the way I use the terms "mainstream" and "alternative" media; and her use of "non-media" means "face-to-face" with a subtext of certain aspects of organizational communication. She recognizes the ambiguity of the various definitions of community, suggesting that no matter how the term is used, "A community has certain boundaries or 'boundary regions' that will be perceived differently by different people." Consequently,

"In any group with common interests (from a family to an 'organized' neighborhood or larger community) there are always divergent or conflicting interests as well as different perceptions of common interests" (Singh, 1982b).

Singh's work has continuities with that of Berrigan. Singh has been concerned in the past with development communication and media systems. However, she stresses issues of leadership in community communication more than Berrigan does. This stress, paradoxically, emerges from her concern with media:

> One of the conclusions of my research was that mass communication has been possible – provided that the message is truly meaningful – without control, or even use, of the mass media. But one of the conditions making it possible has been an approach that is not only multi-media (with special attention to schools and small newspapers) but also multi-modal, with emphasis on organizational and political communication and communication through personal example and life style. (Singh, 1982a)

Singh stresses, as Berrigan does, the importance of considering "horizontal" communication processes; Singh labels this "lateral communication," and, at the community level, she has a particular interest in "bottom-sideways" communication. She counterpoints this type of interaction with an emphasis on "top-down, bottom-up" relationships, which perpetuate elitist, authoritarian, and charismatic (a term she uses negatively) leadership styles. "To be truly democratic," she writes, "leaders must develop alternatives to hierarchic, elitist, bureaucratic, charismatic and macho styles of behavior" (Singh, 1982a).

Bottom-sideways communication "is oriented toward developing common purposefulness," just as top-sideways communication is. But the fundamental reason for the communication is different. The bottom-sideways approach aims "to democratize the structure of money and power ... [by countering] the immobilizing effects of most mass media ... by message systems that mobilize and energize" (Singh, 1983). For Singh such interaction is the place to begin in the action-research of community communication. Like Berrigan, her work is political, as well as expansive from the local to the global. In the syllabus for a community communication course she co-taught in 1983, she states the goal explicitly: "We shall start with the problems of fragmentation in the small communities we are closest to – and work outward" (Singh, 1982c).

Perhaps the best summary of the conceptualization that Singh has brought to community communication is to reproduce her statement on hypotheses. In several instances researchers have adopted these "significant hypotheses" to use them in continuing projects. This is, in a direct sense, then, one of the possible research agendas for community communication at this stage of development of Singh's model.

> In the natural sciences an hypothesis is a generalization that is subject to disproof. In the social sciences, only trivial hypotheses can be firmly proved or

disproved. More significant hypotheses are necessarily controversial and may be regarded as conjectures or speculations. One of the purposes in using such hypotheses is to improve – rather than conclusively prove or disprove – them.

1) In many local communities the underlying sense of common interests tends to be displaced by various forms of social fragmentation and intra-community competition.

2) The big media tend to promote social fragmentation by displacing interpersonal communication by serious under-attention to selected local problems, events and news.

3) Most community groups and leaders have little or no access to the big media.

4) Successful efforts to bring a community closer together depend upon the communication styles of community leaders – particularly on their ability to use non-media channels and the small media.

5) Many of the more effective community leaders tend to be narrowly parochial and provincial, having little or no communication with other communities in the same area or across the state and country.

6) Much contact among different communities and their leaders is lateral, top-top communication among elites.

7) More autocratic leaders act mainly in terms of top-down communication with their members or followers, with bottom-up communication tending to reinforce vertical relations.

8) More democratic leaders give more attention to lateral – or "bottom-sideways" – communication among ordinary people. (Singh, 1982a)

Community Communication Future: Where Are We Headed?

The fate of community communication is tied to the future of critical research and scholarship in the communications field. Community communication itself involves several concrete, specific issues, but first some of the broader issues, such as the alternative/mainstream dispute as it will be debated into the future, call for examination.

The positing of a mainstream/alternative split has its linguistic limitations but it is still a useful tool of strategic inquiry for viewing the concrete differences in the variants of communication research defined by Dallas Smythe and Tran Van Dinh as "critical" and "administrative" (Smythe and Dinh, 1983). This is where the action in the debate over research and its results will be. And it is on the level of research problems and methods that critical communication theory identifies a scope of approaches and, perhaps more important, an intention of result that differentiates it from the mainstream research tradition. Given the diversity of worldviews included in the domain of critical scholarship, it is no surprise that there are many constructions, and not a few deconstructions, of the "proper research questions" to be considered by critical scholars.

It is becoming apparent that critical research perspectives are on the ascendancy in much of the world outside the United States. Almost two decades ago Kaarle Nordenstreng, an important Finnish critical communications scholar, identified the "global trends in the field of mass communications research" in terms of two tendencies: a more holistic framework and a policy orientation (Nordenstreng, 1974).

Critical research, then, is an eclectic amalgam of perspectives and positions that blend together to form a strategy that aims to ask the right questions about social reality. Once the questions are posed, innovative methods to seek answers (or to refine the questions) are the next goal for the critical researcher – at present and into the future. So far there has been little material provided on this matter in books, journals, or theses – but the few publications that do exist are clearly the beginnings of a field. For example, before my own 1986 dissertation, there had been one master's thesis and one doctoral dissertation with "community communication" in the title – and it is in these academic studies that citations germinate. Next will come a scholarly journal to replace Community Memory's *Journal of Community Communications*, a conference funded by a major liberal foundation, and a book or two – one yearns for something with more crisp analysis than Scott Peck's *The Different Drum: Community Making and Peace* (1987), for example.

Several issues can be identified as "odds-on favourites" to become the new categories that will draw the field's principal attention into the next century. In the communications dimension the issue that needs comprehensive examination involves the demarcation of the community communication category from other, related categories. Three of those other categories ripe for study are alternative communication, democratic communication, and *communicación popular.*

Alternative communication as it has been formulated extends beyond the alternative media aspects into other questions. In an important essay, "New Means of Communication: New Questions for the Left," Armand Mattelart and Jeanne-Marie Piemme surveyed the technology that progressive media workers were touting as "revolutionary," including community video and free radio. They found both the technologies and the analyses lacking a truly transformative substance (Mattelart and Piemme, 1980).

The agenda of questions and social practices that a study of alternative communication proposes, it is clear, overlaps with the agenda of community communication. In access, participation, and self-management, for example, are both the seeds of an alternative system and the foundation of the communications system of the healthy community.

After the question of alternative communication, the next more pertinent aspect is the relation between community communication and democratic communication. The term democratic communication has been used in so many different ways that its usefulness as a tool to point sharply to a referent has been overwhelmed. There is, however, a substantive meaning to the term, and it will link with community communication as both develop into mature studies.

The two issues of information equity and lateral communication seem to be the crux of this category. By "information equity," I am evoking the debates that are a part of the struggle for a new world information and communication order. Over the last decade, there have been numerous important treatments of these issues. The correspondence in the new world order debate to the developmental communication aspects of community communication, as Berrigan has stated them, is significant and not a coincidence. The issue of an anti-colonialist communication for Third World communities demands further discussion. I am convinced that the new world information order controversy, which led in part to Reagan pulling the United States out of UNESCO, is the key arena of democratic communication struggle for this last decade of the century, and perhaps beyond.

As well, where those new world information and communication order debates connect directly to internal U.S. issues, as they do with the issue of gentrification of central cities, the questions become crucial for community communication research.

Lateral or horizontal communication is a second dimension of international struggle that directly impinges upon community communication. For our purposes, we are concerned less with the top-top variety but instead with the bottom-sideways dimension discussed in Singh's work. This type of communication is the fundamental component of the "right to communicate" – another term from the new world information and communication order arena. It comes up in the notion of "dialogical communication," part of the influential work of Paulo Freire to situate a democratic communication process outside the "extension" variety of interaction, which is monologic, monolithic, and oppressive (Freire, 1973).

Robert White contends with a third aspect of this definitional problematic in working out the consequences of *communicación popular*. Distinguishing the social origins of the term outside the traditional use of "popular," in the mass culture industry, White places the kind of communication identified as being in the alternative communication of the small communities of Latin America and other parts of the Third World. *Communicación popular* incorporates elements of the folk culture of a region, as well as horizonal channels, but its most dynamic characteristic is that it "arises within a lower-status movement for social change, often in opposition to the stable structure of small communities and to the established local media" (White, 1980).

White's discussion of *communicación popular* and the attention of other scholars to the concepts that define alternative and democratic communication lead organically to the set of issues that go beyond the community and communication issues in their challenge to a community communication theory. These are issues submerged throughout the literature of community communication as it has developed, issues that have not yet been adequately addressed. If it is to take up a mature perspective (or I might have written "paradigm"), community communication has to have satisfactory responses to these issues, which have now surfaced for confrontation:

- Does an area of study for community communication really exist?
- Is community communication a part of critical communication theory?
- What is the appropriate method of inquiry for community communication research?

Does community communication exist? There can be no doubt that the phenomenon exists. The unit of analysis of a neighbourhood or commonage can be marked off, and the relationships of information-sharing within that unit can be identified. Those relationships must be different than any other extant set of phenomena already considered within communication studies to respond to this question affirmatively.

Mainstream communication studies divide the phenomena of human communication into intrapersonal, interpersonal, small-group, organizational, and mass communication. While some authors use different names, the categories hold across the range of mainstream approaches. Intrapersonal and interpersonal studies focus on the individual in his or her relationship to others. "Intrapersonal" is biological or psychological, ascertaining how the human body processes information, or the internal dimension of communication. "Interpersonal" generally limits its analysis to the two-way, face-to-face interactions; it is thus social-psychological in its orientation. Small-group and organizational studies situate the person within larger social structures. Their domain spreads from the social-psychological to the sociological by working in contexts of people interacting in more than a dyad but still within the boundaries of proximate interaction. When technology intervenes and renders the communication one-way and heterogeneous, the phenomenon falls into the domain of "mass communication."

Given this structure, one dilemma for mainstream theory has been the placement of interaction over the telephone, or, as more recent phenomena, the Citizen's Band radio and computer teleconferencing, which fit poorly within any of these categories. Nevertheless, the mainstream enterprise has stuck with this well-developed (one might say overdetermined) schema for nearly half a century.

It would not be impossible for community communication to slide into a modified schema of postmodern mainstream communication studies. One could, for instance, subdivide human communication into an interpersonal, community/organizational, and mediated continuum. Granting overlap at the edges of each category, the elegance of being able to cruise among these phenomena is an inviting prospect – especially if, using community communications research such as the Mott study (Carpenter, 1981), we could also overcome some of the inadequacies of the old sort through a more fluid analysis.

It seems no longer an issue as to whether there is a discrete region that can be labelled community communication. There is such a region. Why it has not been labelled as such until now seems the more pertinent question. However, in some ways that would be the wrong question. It is like asking why there was no subatomic physics until the twentieth century, or why there was no anti-capitalist social movement during the feudal centuries, or why Christianity only came into being after Christ. Community communication, more humble and more limited in its scope than any of the paradigm-shifting events, nevertheless shares with them the *sine qua non* of any intellectual phenomenon: The material conditions for the emergence of the event are its essential precondition.

For a new physics, that was a metaphysics before the old physics; for anti-capitalism, it meant capitalism after feudalism; for Christianity, it meant a mythos of Christ on which to build the ideology of the emerging social and political realities. For community communication, there had to be the precondition of a field of communication. And with the communication discipline we are looking at a young field, one of the newest of the social sciences, really only a development of consequence for the last fifty or sixty years. So it is not surprising that community communication is so undefined when its antecedents themselves are still in the process of forming as distinct fields.

The ferment that communication scholars identify as the dominant tendency in the field demonstrates this state of the art. But there are problems with defining community communication as a legitimate intellectual endeavour. They are epistemological: How do we overcome the self-evident nature of some of the assumptions in the field, which has more than its share of tautologies?

In addition the problems are also semantic: Carving out a separate and justifiable area with agreed-upon boundaries remains an issue in community communication. Further, there is the referential aspect: The domain that community communication intends to study may be too large, too overwhelming – where are the manageable conceptual categories to employ in analysis?

Lastly, and probably most significantly, there are the political questions: As in the UNESCO debates, community communication is perceived as an oppositional tendency within communication studies.

Lest I leave the impression here that there are no satisfactory answers to these questions, I want to affirm that in my view community communication is a legitimate field of inquiry, and that further study in the field can provide responses to these challenges to its legitimacy. In fact, I think the field is remarkably far along the road to solidity and clarity given its decade or two of existence.

But, leaving aside the epistemological, semantic, and referential questions for more thorough exploration in the future, we can tarry a moment longer in the political realm. Is community communication, de jure or de facto, an example of critical communication scholarship? I see no intellectually verifiable way to identify any field of inquiry as, by its internal nature, either "mainstream" or "critical." To do so is to reify social research as a transhistorical, transcontextual construct: and we know enough, after Thomas Kuhn (1970) if no one else, to reject the idea that ideas are separate from their moment in history and cultural context. Therefore, community communication can claim no privilege to status within the critical perspective merely by its assumptive universe.

There is a prior question here, of course. Does community communication desire to be "critical," given the likelihood that the mainstream awaits it with open arms? But that is a question for the future: It cannot be answered until tomorrow, though we can look for clues today.

The simple response to the issue of community communication's critical theo-retical nature is to cite its past practice. There is little quarrel that the construc-tion of assumptions and principles that its scholars and activists have accepted has been in the critical – one might even venture to say emancipatory – discourse. The Berrigan and Singh models substantiate this claim.

But there is also an aspect that tends away from a straightforward critical stance. There is a variety of community/communication thinking that is "soft path," looking to the warm and friendly connecting point in a ritualistic sensibil-ity, such as in Peck's (1987) formulations. Robert White also reveals this dimen-sion in his construct *communicación popular*, expressing the desire to substitute "communion" for "access," in "a ritual model of communication ... not directed toward extension of messages in time and space in order to influence, but toward the creation, representation and celebration of shared belief" (White, 1980).

Tetsuo Kogawa also cites this almost mystical invocation of communion as part of free radio ideology, under the influence of a Merleau-Pontian phenomeno-logical "redefinition of communication" (Kogawa, 1985).

To be blunt, the ritual-communion community communication perspective is not one I share. As a materialist on the issue, I find the communionists within community communication too idealistic in their ritualistic views. But there is room within the critical perspective for that position as well as my own. The de-bate within critical theory and community communication studies, a class strug-gle of sorts, will continue for an indefinite time. Within the field this can be – and, if critical scholars act responsibly, it will be – a healthy tension that leads to syn-theses and renewed energy.

In this line of inquiry, too, it remains to be seen if community communication can be identified as Marxian in its essential perspective, recognizing that "Marx-ist" and "critical" are not synonymous. It has not been my political purpose in this project to construct and defend a precise (or even imprecise) Marxian community communication. At this historical moment, that would be counterproductive to the young field's development.

In sum, the answer to the question "Is community communication a critical theory?" is, at this moment, yes. We mean by "critical" that it takes its sustenance from oppositional concepts outside the mainstream and that its main proponents are themselves self-identified critical scholars.

Our last submerged issue is the one most in need of elaboration: Granting that community communication is a critical field of study, just how does one do it? We have some answers, both concrete and more general. Some of the British commu-nity communications work includes methodological information that advances our research strategies. Richard Reynish, for example, has offered some sugges-tions in "Notes on the Politics of Information," in which he organizes the media of community interaction around the concepts of community structures (Reynish, 1975).

Some of the recent French research – with Mattelart and Piemme (1980) one example touched upon here – provides direction for our work. Francis Balle and

Idaline Carpe de Baillon report on the future directions of mass media in France, postulating a matrix that allows categories of mediated communication to aid a clarification of "the multiple reciprocal relations of influence, complementarity, exclusion, and substitution existing between the various forms of social exchange." Their four-part typology includes a matrix cell for "media as community amplifier," which allows us to proceed heuristically to extend our understanding of mediated communication in communities (Balle and Baillon, 1983).

John Carpenter's five-category device to sort the elements of community communication systems (1981) can prove a useful strategic tool for research. In her work in community communication, Berrigan has not only made theoretical contributions but has also suggested methods. The chapter in *Community Communications* devoted to "An Appropriate Methodology for Development" proposes an eight-step "possible procedure for the development of community media projects" (Berrigan, 1981).

Berrigan, Singh, and other community communication scholars, as well as the dozens of critical, alternative, and democratic communicators, have all been inspirational. The task we next set for ourselves is the next step for the maturation of the discipline: to generalize from the specific analysis of projects to a building of theory in community communication.

And we are not alone. The mode of inquiry in which we may situate our own development of theory is what Clifford Geertz has called the "refiguration of social thought." This is an organic, and perhaps obvious, place to grow a community communication perspective: It is eclectic, critical, new, and oppositional.

As community communication scholars, then, we must accept as part of our responsibility for the future the task of making a contribution to the "how to do it" of communication studies *and* the behavioural sciences, not just limiting ourselves to our particular corner of those disciplines. Our research strategy, however diverse and multidimensional, must consciously build the movement towards a new paradigm to study social reality – and our goal is not just study but transformation.

References

Balle, Francis and Idaline Carpe de Baillon (1983). "Mass Media Research in France: An Emerging Discipline," *Journal of Communication*, Summer:146-156.

Berrigan, Frances S., ed. (1977). *Access: Some Western Models of Community Media*. Paris: UNESCO Press.

Berrigan, Frances (1981). *Community Communications: The Role of Community Media in Development*. Paris: UNESCO Press.

Carpenter, John (1981). "Community Communications: An Assessment of Local Media in the 80's." Unpublished foundation report.

Eagleton, Terry (1983). *Literary Theory: An Introduction*. Minneapolis: University of Minnesota Press.

Freire, Paulo (1973). *Education for Critical Consciousness*. New York: Seabury/Continuum.

Kogawa, Tetsuo (1985). "Free Radio in Japan." Mimeo.

Kuhn, Thomas S. (1970). *The Structure of Scientific Revolutions.* Second edition. Chicago: University of Chicago Press.

Mattelart, Armand and Jeanne-Marie Piemme (1980). "New Means of Communication: New Questions for the Left," *Media, Culture and Society,* October:321-339.

Nordenstreng, Kaarle (1974). *From Mass Media to Mass Consciousness: Current Thinking in Scandinavia.* Tampere, Finland: University of Tampere.

Peck, M. Scott (1987). *The Different Drum: Community Making and Peace.* New York: Simon and Schuster.

Reynish, Richard (1975). "Notes on the Politics of Information," *Journal of the Center for Advanced Television Studies,* 3,1:2-8.

Schulman, Mark (1986). "Neighborhood Radio as Community Communication." Unpublished doctoral dissertation.

Singh, Kusum (1981). "Community Communication Research." Mimeo.

Singh, Kusum (1982a). "A Note on Research Activities." Mimeo.

Singh, Kusum (1982b). "Some Guidelines for Research and Action on Community Communication." Mimeo.

Singh, Kusum and Bert Gross (1982). "Syllabus for Community Communication: Saint Mary's in the World Community." Mimeo. Moraga, Cal.: Saint Mary's College of California.

Singh, Kusum and Bert Gross (1983). "Democratic Planning: The Bottom-Sideways Approach." Manuscript of book chapter.

Smythe, Dallas and Tran Van Dinh (1983). "On Critical and Administrative Research: A New Critical Analysis," *Journal of Communication,* Summer:117-127.

White, Robert A. (1980) "Communicación Popular; Language of Liberation," *Media Development,* March 3-5.

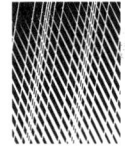

Elitist vs. Democratic Communication: Ronald Reagan and Mohandas Gandhi

Kusum Singh

So in what was nominally a democracy, power was really in the hands of the first citizen.
— *Thucydides*, The Peloponnesian Wars

IN THE TECHNOCRATIC WORLD of information management, the idea of "democracy" is an unwelcome stranger. It suggests the intrusion into top-level decision-making of untutored minds that have not yet learned the difference between a bit and a byte or plumbed the essence of front-end and friendly systems. Democracy may even suggest human values, interests, and needs, all those intangible basics that make human beings different from machines and that, if taken seriously, may lead Have Nots and Have Littles to claim human rights and freedoms that elites feel should be their exclusive privileges.

With enough money and top-top teamwork, however, information managers can program any formal system of representative democracy to sidetrack unfriendly intrusions by non-elites. The inexpert, unrich, unwhite, and even unmale multitudes can be held at bay by selective co-optation, divide-and-conquer strategies, and well-polished imagery. Thus can *representative* democracy, with its constitutional machinery for the bottom-up selection of top leaders, be converted into *image* democracy. Elected officials can then represent a minority of self-serving elites who finance electoral and lobbying campaigns while feeding the majority of people symbolic representation suggesting selfless service to their country.

The most revolutionary technology of our age is not the computer, atomic bomb, outer space travel, or bio-engineering. It is a new technology of undemocratic communication. A new breed of experts has devised effective techniques of manufacturing and disseminating images that undermine democracy by providing people with deceptive information about leaders, events, and countries.

These images invariably cast a mantle of benevolence and high moral commitment around the heads of the most visible political leaders in the "West," "East," and "South." They distract attention from corporatist establishments in which power is concentrated in the hands of behind-the-scene elites who run the machinery.

This corporatist-elitist-imagery apparatus tends to centralize power through undemocratic control of what – in the words of Thucydides – may be "nominally a democracy" (Warner, 1974:164).[1] Entrenched minorities can manipulate elections, legislatures, courts, political parties, and referenda. Westerners are quick to see how this worked in the Soviet Union and other countries with little experience of democratic institutions. But they are often blind to dangerously antidemocratic trends in the countries of democratic capitalism. Indeed, many of the best Western analysts of TV imagery confine themselves to "safe" studies that ignore the imagery that cloaks the highest citadels of power. In trying to avoid controversy, these analysts accept distorted establishment statistics as a touchstone of reality. "Why is it," asks Charles Henry, professor of African-American Studies at the University of California at Berkeley, "that so many American experts on human rights in other countries often close their eyes to the denials of basic rights in their own country?" One answer may be found in Daniel Boorstin's observation that "We are the most illusioned people on earth. Yet we dare not become disillusioned because our illusions are the very house in which we live; they are our news, our heroes, our adventure, our forms of art, our very experience" (Boorstin, 1985:240).

In *Understanding Media* Marshall McLuhan (1965) called television "cool." By that he meant that the "receptor" is drawn into the picture and "thus reaches a high level of involvement." Similarly, even liberals and radicals – along with conservatives and reactionaries – are sometimes sucked into the "cool" corporatist-elitist imagery. The majority of people, in turn, are mobilized as spectators to be titillated and as "human resources" to be shaped, stored, and exploited.

The reelection of Ronald Reagan by popular choice in 1984 is said to be due to "mastery of television." So we are told by many expert commentators who, in crediting or blaming the electronic media, ignore the impact of the substantive images that the Reagan administration had projected through the media. This approach gives the false impression that the technical mastery of television is the secret of image creation. It ignores the creative dramaturgy displayed by teams of competing political consultants, make-up artists, speech writers, policy analysts, researchers, and spokespersons. For a price, these people manufacture images that appeal to the subconscious aspirations, deep emotions, and latent values of target audiences. James Carey, on the other hand, sees a broader problem: "Reagan is not programmed by a conspiratorial class but by the entire culture of the mass media that has contained the real world of experience, politics and people"(Carey, 1987). The images of the Reagan presidency were indeed outstanding in this respect. Political observers are still puzzled by Reagan's personal popularity (even after the Iran-Contra scandal) among large groups of people who rejected most of his policies. One possible explanation is the enormous appeal of a few deeply held values, simply presented, as contrasted with the confusing complexity of such basic issues as war, racism, sexism, poverty, taxation, underemployment, environmental degradation, homophobia, hunger, and homelessness.

"What are the values projected by the political image-makers?" This question can best be answered by applying to political speeches and campaign spectacles the same powerful tools of analysis pioneered by George Gerbner, Larry Gross, and their colleagues in probing imagery and violence in American TV entertainment. As founders of the "cultural indicators" school, these critics have sought to arrive at the "meaning structure" of dominant forms of television output by way of a systematic quantitative analysis of the overt elements of television representation (Gerbner and Gross, 1976; see also Gerbner, 1986). This requires the careful selection of symbols and theme and the development of imaginative hypotheses that can be tested, improved, or disproved by careful monitoring.

Image-makers and their Creations

The devices by which oligarchies deceive the people are five in number ... the assembly, the magistracies, the courts of law, the use of arms, and gymnastic exercises.

– Aristotle, Politics

Today's political scientists often proclaim the decline of old-style party machines without noticing the rise of the more powerful political machinery guarded by the image-makers. Or they debate party realignment while closing their eyes to the realignment of forces in modern corporatism.

If Aristotle were alive today, I suspect he might brush past the bodyguards of imagery and unveil the new corporatist devices of oligarchic control. The devices he enumerated 2,400 years ago still exist. But only the armed forces come near the top of the pyramid. Aristotle's legislators, bureaucrats, courts, and sports are subordinated to superior organs. Nor can any military-industrial complex stand by itself. Rather, it is always part of a broader establishment supported – and at times led – by other powerful components:

Military Leaders	Big Business	Top Politicians
Police	Communication	Welfare
	Science	

The business-military-political elements appear in varying combinations.[2] In a Chile under Pinochet or a Pakistan under General Zia the military chieftains become the top politicians; the most powerful business interests are foreign companies. In most "state socialist" nations, despite the strength of the military and government monopolies, the party is usually top dog. In NATO countries the Big Three sleep together in close embrace.

In all countries the police are available as iron fists for domestic control. The media disseminate velvety myths that both hide and guide human behaviour. In

capitalist countries dissent and unrest are diffused by co-optation, mind management (Schiller, 1973), and varying levels of "welfare" benefits, such as income,
medical services, education, or housing. In communist countries, even more extensive "welfare" benefits did not succeed in crushing dissent and unrest. In
"Third World" democracies and dictatorships alike, the impoverished majorities
are weakened by massive unemployment, poverty, hunger, and ill-health, with
cinema, radio, and now TV being used to cultivate apathy, providing the masses
with an escape from reality. In all countries, science – indigenous or borrowed as
well as applied – underlies the growing forces of production, distribution, and
destruction.

In such labyrinthine establishments, obviously, there can be no all-powerful or
all-knowing Big Brother. If Orwell were to return to the post-1984 world, he
would probably write about a *multiplicity* of Big Brothers. He might even note the
hundreds of faceless *little* brothers operating above, alongside, inside, and below
the machinery of nominal democracy.

In the nominal democracy of Athens, power was in the hands of rich elites (like
Pericles and his fellow slave-owners) who treated other power holders with democratic deference. But neither in peace nor in war would these elites allow the great
majority of slaves, foreign workers, or women to enter the exclusive circle of open
discussion and majority voting. Centuries later a new aristocracy of industrial
elites pushed its way into the charmed circle of representative democracy.

More recently, peasants, workers, peasant and working-class leaders, professionals, technicians, ethnic minorities, and women have insisted that what was
good for VIPs would be good for them also: *democracy for everyone.* But their main
impact, unfortunately, has been to help specialized – and usually docile – elites
enter the exclusive circles. Thus representative democracy usually remains (in
Michael Parenti's words) *democracy for the few* – government of the many by the
few for just a few more (Parenti, 1980).

Moreover, the spirit of technocratic elitism pervades work, education, religion,
politics, and science (Singh, 1977). A foreman, division head, dean, bishop, chair
person, or president enjoys ascribed superiority over his or her "inferiors." The
superiority of the "superiors" is symbolized by more pay, fringe benefits, services,
and respect. As certified specialists in economics, medicine, psychiatry, and law
learn more and more about less and less, they win docile homage from "ordinary"
people. Election campaigners speak the language of ego inflation: "*I* shall be a
strong leader" or "*My* administration will do this or that ..." In so-called Marxist
countries self-selected politburo big shots – now being put to the real test of direct elections – can hardly sit comfortably on super-elitist Olympian heights.

Reagan's Imagery
*I submit to you that I had told the truth.... The truth got there, and in other words, it can
be attractively packaged.*

                                    – *Ronald Reagan,* The New York Times, *June 17, 1976*

The Reagan presidency set a high standard of well-designed and brilliantly executed imagery. A preliminary monitoring of Reagan's major addresses during
most of his two terms as U.S. president reveals at least five images of powerful
emotional appeal: strength, freedom, individualism, patriotism, and sincerity. Using these images Reagan captured the "high ground" from any critics or opponents who countered in terms only of complex policy details or mundane facts. As
far back as 1962, as governor of California, Ronald Reagan stated in his inaugural
message: "For many years now, you and I have been shushed like children and
told there are no simple answers to the complex problems which are beyond our
comprehension. Well, the truth is, there are simple answers."

I have a few preliminary hypotheses regarding the Reagan imagery – hypotheses that, with some adjustment, could be applied to leaders in many other countries. I present them with unrestrained candour with respect to my own images of
political reality. In other words, I reject the image of value-free objectivity as projected by positivist social "scientists." Instead, I think we should develop ways to
unmask the deceptions often projected by all power structures, whether radical,
liberal, or conservative. Such analysis involves transcending the manifest content
of issues and probing into latent images that win support for a leader based on
imagery rather than substance.

Strength. "Standing tall" has been one Ronald Reagan image. His "merry
eyes and open smile" were combined with the confident jutting of his jaw, the
thoughtful tilting of his head, and his quasi-athletic stance to project a well-acted
image of strength. This image masked sustained subservience to corporate lobbies
seeking larger war contracts. For seven long years the image flaunted the ma-
chismo of the nuclear and non-nuclear (but no longer conventional) arms race.
Over two thousand years ago, the Athenian generals at Melos, confident of their
military might, told the people there: "We have the right to our empire.... It is a
general and necessary law of nature to rule whatever one can" (Werner, 1974:400-
408).[3] Similarly, Ronald Reagan exalted the power of an increasingly expensive
and enormously destructive weaponry. But behind the image of nuclear might lies
the reality of weakness. The men in the White House or the Kremlin or the other
countries stockpiling atomic weapons could not use this might without destroying themselves along with the rest of humanity. Nor could either of the so-called
superpowers subdue small, "backward" countries on or near their borders – not
Afghanistan and not Nicaragua.

Reagan mimicry has not been limited to conservative leaders in Britain, Canada,
West Germany, and Japan. Mitterand in France and Gonzalez in Spain weakly
kow-tow before the new gods of "high-tech" militarism. In India and Pakistan,
Rajiv Gandhi and the Pakistani militarists built up their images as strong men
while meekly submitting to the pressures of transnational corporations, the desires
of home-grown militarists, and the worst instincts of Hindu and Moslem extremists.

Freedom. The wolf and the sheep, wrote Abraham Lincoln long ago, seldom
agree on the nature of freedom.

Today's wolves wear sheep's clothing designed by experts. Economists like Milton Friedman weave "free market" and "free trade" disguises. With their help, business oligarchies have more freedom to rig prices, swallow up small businesses, and devastate entire communities by moving to countries with the most efficient anti-labour dictatorships.

Western communications experts use the rhetoric of the "free flow of information." Behind this disguise, Western media disseminate the cultural values of Superman, Mission Impossible, and the NATO-dominated marketplace. They make the false charge that UNESCO is trying to licence journalists. At UNESCO, Second and Third World experts call for a "balanced flow" to provide more positive images of the East and South. But in "Third World countries dominated by repressive minority regimes" (to use the words of Gabriel Garcia Marquez of Colombia and Juan Somavia, a Chilean refugee), "balance" means censorship – often with the avowed purpose of suppressing unfavourable information (Singh and Gross, 1984; see also UNESCO, 1980). In India, after 2,500 people were officially reported dead due to the leak at the Union Carbide plant in Bhopal, the local government stopped issuing death certificates. At Union Carbide headquarters in the United States, Burston-Marstellar – one of the world's largest public-relations firms – developed a doctrine of apparent candour to guide the company's public statements (Everest, 1986).

Throughout the world transnational corporations have spent millions to prevent the free flow of information on their use of chemicals that damage workers, consumers, and the environment or on the trickery in their pricing and tax evasion schemes. This helps expand their own freedom to cultivate a high-cost executive addiction to power and privilege. Their efforts are helped by statistical misinformation on the true extent of unemployment and underemployment, particularly in Third World countries. In turn, labour movements have helped out by abandoning serious efforts to organize the unemployed, raise the banner of "the right to earn a living," or mobilize people behind full employment programs (Gross, 1987). This failure is particularly striking in countries such as India, China, Yugoslavia, and Mexico, where underemployment is of massive proportions and appears to be getting worse.

Meanwhile, the great majority of people also have different freedoms. The jobless and the underemployed are free to "take it or leave it." They are free to starve, languish on public assistance (where available), or risk life and limb in the "underground economy." In most countries everyone is free to vote. In some countries people are free to vote for only one candidate and in other countries they are free to choose among opposing candidates with converging policies. In the United States, they are also free not to vote – and in 1984 47 per cent of potential voters used this freedom. Thus, in 1984, with 59 per cent of the votes actually cast, Reagan was supported by less than 32 per cent of the voting-age population. Some 68 per cent of the voting-age population voted for either Democratic candidate Walter Mondale or nobody – with many having little idea of the difference between the two. In 1988, Michael Dukakis's imagery concentrated on technical issues rather than values, while George Bush, with the brilliant help of Lee Atwater and other media manipulators, pinned on Dukakis the image of an unpatriotic bureaucrat who was weak on crime, defence, and even saluting the flag.

Individualism. "Look out for Number One." This individual-as-hero image is a favourite of free-market ideologues. It helps mask the political and economic networks that nurture the accumulation of wealth and power in Silicon Valleys and military-industrial complexes. It also promotes the social fragmentation that diminishes the power of all others. Already divided by galloping specialization, people in both the middle and lower classes are further divided into single-issue interest groups and then privatized down to narcissistic "me First" atoms.

In an overcomputerized world, everyone (like adults in many countries today) will have a unique identification number. But in terms of political power, a few billion people could end up with numbers even lower than the rights of three-fifths of a person granted to slaves in the U.S. constitution of 1789. Many might even be close to ZERO.

People are already learning how to survive as near-zeros. TV, films, and music – along with high dosages of alcohol, drugs, and pornography – suck people up into delusions of individual power: superconsumerism, supercharm, supercleverness, and – hurrah – supersex. Some people feel they are only half-zeros, trying to work their way up to full-zero status.

Outside this dream world, some people compensate for a sense of inadequacy by adopting nightmarish stereotypes that demonize WASPS, "uppity blacks," "pushy females," "money-grubbing Jews," "drunken Irish," "stupid Poles," or Third World "rabble." These racist, sexist, and chauvinist horrors are outdone by the atomization of entire populations through state terrorism in Central America, "religious" wars like the one between Iraq and Iran, and the "state socialist" wars that devastated Afghanistan, Cambodia, and Ethiopia.

Patriotism. "Patriotism," wrote Samuel Johnson, "is the last refuge of a scoundrel." Ambrose Bierce retorted: "I beg to submit it is the first" (cited in Gross, 1988).

I submit that they were both wrong. Like some of the people I know, Johnson and Bierce were reluctant to express their own love of country. They each made the mistake of equating militarism, chauvinism, or xenophobia with love of country. They failed to detect the difference between genuine patriotism and the "pretended patriotism" that George Washington warned against in his farewell address.

In both West and East, North and South, flag-waving is a favourite way to project vested interests as national interests and protect them from criticism. To the extent that this strategy is successful, bogus patriots can then mobilize support for imperial adventures that distract attention from domestic failures. They can condemn as disloyal any genuine patriots whose loyalty to country surpasses their tolerance of self-serving leaders.

George Orwell pointed much of this out decades ago:

One cannot see the modern world as it is unless one recognises the over-whelming strength of patriotism, national loyalty.... As a *positive* force there is nothing to set beside it. Christianity and international Socialism are as weak as straw in comparison with it. Hitler and Mussolini rose to power in their own countries very largely because they could grasp this fact and their opponents could not. (Orwell, 1941:75)

For the Soviet militarists, patriotic flag-waving justified for decades their special privileges at the cost of inflicting death and destruction on the people of Afghani-stan and more sluggishness on the Soviet economy. For the leaders of Commu-nist China, brutal suppression of non-violent student demonstrations for reform and democracy was justified on the ground that the demonstrations were under-mining national interests. For the United States, flag-waving helps justify the ex-cessive military spending that bolstered the U.S. economy while wrecking the economies of Southeast Asia and Central America – and slaughtering tens of thou-sands of people there.

Sincerity. Reagan's sincerity flowed from a well-acted illusion of deep thought and conviction. He appeared to believe the illusions he himself helped create. This ability is not surprising considering that he was an actor before being a politician. Actors succeed or fail, one would think, based not on the truth of what they say but rather on the effect of the lines scripted for them by others. Any viewer of network news will recognize "Reagan's choreography of candour" (Wills, 1987). Reagan explained it in his autobiography, *Where's The Rest of Me?*: "So much of our profession is taken up with pretending that an actor must spend at least half of his waking hours in a fantasy" (Reagan and Hubler, 1965). Has Reagan helped U.S. politics to cross some invisible line between reality and im-agery? John Buckley, a Republican political consultant, maintains: "There is no longer a value judgment on the need to tailor a message to television. It's now a matter of survival, not a matter of ethics or intellectual honesty" (*The New York Times*, October 2, 1988).

This need might also justify Reagan's remarkable capacity to mould all infor-mation to fit his ideological conviction. Stories that demean welfare recipients were accepted as true while information detrimental to the Pentagon was held suspect. He would rather change facts than his mind (Green and MacColl, 1983). Was Reagan, then, insincere or negligent with the truth? Did he really believe that he had never favoured voluntary social security, or that he had never expressed indifference to nuclear proliferation, or that he had appointed more women to government posts than his predecessor, or that he had vastly reduced the welfare rolls in California? In a triumph of belief over reality, Reagan seemed to have per-suaded himself that he was forever stating nothing but the truth. "It is a psycho-drama starring President Reagan and bringing his listeners into communion with his experience of interpreting the original texts" (Erickson, 1985).

Comparing Reagan With Gandhi

Mohandas Gandhi, who came to be known as the Mahatma (great soul), provides an intriguing, if somewhat startling, comparison to Reagan's imagery and style of leadership. There are, of course, fundamental sociocultural and political differences, not only between India and the United States but also between the two men themselves. Reagan was tall and handsome, with a strong, square jaw, broad forehead, clear almond-shaped eyes, and dark eyebrows. Gandhi, on the other hand, was tiny, barely five feet tall, with "his ears flared out from his oversized head like the handles of a sugar bowl." Obviously, nature had not meant him to belong to the distinguished galaxy of "politically attractive" leaders. And yet Gandhi, in a century of ranting demagogues and shrieking dictators, captivated not only the foreign press but also people around the world through sheer moral force – and without raising his voice.

My review of Gandhi's imagery may appear to some critics as more "friendly" than critical. I recognize the fact that leaders, like most of us, have both good and bad characteristics. Therefore, conclusions based on a "critical" review of Gandhi's imagery could be quite different, as they would be coming from a "friendly" review of Reagan's imagery. More importantly, Gandhi's relationship with his people was influenced by the fact that he was leading a national liberation movement against a powerful foreign enemy, whereas Reagan, as leader of a "superpower," was more preoccupied with remaining *in* power. However, in today's precarious post-Cold War world, Gandhi's legacy of non-violent activism is of special interest and of some relevance for people around the world. It was Gandhi, the little old man whom Winston Churchill had called "the naked fakir," who shook the power of the imperialists in India by leading a non-violent movement against their military might. How was this "communication miracle" achieved by Gandhi and his associates when they had almost no access to the media of communication: the press, the radio, the schools, and the major bureaucratic organizations? Their genius lay in the fact that they set out to develop a more effective means of communication through interpersonal, mass, and political organizations that enabled them to transcend the divisions imposed by religion, caste, language, gender, and social role. To the extent that this bottom-sideways outreach was successful in reaching hundreds of millions of illiterate peasants, workers, and tradesmen across the country, Gandhi's messages up the ladder of the British monarchy were no longer humble petitions from submissive subjects: they had people's power behind them.

Comparing Reagan with Gandhi might help reveal some fundamental symbolic behaviour of politicians whose substantive meaning may be strikingly different. At the risk of simplifying a complex process, the question that needs to be addressed is: How do we identify the genuine democratic characteristics of a leader from that of an elitist one? What styles of leadership encourage the dependency of followers on the leader and what kind of behaviour and action on the part of a leader encourages the self-reliance and self-confidence of followers in doing things in co-operation with other people?

In Europe and North America the popular image of Gandhi is that he was a charismatic leader. This is correct only for Gandhi's image after he was killed in 1948. From that time, he was deified. But during his long struggle for liberation – particularly during the 1930s and the 1940s – the strength of Gandhi's leadership derived from the fact that his image was that of an ordinary person, a common man with a common touch. And this image was based on reality, not on ingenious concoction. He developed a style of democratic leadership that was not quite in keeping with the elitist traditions of the Indian Congress Party. While the Indian intellectuals discussed and wrote papers and articles about how to approach problems and organize the masses, Gandhi and his associates were out among the people, sharing their daily hardships and poverty and speaking a language that the people understood. Thus Gandhi was able to transform an elite struggle into an open popular movement.

There is no doubt that both Reagan and Gandhi captured the "high ground" from their adversaries through strong symbolic appeal. They enunciated positions that were strongly held and simply formulated. Both performed well on the world stage and were hailed as "Great Communicators" by supporters and opponents alike. While Reagan was a successful deliverer of homilies off a Teleprompter, Gandhi used the foreign press (and to some extent the anti-Gandhi national press) to make the world his confessor in matters large and small, from his inmost spiritual longings to the life of the bed and the latrine. While Reagan had at his disposal the most sophisticated communication technologies and professional advice, Gandhi relied on the extremely primitive but intimate human system of mass communication. As Gandhi declared in his newspaper, *Harijan*, which was often shut down by the British, "Let everyone become his walking newspaper and carry the good news from mouth to mouth.... This no government can suppress. It is the cheapest newspaper yet devised, and it defies the wit of government, however clever it may be" (October 24, 1940).

Gandhi exercised his authority from an *ashram* that had no radio, electricity, or running water, and the nearest telephone was thirty miles or so away by foot.[4] Yet his message reached the remote corners of an enormous continent. He used his life as a great drama and kept the world's attention on his historic marches and fasts against the injustices inflicted on the "poorest of the poor" by the Indian elite and the British regime.[5] One can only speculate how he would have used television and the new technologies of communication. It is safe to assume that he would not have fallen a prey to the merely "photo opportunity" gimmickry of the media at the expense of addressing the serious human and political problems of our times.

Furthermore, Gandhi, unlike Reagan, believed that ends and means were inseparable, which precluded the possibility of using violence. His principle of *satyagraha* (truth-force) helped build a political movement based on "soul-force" rather than "physical force," a movement concerned with reaching the heart and the conscience of an opponent through the activist's own personal suffering and self-sacrifice. Gandhi's struggle, in other words, was firmly based on the principle of conversion, not domination.[6]

The clue to the sharply different qualities of Gandhi's leadership is suggested by his own often repeated remark that "He was all the time fighting on three fronts – against himself, against Indians, and against the British" (Joshi, 1980; Singh, 1979). The key to the achievement of national freedom, Gandhi pointed out, lay in remoulding national character and in developing the capacity for self-governance. And the remoulding of national character required much more than struggle against the enemy outside (that is, the colonial system of exploitation); it required continuous struggle against the enemy inside (against the ignorance, selfishness, cowardice, and moral degradation of people and leaders alike).

How are we to differentiate Gandhi's sincerity from that of Reagan's? A "critical" analysis of latent images might reveal that Gandhi was indeed a shrewd politician who was able to win over the illiterate peasants by appealing to the spiritual heritage of the Indian culture. As one of my students very wisely inquired, "Wasn't Gandhi tricking people when he changed his clothing from western dress to that of a loin cloth?"[7] It would indeed be easy to perceive of this transformation as a confidence trick, if it were not for the fact that Gandhi did more than merely change his clothes: He risked his own life in non-violent combat against the military might of the British (Singh, 1984; for more detail, Singh, 1978). It was this personal example of courage that aroused the moral conscience of most followers and even of many adversaries. Indeed, it was this example that inspired a spirit of trust and fearless initiative among the so-called powerless people of India, which in turn brought about the overthrow of a ruthless imperial power through non-violent action.

Replacing Elitist Imagery

This leads me to examine those truly democratic currents in American life today that Mohandas Gandhi would certainly applaud, if he were alive. Although still weak and fragmented, nevertheless these currents have the potential of replacing present-day elitism, corporatism, and false imagery.

There are many people today in the United States who are trying to organize effective movements on behalf of extremely important, even structural, reforms in the social order. The most effective thus far have been people struggling for women's liberation, labour, civil rights, the rights of the disabled, environmental protection, and the cessation of U.S. intervention in certain other countries. Many people have been actively trying to build stronger movements in the fields of peace, gay and lesbian rights, reproductive rights, the "right to life," crime prevention, victims' rights, and drug addiction. A new spirit of initiative and self-help seems to be arising to counterbalance the power of foremen, know-it-all professionals, politicians, bureaucrats and plutocrats, hierarchs and husbands. They are trying to cure themselves as well as others of deep-rooted social diseases: sexism, racism, ageism, anti-semitism, and homophobia. Without falling into the laissez-faire trap of "everybody do your own thing," they are inventing new styles of democratic and accountable leadership. They are trying to organize the unorganized in ways that might counter inevitable tendencies towards oligarchy. "We too," they say, "are smart enough to take charge of our own lives."

There are also important examples of resistance to corporatism: for instance, the displacement of dictatorial or authoritarian right-wing regimes in Argentina, Haiti, the Philippines, and Uruguay, and the anti-apartheid movement in South Africa. More recent examples are the dramatic pro-democracy movements in China, Poland, Hungary, and South Korea, and in East European countries where people have displaced well-armed dictatorships. In some countries of constitutional capitalism a new idea is arising: a *democratic* corporatism to replace behind-the-scenes planning by the exclusive corporatists. In this idea, labour would win senior, not junior, status – something possible only if labour can become stronger, more transnational, and more democratic. The bottom-sideways-and-up machinery of formal representation can yield more genuine representation when people and groups reach out to each other across many boundaries that divide them.

At a time of moral disarray, new attention is being given to basic moral values as a guide to policy on specific issues. The high ideals of justice and community have long been professed – but often forgotten – by Christians, Jews, Hindus, Moslems, and Buddhists. In Latin America, liberation theologians have revived them in reaction against oppression and poverty. In more positive terms, the American Catholic bishops have tried to apply them to the United States. They hope to spark a popular movement against (in the Bishops' words) "the sins of indifference and greed."[8]

Finally, there are many – uncelebrated by the media and virtually unknown to everyone except those among whom they live – who are making more democratic use of media as well as reviving non-media (people to people) communication. In India, after the British were thrown out and Gandhi assassinated, there were still thousands of Gandhi's followers who wanted to continue in Gandhi's tradition. But they were overwhelmed by a new surge coming from the new elites of modern India to convert Gandhi into a unique charismatic leader (Willner, 1984).[9] Today, however, some progress has been made in developing both the philosophy and practice of non-commercial communication through decentralized use of small-scale, low-cost, and intermediate technologies.

Basically, the central potentiality for the emergence of more democratic leaders lies in the scepticism of those who reject the notion of charismatic solutions to democratic problems (Singh, 1981). After the experience of Vietnam, Cambodia, Watergate, and the Iran-Contra affair, people have become wary of inflated claims of elitist superiority on the part of today's leaders. Fortunately, this negative opposition is shaping into something more positive. The moral vision that Gandhi envisioned can move the hearts and souls of people and would surely include:

- the *strength* that utterly rejects the tradition that Might (in the form of violence) Makes Right and is based rather on non-violent resistance to militarism and aggression;

- the *freedom* that consists of a fabric of rights and rules that, as Gandhi put it, "guarantee to our opponents the same freedom we claim for ourselves";
- the genuine *individualism* that can thrive healthily among persons who see themselves as part of a human community rather than lonely specks of dust;
- the true *patriotism* that recognizes interdependent interests in a deeply divided world and, in Gandhi's words, "admits of no enmity or ill-will" towards people of other nations and is based upon open debate concerning national interests rather than blind acceptance of the narrow interests of self-serving leaders;
- *sincerity* reflecting deep conviction and selfless action towards the building of a solid democratic society.

Could action based on these values not only save people from the destructive policies but in fact save the elites and corporatist leaders themselves?

"Improbable!" is the first response. The hopeful currents seem hopelessly divided. They are fragmented by single-issue myopia, by localism, by nationalism – and, alas, by sexism, racism, and religious prejudice. This is a tragedy of our era.

Can intellectuals help reverse this trend?

In part, without doubt. Many communication researchers have already shown remarkable strength – both intellectual and moral – in exposing the myriad misuses of the media. Where would we be today without the contributions – to mention but a few – of Ben Bagdikian, Eric Barnouw, Luis Ramiro Beltran, Noam Chomsky, K.E. Eapen, George Gerbner, Larry Gross, Cees Hamelink, Kaarle Nordenstreng, Colleen Roach, Juan Somavia, Herbert Schiller, and Janet Wasko?

But there are also obvious difficulties. The best work of these and hundreds of less well-known researchers has been "against the stream," underfunded, and – as one might expect – either ignored or distorted by the mass media. Moreover, it is not easy for any researcher to escape the dead hand of value-free positivism and face up openly to the value premises that guide all research. It is not easy to invigorate creative thought and observation by openly participating in the great debates and struggles of our era. I would like to think that most mass communication researchers will surmount these difficulties, and get engaged in serious image analysis, as suggested by Kenneth Boulding (1956).[10] These days we hear a great deal about the power of image, but very few have yet admitted that this power expresses an important change in our way of thinking.[11] What are the epistemological and philosophical implications of this change?

Apart from the natural beauty of our planet, good things have always been improbable. For millennia human life on earth was itself improbable. So, for centuries, was freedom from slavery and serfdom. So was the beginning of women's emancipation and of civil rights for African Americans. In 1972 we saw the "impossible" come to pass, as the fiercest anti-communist in the United States suddenly went to China and then signed the first détente agreements with Leonid Brezhnev. More recently a Soviet leader who had worked loyally under Brezhnev slowly emerged as the spokesman for a new generation of Soviet intellectuals and workers who were fed up with the Brezhnev version of Stalinism. And in slow response to Gorbachev's *glasnost* and *perestroika*, Ronald Reagan started to put some new content into his old-time symbolism. After astounding his militarist constituents by advocating the elimination of all nuclear weapons, he backed an INF treaty that won more support from Democrats than from Republicans. Above all, he helped usher in a new era in which the "cold war" confrontation with the Soviet Union began to wind down. Under these new circumstances, many hawks and doves – and even the academic owls who study and teach communications in departments of literature, drama, politics, anthropology, sociology – are struggling to reconceptualize, in the timeless phrase of Justice Oliver Wendell Holmes, Jr. – their "inarticulate major premises."

Notes

1. As an aristocratic critic of Athenian democracy, Thucydides helped establish the tradition of exaggerating. He suggested that the power was really in the hands of "the first citizen," namely Pericles. While this argument ignored the elite companions of Pericles, it also had the great historic merit (thus far ignored by most commentators on the classics) of making the first recorded distinction between "nominal" and "real" or "true" democracy.
2. The chart is an oversimplified summation of the more complex presentation in Gross (1982).
3. In *The Republic* Plato has Callicles "declaring openly what the rest of the world think, but do not like to say": namely, that the strong rule the weak. In addition to arguing this point stubbornly, Callicles quotes the poet Pindar to the effect that *law itself* "makes might to be right."
4. The *ashram* was a communal settlement under Gandhi's direction and devoted to the purification of its members. Through spinning, vegetarianism, and asceticism, the members of the settlement were to become servants of truth.
5. For example, on April 6, 1930, when Gandhi picked up a few grains of salt from the Dandi beach and thereby broke the law, the eyes of the nation followed his every move. His simple symbolic gesture told India what it must do, while the foreign press held its breath to see what the British would do.
6. In the United States, Martin Luther King, Jr. embraced *satyagraha* as the only moral and practical way for oppressed people to struggle against social injustice. See Oates (1982).
7. This question came up in my January 1987 interdisciplinary course on "Two Faces of Charisma" at Saint Mary's College of California. It was further analyzed by the Communication seniors in the following spring semester course, "Image and Charisma."
8. In their pastoral letter on the U.S. economy the Bishops called for "a new American experiment" in overall planning based on the ethics of social justice and community solidarity. They united morality with economic policy through the principle that "All persons have rights in the economic sphere." They advocated a package of full employment policies to guarantee the right to earn a living at good wages. Beyond this, they affirmed most of the rights formally accepted (but largely deserted) by the many signatories to the UN Covenant on Economic and Social Rights.
9. In my courses on charisma, while I used the classic writings of Max Weber and many other authors (including the writers on the religious aspects of the subject), the students found that Willner (1984) not only provided the best overview of the subject but was also the only text that went far beyond Weber.

10. The concept of image in Boulding (1956) relates basically to anything that is *perceived*, as distinguished from Boorstin's concept, which relates only to those images defined by him as "pseudo-events."
11. Brian McNair (1988) looks at recent developments associated with the rise of Mikhail Gorbachev in the Soviet Union and their effects on Western media coverage of Soviet affairs.

References

Boorstin, Daniel J. (1985). *The Image: A Guide to Pseudo-Events in America*. New York: Atheneum.

Boulding, Kenneth (1956). *The Image*. Ann Arbor: University of Michigan Press.

Carey, James (1987). "Reagan and the Mythology of the American Childhood," *In These Times*, August 19-September 1.

Erickson, Paul D. (1985). *Reagan Speaks: The Making of an American Myth*. New York: New York University Press.

Everest, Larry (1986). *Behind the Poison Cloud: Union Carbide's Bhopal Massacre*. Chicago: Banner Press.

Gerbner, George (1986). "Television Imagery and the New Populism." Paper presented at the International Association for Mass Communications Research, New Delhi, August 29.

Gerbner, George and Larry Gross (1976). "Living with Television: The Violence Profile," *Journal of Communication*, 26,2:172-199.

Gerbner, George and Marsha Siefert, eds. (1984). *World Communication: A Handbook*. New York: Longman.

Green, Mark and Gail MacColl (1983). *There He Goes Again: Reagan's Reign of Terror*. New York: Longman.

Gross, Bertram (1982). "The Mysterious Establishment." In *Friendly Fascism: The New Face of Power*. Boston: South End Press.

Gross, Bertram (1987). "Toward Global Action." In Bertram Gross and Alfred Pfaller, eds., *Unemployment: A Global Challenge*. The Annals of the American Academy of Political and Social Science, July.

Gross, Bertram (1988). "Loving the Best of America, Changing the Worst," *New Patriot*, May.

Joshi, P.C. (1980). "Gandhi and Today's Mass Politics," *Mainstream*, October 25.

MacBride Report (1980). *Many Voices, One World: Communication and Society, Today and Tomorrow: Towards a More Just and More Efficient World Information and Communication Order*. "Report by the International Commission for the Study of Communication Problems." London: K. Page.

McLuhan, Marshall (1965). *Understanding Media: The Extensions of Man*. New York: New American Library.

McNair, Brian (1988). *Images of the Enemy*. London: Routledge.

Miller, William Lee (1975). *Of Thee, Nevertheless, I Sing: An Essay on American Political Values*. New York: Harcourt Brace Jovanovich.

Oates, Stephen B. (1982). *Let the Trumpet Sound: The Life of Martin Luther King, Jr.* New York: Harper & Row.

Orwell, George (1941). "The Lion and the Unicorn." In *The Collected Essays, Journalism and Letters of George Orwell*, Vol.2, *My Country Right or Left*. Harmondsworth, Middlesex: Penguin Books, 1970.

Parenti, Michael (1980). *Democracy for the Few*. New York: St. Martin's Press.

Reagan, Ronald and Richard G. Hubler (1965). *Where's the Rest of Me?* New York: Duell, Sloan and Pearce.

Schiller, Herbert (1973). *Mind Management*. Boston: Beacon Press.
Singh, Kusum (1977). "Elite Control and Challenge in Changing India." In George Gerbner, ed., *Mass Media Policies in Changing Cultures*. New York: John Wiley & Sons.
Singh, Kusum (1978). "Gandhi and Mao as Communicators: A Comparative Study of Practice and Theory." Dissertation, University of Pennsylvania.
Singh, Kusum (1981). "People Against Charisma," *Communicator*, October.
Singh, Kusum (1984). "Mass Line Communication: Liberation Movements in China and India." In Gerbner and Siefert (1984).
Singh, Kusum and Bertram Gross (1984). "The MacBride Report: The Results and Response." In Gerbner and Siefert (1984).
Warner, Rex, tr. (1974). *The Peloponnesian Wars*. London: Penguin Books.
Willner, Ann Ruth (1984). *The Spellbinders: Charismatic Political Leadership*. New Haven, Conn.: Yale University Press.
Wills, Gary (1987). *Reagan's America: Innocents at Home*. New York: Doubleday & Company.

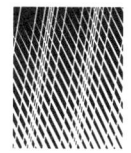

Part II

Information Age Technologies: New Promises, Old Problems

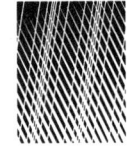

Gulf War in the Global Village: CNN, Democracy, and the Information Age

Dwayne Winseck

AFUNDAMENTAL FEATURE of the emerging information age is the evolution of large-scale international media organizations. During the 1980s, media moguls and pundits alike repeatedly suggested that the future is likely to see worldwide news and cultural production controlled by a handful of large media organizations with a wide range of intra- and extra-media ties (see, for example, Bagdikian, 1990:6; Murdock, 1982). One such relatively new media giant in this so-called information age is Cable News Network (CNN).

CNN has been proffered by the popular press as the incarnation of public benefits in the information age. As *Newsweek* suggests, the twenty-four-hour "all news" channel has brought to fruition Marshall McLuhan's Global Village (Alter, 1990:48). Meanwhile, the cable channel itself rides the euphoria surrounding the futuristic notions of the "global village" when it promises to take us "around the world in thirty minutes."

Throughout the Gulf War of 1991, CNN solidified these sentiments economically and ideologically. In early 1991 *Time* magazine called it the "undisputed star of [Gulf War] coverage, affirming its credibility and world wide clout with new authority" (Zoglin, 1991:69). CNN emerged from the Gulf War increasingly represented as a positive new convergence of technology, communication, entrepreneurship, and democracy in the unfolding "information age." This representation extended prevailing opinion among journalists, academics, and policy-makers, who consistently cite the network as a concrete exemplar of what the public should come to expect from developments in communications technology, a free-market press, and the information age in general (United States Subcommittee on Communications, 1989a, 1989b; Wallace and Baran, 1990).

That the news network was prominent in this period and took on immense proportions underscores the importance of this analysis. As numerous studies have found, given events in which people lack preexistent cognitive structures to absorb new knowledge, the operations of news organizations like CNN become decisive in the formation of public opinion (Lippmann, 1922/81; Park, 1974; Gitlin, 1978). Indeed, the relative ambivalence and opinion swings expressed in public-opinion polls leading up to the outbreak of the Gulf War provide support for arguments based on media dependence.[1] Indeed, researchers Sut Jhally, Justin Lewis, and Michael Morgan have recently demonstrated an inverse correlation between television viewership and knowledge of fundamental issues underlying the war, and about the Middle East in general (cited in "TV: The More You Watch ...", 1991:11). In another survey, 73 per cent of the respondents were unaware that just a few years earlier, "The U.S. had supplied arms to Iraq during its war with Iran" ("TV: The More You Watch ...", 1991:8).

Of course, a counterargument can be raised that this "ignorance factor" can be rectified by abundant and competing sources of information. However, this claim, for the most part, can be challenged by three features of media coverage in the Gulf War: (a) the press pool; (b) CNN's supply of information to other news organizations; and (c) CNN's agenda-setting role. In addition, it can be argued that these are only the focused phenomenon of continuing developments in North American media.

The Political Economy of CNN

A political-economic analysis of CNN in the context of its Gulf War coverage can identify some of the structural possibilities for democratic communication in the information age. Such a study identifies the structural relations of the network, outlines its emerging function within the U.S. media system, and illustrates the structures and practices undergirding its "mode of information production."

Cowboy or Corporate Capitalism?

Turner Broadcasting Systems (TBS), the parent company of CNN, is an international media enterprise with extensive structural ties to the rest of the U.S. media industry. TBS itself consists of CNN, Turner Network Television, SuperStation WTBS, CNN Radio Network, Turner Film Library, joint ownership with HBO of two satellite transponders, as well as real estate holdings. In 1990 its revenues surpassed $1 billion (TBS, 1990:13). Of all of the operations, CNN was the largest source of revenue, bringing in about $417 million. This made CNN the second-largest cable programming service in the United States (TBS, 1989:46).[2]

In international operations CNN has committed substantial resources to news gathering. It has twenty news bureaus, nine of them located in the United States, with the rest overseas (Beijing, Cairo, Frankfurt, Jerusalem, London, Managua, Moscow, Nairobi, Paris, Rome, and Tokyo) (TBS, 1990). From each of its news bureaus, sophisticated news gathering equipment and satellite transmission enable the staff to go live immediately. The network can reach 162 countries. To operate this system CNN has a staff of 1,278 news employees, who remain mostly non-unionized, despite attempts by the National Association of Broadcast Employees and Technicians (NABET) to organize TBS staff (TBS, 1989:15). To bolster its news collection capabilities the network also uses other news services and some freelance journalists. In the United States CNN has also become a full-fledged member of the White House Press Corps.

It has been suggested that CNN's international news operations are not those of a typical news network but are more similar to a "video wire service" (Anderson and Carpignano, 1991:12). This appearance of an international video wire service stems from "barter agreements" and the sale of its news on a national and international basis. Through such agreements local stations bypass network affiliates; and foreign broadcasters, instead of gathering their own news, pay "annual subscription fees" for content provided by CNN. For example, Swedish Television pays an annual fee of $160,000 to use one hour of CNN news per day (Wallace and Baran, 1990:87). Additionally, a number of foreign hotels and embassies also subscribe (106). This international "subscriber base" is accomplished through a system of sales agents with sales offices in three U.S. cities and seven abroad. This international and domestic network of subscribers became increasingly active during the Gulf War, underscoring the importance of CNN's performance during that time.[3]

Through the revenues generated by this extensive international network, TBS qualified for membership to the Fortune 500 in 1990 (Kretchmar and Labate, 1990:298). Contrary to notions in the popular press and promulgated by TBS, however, CNN is not solely an extension of Ted Turner or the product of "cowboy capitalism." Although Turner promotes this image when he invites the public to be partners in CNN for only $15 (per share), the economic organization and concentration of power at TBS is contained in the hands of a few familiar media elites ("Ownership Opportunity," 1991:84).

While Turner retains ultimate control of TBS operations, responsibility for the media empire is shared with two major as well as two lesser communication companies. These four companies are: Time Warner Inc., the largest media organization in the world (Kellner, 1990:66); Tele-Communications Inc. (TCI), the largest vertically integrated cable company in the United States; Continental Communications, the third largest cable company in the country; and Comcast, the fourth largest cable company ("Field Guide," 1991:48).

Two key measures are helpful in understanding where corporate control lies at CNN: share ownership and representation on the Board of Directors. First of all, TBS has over seventy-five million shares of stock outstanding. About 65 per cent of these shares are held by Turner, TCI, and Time Warner Inc. (TBS, 1990:7-8). When the Continental and Comcast stock ownership is added, 75 per cent of all stock is owned by five companies (TBS, 1990:12).

If only those shares with voting privileges are tabulated, the five companies own 85 per cent of such stock. Furthermore, the authority of Turner's 45 per cent ownership share is tempered by stockholder rules that concentrate veto power in a class of stock overwhelmingly owned by TCI and Time Warner Inc. This rule accentuates the power of TCI and Time Warner Inc. over corporate policy-making at TBS (TBS, 1990:2,7,8). Thus, three factors are apparent. First, TBS is not a widely held company. Second, control of its operations is concentrated. Third, the structure of stock ownership in the company constrains unilateral action by Turner.

The importance of this concentration becomes increasingly apparent given the ability to translate stock ownership into effective representation on the Board of Directors. Out of sixteen Board of Director positions, nine are controlled by Turner and the remaining seven are shared by the other companies (TBS, 1990). The positions held by the outside directors can be translated into *real* power, as shown by recent events when the president of TCI, John Malone, proved instrumental in aborting CNN's attempt to acquire the Financial News Network (Mahar, 1989:18).

"Private Ministries of Information" and the United States Information Agency

These structural ties between CNN, Time Warner Inc., TCI, Continental Cable Co., and Comcast are particularly revealing because the information and cultural products offered by these companies, once amalgamated, account for a significant portion of what people in the United States, and increasingly the rest of the world, watch, listen, and read each day. This is one aspect of what Ben Bagdikian has called the Private Ministry of Information and Culture. As Bagdikian states, "Today fifty corporations own most of the output of daily newspapers and most of the sales and audience in magazines, broadcasting, books and movies. The fifty men and women who head these corporations would fit in a large room. They constitute the Private Ministry of Information and Culture" (1990:xx). It seems clear, from the evidence presented here, that CNN, especially through its ties to the largest U.S. media corporations, is a member of this "Private Ministry of Information and Culture."

Through their cable operations, the companies affiliated with CNN gain access to 25.2 million homes in the United States, or about half of the nation's cable subscribers ("Cable's Top 50 MSO's," 1990:54; "Field Guide," 1991:48). In addition, the companies, mostly through TCI, have an interest in at least twenty television stations and fifteen radio stations. They also have varying degrees of ownership in four out of the top five pay cable networks, representing nearly 90 per cent of the pay cable networks' subscriber base. In pay-per-view programming services, the four companies again dominate, securing subscriptions from over 50 per cent of pay-per-view subscribers.

From all of these operations in 1986, TBS, Time Warner Inc., TCI, and Continental Cable earned $5.1 billion.[4] This was about 25 per cent of all revenue generated by the top twenty-five electronic media corporations that year ("Field Guide," 1991:47-51). By 1990, total revenues for these four companies were estimated at $7 billion.[5] If, as Bagdikian asserts, "Seventeen firms receive half or more of all [industry] revenue," these companies could be conservatively estimated as controlling between 12 and 15 per cent of all electronic media revenues (Bagdikian, 1990:18-19). This figure would cross the 10 per cent threshold commonly used to analyze and diagnose market competitiveness (Zeitlin, 1974; Wasko, 1984).

More Control: Following the Thread that Binds

Although this analysis reveals the extensive integration of CNN and dominant U.S. media, additional sources of potential influence arise. These stem from a number of mutually beneficial reciprocal agreements between TBS, Time Warner Inc., TCI, Continental Cable, and Comcast. These agreements are basically of three kinds: (1) carriage and subscription-fee remittance contracts; (2) advertising contracts; and (3) shared entertainment and informational material (TBS, 1990:12-13).

The importance of carriage and subscription-fee remittance contracts can be grasped by noting the reliance of TBS on these affiliated companies' cable systems. Between 61 and 77 per cent of TBS programming service audiences are subscribers to the cable systems of these companies (TBS, 1989:44). For example, TBS received $36 million in subscription fees from the eleven million subscribers to TCI cable systems in 1989 (TCI,1989:1,24). In the same year TBS received an additional $19 million in subscription fees from Time Warner cable systems (TBS, 1990:12). When the $4.8 million and $8.4 million in subscription fees from Comcast and Continental Communications are added, the four companies contributed about $67 million to TBS, close to 50 per cent of its subscriber fees (TBS, 1989:44). In addition, some TBS services, such as the SuperStation, are granted free carriage on Southern Satellite Systems, which is owned and operated by TCI.

Formal advertising agreements also exist between TBS, Time Warner Inc., and TCI, allowing preferential advertising rates on their respective services. Through such an agreement, Time Warner Inc. provided the various services of TBS with over $6.2 million in 1989, as well as underwriting a portion of the Turner-sponsored Goodwill Games with another $1 million. Altogether, about 50 per cent of TBS's advertising revenues come from these four companies (TBS, 1989:56). In short, the synchronized allocative policies of TBS's major stockholders benefit each of their respective services at the expense of those without such corporate interlocks. Each example of shared advertising and transfer of subscription fees is an example of revenue derived from other media industry competitors – revenue that is thus a threat to competition.

These companies support each other not only with subscriber fee remittance and advertising contracts but also by sharing entertainment and informational material. Services such as Turner Network Television, Home Box Office (Time Warner) and Showtime (TCI/Viacom) each use the Turner Film Library, which consists mostly of films acquired in TBS's earlier purchase of MGM/UA. Three channels, TNT, HBO, and Showtime, each supposedly representing independent competitors, share the same pool of "cultural" material (TBS, 1990:13). From this sharing agreement TBS received $30 million from Time Warner Inc. in 1988 alone.

TBS's own pool of cultural material is rather restricted, since 70 per cent of the material, other than that drawn from its own library, is purchased from three of the Hollywood majors: Columbia, 20th Century Fox, and Paramount (TBS, 1989:3). For the TBS pay-TV service TNT, for example, less than 3 per cent of the programming was "produced specifically for the company, either internally or by others under contract" (TBS, 1989:4).

The relationships between these companies, thus, become particularly important in the formation of vertically and horizontally integrated operations. This is a strong motivating factor behind CNN's status as the second-largest cable programming service in the country (TBS, 1989:7). By eliminating each other as potential competitors, the companies establish mutually beneficial and reinforcing partnerships. The synergy created by the exchange and combination of each other's "software" and "hardware" also allows these companies to be the primary beneficiaries of the "pay-per" media landscape emerging since the onslaught of Reaganomics and deregulation (Mosco, 1989).

CNN: Official Propaganda Agency?

It is through interlocking directors that CNN becomes fully integrated into the upper echelons of a closely integrated corporate media elite in the United States, becoming part of the "Private Ministry of Information and Culture." Yet the tentacles of this ministry are not only confined to corporate America but also *formally* extend to the official propaganda agency of the U.S. government, the United States Information Agency (USIA).

Through interlocking directorships with Time Warner Inc. and TCI, CNN is officially represented on USIA consultative committees. Representatives on these committees include Reginald Brack (Chief Executive Officer, Time Warner Inc.), Michael Solomon (President, Warner Bros. Intl.), Salem Hassanein (Warner Brothers International Theatres Co.), Beverly Sills Greensborough (Director, Time Warner Inc.), Anne Sutherland Fuchs (publisher, Time Warner's *Elle* magazine and related to TBS director Michael Fuchs), and Robert Johnson (president of BET, partially owned by Time and TCI). A more tenuous tie exists with USIA consultative committee member Jean Firstenberg, a member of the Peabody Broadcasting Awards committee which recently honoured CNN for its coverage of the war.[6] Each of these private-sector representatives meets periodically with the USIA executive "to share ideas and to identify common interests" (USIA, 1990:3).

These individuals and private-sector representatives also make "cash and in-kind contributions to [USIA] programs" such as audio visual material, satellite dishes, books, data, and consultations (USIA, 1990:4-6). The value of these contributions from the private sector is well recognized and applauded by the agency. (USIA, 1990:7). Thus, through share ownership and Board of Director positions held by Time Warner Inc. and TCI at TBS, CNN has access not only to the corridors of U.S. corporate power but also to the political power structure guiding, informing, and disseminating U.S. domestic and foreign policy.

The Political Economy of CNN, News Gathering, and the First Amendment

The above analysis establishes the extent of CNN's integration into the economic and political hierarchy guiding the U.S. media system. This section discusses the performance of this system in the context of the Gulf War by considering: the "press pool"; the media market; and news production.

CNN, War, and the Press Pool

Throughout the 1980s, restrictions on international news gathering by U.S. media have been retained and entrenched by the U.S. government. These restrictions are the "old guards" of the Cold War. They include legislation such as the McCarran-Walter Act, Defense Department rules governing the press during outbreaks of war, the Foreign Agents Registration Act, and certification of films by the USIA for export and duty-free status under the Beirut Agreement. Three recent and popular instances of the regulations in action are: (i) the problems ABC encountered covering the Pan American games held in Cuba; (ii) CNN's exemption from the provisions of the McCarran-Walter Act for its activities in Vietnam; and (iii) its exemption from the same law to cover the Gulf War from Iraq ("Conservatives want U.S. to Force CNN out of Iraq," 1991).

The implementation of a "press pool" during the Gulf War must be contextualized within this rather static legal environment. Furthermore, it must be considered as an ongoing extension of a pattern steeped in the history of the Vietnam War. As the government has noted, the regulations enacting the press pool were "adopted after the Vietnam War, [and] were in effect in some form during the Grenada and Panama military operations" (1991 U.S. Dist. Lexis 4853:3).

The rules governing the press's actions during the Gulf War were specifically intended to manage the flow of information on which public support for the war greatly depended. During the war, press rules were adopted requiring journalists to be under constant military escort, barring reporting on allied deaths and casualties, and dictating that all reports be passed through military censors before being presented for public consumption (1991 U.S. Dist. Lexis 4853). Journalists found "working outside the press pool" were "seized and detained by U.S. military guards" (Lederer, 1991:10).

These policies ensured that the war would not only be a glorification of technology and defence spending but also a celebration of war's "cleanliness." As pointed out in an article by Steve Tesich (1991), this approach appears to be an important factor in an era of "rapid deployment" warfare that will increasingly take place in the Third World (see also Mosco, 1989).

According to the rules of CENTCOM (the umbrella U.S. co-ordinating agency for the Gulf War), the so-called "press pools" were limited to "media principally serving the American public" and to media "organizations rather than ... individual press representative[s]," and they "have a long term presence covering Department of Defense military operations.... Participants were [also] required to share all media products within their medium to pool members, but were not required ... to distribute information to non-pool members" (1991 U.S. Dist. Lexis 4853:8). Furthermore, pool members were also required to submit all reports for military review in English. These capricious criteria impeded access to a number of journalists, hindered the news gathering efforts of those admitted into the pool, and were particularly disadvantageous to foreign journalists. One of the major consequences was that control over defining the war and its salient aspects was retained by a few Western media organizations.

The mainstream press, of course, criticized the press pool. However, CNN and the others qualifying for admittance to the pool were conspicuously absent when the press pool was challenged on First Amendment grounds in a U.S. District Court (1991 U.S. Dist. Lexis 4853). Those launching the suit against the pool included Agence France Press, *The Nation*, *Mother Jones*, *The Progressive*, and a number of independent journalists from the mainstream press, such as *Newsweek*. On April 16, 1991, the Court dismissed the case as moot.

Yet the Court acknowledged that the questions raised would persist since the rules "may be reactivated" and "the government concedes it is likely to follow this format in the future" (1991 U.S. Dist. Lexis 4853:14). The prevalence of the "Vietnam theory of media" evident in the recent spate of press pools ensures that the First Amendment issues raised are indeed not dead. There is also some undeserving support for this theory in academia (see, for example, Tunstall, 1972). The failure of CNN to challenge the press pool and these "theories" reveals an inconsistency between the news channel's popularly heralded journalistic success and its dubious commitment to the deeper issues of democratic communication.

Furthermore, we should not view the situations of war as anomalous. War is an amplified instance of deeper, structural developments in the legal structure guiding news gathering and public access to information in the United States. Restrictions on the "free flow of information" at the international level are paralleled at the domestic level. For example, routine access under the Freedom of Information Act became progressively more restricted during the Reagan years (Demac, 1988). This process has been further extended under Bush. General inquiries under the Freedom of Information act, instead of taking 10 days, as mandated by law, on average take 320 days for *approval* and processing (Gersh, 1991:12). As well, commitments to "public-domain" information are also giving way under the stress of intensified information "privatization" and "commodification" (Mosco, 1989; Schiller, 1989). Again, in both these instances the public voice of major media organizations has been conspicuously quiet. If the voice is heard at all, it is during self-aggrandizing propaganda before their audiences and policy-makers on the wonders and benefits of the "information age."

CNN, Free Markets, "Leaky" Information[7] *and News Flow Oligopoly*
The logic underlying these sporadic interventions into the wider issues of democracy, communication, and the Constitution by the media reflects the instrumental

rationality of news gathering and cultural production in the United States: competition and the free market. Restricting the pool proved safe not only to the Defense Department but also to those "qualified" media organizations by providing them with an oligopoly over the flow of information. This was, of course, at the expense of the same competitors involved in the lawsuit and ultimately the public.

One only has to consult the relevant trade publications to find that economic competition was both a compelling and constraining factor in media organizational behaviour during the war. As competition over the commodities of U.S. media – audiences and content – heated up during the Gulf War, pricing and contracts between advertisers and the media became extremely fluid (Walley, 1991:35). Second, there was a rapid increase in the intra-media exchange and sharing of information, most often involving CNN providing feeds to other networks, network affiliates, and independent stations. CNN profited from both of these developments, ideologically and economically.

Although neither the media nor advertisers acknowledge bowing directly to right-wing media critic groups (such as Accuracy In Media [AIM]), politicians, and the military, who questioned the "patriotic alliance" of U.S. journalists such as CNN's Peter Arnett, it appears, however, that advertisers did express their concerns with CNN (Colford, 1991:1). Though there was little direct contact between the media and advertisers, the need for anything more was negligible as major advertisers such as Procter and Gamble, McDonald's, Ford Motors, Sears Roebuck, and American Express, among others, pulled their ads from war-related "news," citing an environment not conducive to purchasing ("Marketers Slash Ads ...," 1991:1). Thus Corporate America sent the media a clear message not to overdo its war coverage and to provide more "regularly scheduled programming" where the advertisers would "continue to run advertising." The major networks returned to their regularly scheduled programs forty-two hours after the war commenced and CNN did so shortly thereafter. All in all, however, as one advertising executive enthusiastically commented, the war has, been "terrific for CNN and their credibility" (Walley, 1991:52).

The ideological significance of CNN's response to this "flak"[8] in terms of justifying its role as a full-fledged member of the independent "fourth estate" should not be lost (for example, see Zoglin, 1991:52, *Broadcasting*, February 18, March 4, March 25; *The Globe and Mail*, (Toronto), February 13; *MacNeil/Lehrer Newshour*, PBS, February 14). Instead of engaging in the "real" constitutional battle on behalf of the First Amendment in a court of law, CNN chose to make minimal public representations on its own stage and in the popular press. Thus, in a serious challenge ostensibly between legal confrontation and irate, conservative political and military officials, CNN sought out control over the discourse on its own terms. Such inconsequential commitments to the First Amendment substantiated its ideological claim to independence, impartiality, and public service but leave behind questions about its broader role in "democratizing" the U.S. media system.

Not only was CNN's credibility enhanced by the war, but also its economic bottom line. This was also the case for cable companies carrying CNN; they reported a substantial "increased call volume in the early days of the war, as noncable viewers wanted access to CNN" ("CNN's Place in History," 1991:29). During the war, CNN's viewership quadrupled, cable subscriptions increased, and advertising rates rose accordingly (Walley, 1991:35). Unlike other networks, there was no exodus of advertisers from CNN, and the long-term residual effects for CNN were thought of as promising. As one CNN executive reported, "Even if they [ratings] drop off to say 15 or 20 percent above what they were before the war, we'll have benefitted" ("Ratings Drop as CNN Ends War Format," 1991:5A).

Routinizing the Flow of Information
Another benefit for CNN during the Gulf War was the upsurge in news organizations buying and sharing its content. During the war over two hundred stations became new subscribers to CNN. In many cases these were local network affiliates who preempted network coverage in favour of the cable channel. The new subscriber base also included independent stations, which often provide little or no news programming. This raises at least three important questions. First, there is the issue of the quantity, quality, and diversity of information flow in the U.S. media in general and CNN in particular. Second, these developments require an analysis of the structural causes of this phenomenon. Third, it suggests that there is a widening chasm between the mass media and democracy predicated on considerations of who is allowed or denied the privilege to speak and command authority in the media.

First, "news sharing" cannot be considered a new phenomenon. Its increased visibility during the Gulf War is only a magnification of a general reduction in news gathering and public-affairs programming by the national and local media in the United States since deregulation. Therefore, the increased sharing of material during the Gulf War must be seen as an amplified instance of deeper structural developments in U.S. mass media. The evolution of CNN must be seen in relation to these wider, long-term developments.

The "structural causes" contributing to the emergence of CNN can be linked to the cutbacks in international news budgets by the networks and their increasing reliance on new television "wire services" such as CNN and Visnews (Wallace and Baran, 1990). At each of the traditional networks, budgets have been cut, staff eliminated, and full-time workers replaced with part-time employees. For instance, between 1985 and 1990 CBS reduced its staff from 1,500 to around 750. Plans to lay off another 200 employees have also been announced. These staff cuts are paralleled by deep cuts in CBS's news budget. In 1986 alone, $30 million was chopped from the news budget. Similar developments have occurred at the two other major networks. For example, in 1988 NBC cut news budgets by $55 million and eliminated four hundred jobs (Gay, 1988:1; Aufderheide, 1990:51). These examples express the new philosophy of a corporate media that questions the very existence of news programming. As *Variety* magazine paraphrased Bob Wright, president of NBC, General Electric's broadcasting arm: "News execs are systematically questioning virtually every aspect of the operation of the news organization; questioning whether NBC News should even continue to exist" (Gay, 1988:1).

These extraordinary cuts are not limited to the major networks but also extend to local affiliate and independent stations where news and public-affairs programming have been severely curtailed or eliminated altogether. A 1988 study by the Radio Television News Directors' Association (RTNDA) found that news staffs at many of the television stations in the top fifty markets had declined and that "Nearly one half of the independent stations had no one working in news" (cited in Aufderheide, 1990:51; see also Ray, 1990; Kellner, 1990:65-66). It is in the face of these developments that CNN continues to increase its profits by about 24 per cent per year to remain TBS's largest source of revenue, while maintaining a larger news staff than any of the traditional networks (TBS, 1989:15,46). Thus, in very real terms, CNN has filled space abandoned by the networks during an era stressing the bottom line over public service. These developments had a serious adverse effect on the quantity, quality, and diversity of competent journalism during the Gulf War. More analysis is needed of the long-term effects of this retreat from the concept of public service by the traditional networks, local affiliates, and independents.

There are further factors routinizing and diminishing the cost of CNN's news gathering and production. The most salient is the increasing reliance on institutional and official news sources. These are sources such as CNN's "Gen. James Blackwell, who has also served as a consultant to Lockheed, the manufacturer of many of the weapons Blackwell was called upon to praise" during the Gulf War (Naureckas, 1991:4). This reliance on so-called "official" sources is a factor that has become increasingly prevalent throughout the U.S. mass media. The reasons for this development are, as Herman and Chomsky (1988) argue, two-fold. First, official sources "reduce the media's costs of acquiring the raw materials of, and producing, news" (22). Second, as Mark Fishman states, official sources allow the semblance of "credible, competent pieces of knowledge ... amounting to a moral division of labor: Officials have and give the facts; reporters merely get them" (cited in Herman and Chomsky, 1988:19). Unfortunately, the extension of this development to CNN compromises its claim not only to journalistic integrity but also to uniqueness.

Such features undermine the arguments of right-wing critics and conservative media groups that CNN exhibits a left-leaning bias, often attributed to the somewhat eccentric Turner, a criticism that became most vociferous during CNN's coverage of the Gulf War. Yet this feature seems to be a continuous institutionalized feature at CNN. AIM, through its stock ownership, although minuscule, has at least twice put forward motions seeking to compensate for the alleged left-wing bias of CNN and other TBS programming services. Both proposals were rejected but were given rather interesting prominence in annual Proxy Statements, suggesting that they had, at least, an indirect effect (TBS, 1990:18).

Conclusion

In light of these findings, the much touted contribution of CNN to diversity in news and information simply becomes a myth. In addition, the claim that CNN has broken the longstanding oligopoly over news flow only reflects space abandoned by the traditional networks in light of regressive U.S. communications regulatory policy. Furthermore, CNN's possible contribution to a more democratic U.S. media system has been seriously curtailed by: (i) corporate interlocks that reduce its independence in relation to other information providers and the USIA; (ii) economic pressure flowing from the market; (iii) deregulation; (iv) government-imposed regulations associated with the recent press pools and the free flow of ideas; and (v) media capitulation to these restrictions. Consequently, it should not come as a surprise that CNN, along with the rest of the U.S. mainstream media, presented the events and subsequent war in the Gulf predominantly in patriotic, non-critical terms.

Notes

1. For example, see the *Time* poll (August 20, 1990) where a majority of respondents opposed war as an option. Again, five months later, *New York Times/CBS* (January 14, 1991) and *Time* polls still showed strong preference for solutions other than war.
2. This figure used 1988 as a base year and extrapolates to the present total based on annual percentage increases in TBS's 1989 and 1990 *Proxy Statements*.
3. I have only briefly outlined CNN's worldwide operations, and further studies are required. Specifically, research should direct attention to CNN's "worldview" represented by the pattern of international news flow and source identities in its coverage. Such studies might take earlier research on the international flow of news, conducted by the International Association of Mass Communication Researchers under the auspices of UNESCO, as an initial point of comparison (Sreberny-Mohammadi et al., 1984).
4. Mergers and acquisitions were accounted for and included under the revenues of the appropriate company.
5. Compiled from various 1990 Annual Reports and Form 10-Ks from the companies under consideration. Since these sources were not available for Continental and Comcast, I extrapolated Continental's revenues from 1986 and arrived at the 1990 figure by accounting for average industry revenue increases. This is a conservative approximation considering Continental's greater than average growth rate reflected in its higher ranking in *Channels'* (1990) list of the top twenty-five media corporations and the exclusion of Comcast, the fourth largest U.S. cable company. It is also important to note that the figures do not include the revenues gained outside of "electronic media," such as Time Warner's publishing business.
6. The names and associations outlined here are from Time Warner Inc.'s 1989 *Annual Report*, 1989 and 1990 *Form 10-K* and *Annual Reports* from TBS; and from the United States Information Agency publication *Points of Light* (1990). This analysis could have been extended further to include more generalized associations through each of the companies' representation in political action groups such as the National Association of Broadcasters, National Cable Television Association, or Magazine

Publishers Association. These groups, too, have representation at the USIA, as well as lobbying and making financial contributions in the hope of swaying political agendas (USIA, 1990; Bagdikian, 1990:11)

7. In 1985 Cleveland Harland wrote an article that has subsequently been extensively quoted by those suggesting that we are entering a new era in democracy and egalitarianism due to the inherent "leakiness" of information. According to Harland, information is becoming increasingly ubiquitous and uncontrollable. Consequently, he argues, traditional power structures and control over information flow are breaking down in favour of new forms of democracy.

8. "Flak" is the term used by Herman and Chomsky (1988) that "refers to negative responses to a media statement or program" (26). It is criticism that is directed towards the media by right-wing groups such as AIM, Freedom House, and American Legal Foundation, and by the government. These groups work from the premise "that the mass media not only should support any national venture abroad, but should do so with enthusiasm." Furthermore, "They receive respectful attention, and their propagandistic role and links to a larger corporate program are rarely mentioned or analyzed"(28).

References

Alter, Jonathan (1990). "Ted's Global Village," *Newsweek*, June 11.

Anderson, Robin and Paolo Carpignano (1991). "Iraqi Dupes or Pentagon Promoters? CNN Covers the War," *Extra!*, 4,3:11-12.

Aufderheide, Patricia (1990). "After the Fairness Doctrine: Controversial Broadcast Programming and the Public Interest," *Journal of Communication*, 40,3:47-72.

Bagdikian, Ben H. (1990). *The Media Monopoly*. Boston: Beacon Press.

"Cable's Top 50 MSO's" (1991). *Broadcasting*, March 25.

Cleveland, Harland (1985). *The Knowledge Executive*. New York: Dutton.

"CNN's Place in History" (1991). *Broadcasting*, March 4.

Colford, Steven W. (1991). "Protests of CNN Hit Advertisers: Callers Lash Arnett Reports, But Sponsors Support Network," *Advertising Age*, February 18.

"Conservatives Want U.S. to Force CNN out of Iraq" (1991). *The Globe and Mail* (Toronto), February 13.

Demac, Donna (1988). "Hearts and Minds Revisited: The Information Policies of the Reagan Administration." In V. Mosco and J. Wasko, eds., *The Political Economy of Information*. Madison, Wis.: University of Wisconsin Press.

"Field Guide" (1991). *Channels*.

Gay, Verne (1988). "Introspection at NBC: Is No News Good News? *Variety*, 334,11.

Gersh, Debra (1991). "The Bush Administration and the News Media," *Editor and Publisher*, March 23.

Gitlin, Todd (1978). "Media Sociology: The Dominant Paradigm," *Theory and Society*, 6:205-253.

"Group Launches Campaign to 'Pull Plug' on CNN's Arnett" (1991). *Broadcasting*, February 18.

Herman, Edward S. and Noam Chomsky (1988). *Manufacturing Consent: The Political Economy of the Mass Media*. New York: Pantheon Books.

Kellner, Douglas (1990). *Television and the Crisis of Democracy*. Boulder, Col.: Westview Press.

Kretchmar, Laurie and John Labate (1990). "The Fortune Service 500," *Fortune*, 121,13:298-333.

Lederer, Edith (1991). "Press Pool Hassles," *Editor and Publisher*, February 16.

Lippmann, Walter (1922/81). "Stereotypes." In M. Janowitz and P. Hirch, eds., *Reader in Public Opinion and Mass Communication*. Third edition. New York: The Free Press.

Mahar, Maggie (1989). "Turned On, Tuned Out: Ted Turner Wanted FNN; Board Gave It a Bad Reception," *Barron's*, 63,13:18.

"Marketers Slash Ads as War Erupts" (1991). *Advertising Age*, January 21.

Mosco, Vincent (1989). *The Pay-Per Society: Computers and Communication in the Information Age*. Toronto: Garamond Press.

Murdock, Graham (1982). "Large Corporations and the Control of the Communications Industry." In M. Gurevitch, T. Bennett, J. Curran and J. Wollacott, eds., *Culture, Society and the Media*. New York: Methuen.

Naureckas, Jim (1991). "Gulf War Coverage: The Worst Censorship Was at Home," *Extra!*, 4,3:3.

"Ownership Opportunity" (1991). *Broadcasting*, March 4.

Park, Robert E. (1974). *Perspectives in Social Inquiry: Classics, Staples and Precursors in Sociology*. New York: Arno Press.

"Peter Arnett Defends His Baghdad Reporting" (1991). *Broadcasting*, March 18.

"Pete Williams Debriefs the Press" (1991). *Broadcasting*, March 18.

"Ratings Drop as CNN Ends War Format" (1991). *The Register Guard* (Oregon), March 12.

Ray, William B. (1990). *FCC: The Ups and Downs of Radio-TV Regulation*. Iowa: Iowa State University Press.

Schiller, Herbert (1989). *Culture Inc.* New York: Oxford University Press.

Sreberny-Mohammadi, A., Nordenstreng, K., Stevenson, R., Ugboajah, F. (1984). *Foreign News in the Media: International Reporting in 29 Countries*. New York: UNESCO.

Tele-Communications Incorporated (TCI) (1989). *Annual Report*.

Tesich, Steve (1991). "Quick Wars, Quick Fixes: Breaking Away from Ourselves," *The Nation*, 252,10 (March 18):334-336.

Time Warner Incorporated (1989). *Annual Report*.

Turner Broadcasting Systems (TBS), Incorporated (1990). *Proxy Statement*. Filed with U.S. Securities and Exchange Commission.

Turner Broadcasting Systems (1988). *Proxy Statement*. Filed with U.S. Securities and Exchange Commission.

Turner Broadcasting Systems (1988). *Form 10-K*. Filed with U.S. Securities and Exchange Commission.

Tunstall, Jeremy (1971). *Journalists at Work*. London: Constable.

"TV: The More You Watch the Less You Know" (1991). *Extra!*, 4,3:8.

United States Information Agency (USIA)(1990). *Private Sector Committees Annual Report*. Location and identity of publisher not specified.

United States District Court, New York (1991). Lexis 4853.

United States District Court, New York (1988). *World-Wide Free Flow Export-Import of Audio-Visual Materials: Regulations – 22CFR – Part 502*. Reprint from the Code of Federal Regulations, Washington, D.C.: USIA.

United States Subcommittee on Courts, Intellectual Property, and the Administration of Justice of the Committee on the Judiciary House of Representatives (1989). *Free Trade in Ideas: Hearings*. 101st Congress, First Session, Washington, D.C.: Gov't Printing Office.

United States Subcommittee on Communications of the Committee on Commerce, Science and Transportation (1989a). *Media Ownership: Diversity and Concentration Hearings*. 101st Congress, First Session, Washington, D.C.: Gov't Printing Office.

United States Subcommittee on Communications of the Committee on Commerce, Science and Transportation (1989b). *Oversight of Cable*. 101st Congress, First Session, Washington, D.C.: Gov't Printing Office.

Wallace, Roger and Stanley Baran (1990). *The Known World of Broadcast News*. New York: Routledge.

Walley, Wayne (1991). "CNN Has Its Shining Moment, But Can All Those 'News Junkies' It Hooked Really Translate into Growth?" *Advertising Age*, 62,13.

"War of Words Over Coverage Continues" (1991). *Broadcasting*, March 25.

Wasko, Janet (1984). "New Methods of Analyzing Media Concentration." In V. Mosco, ed., *Policy Research in Telecommunications*. Norwood, N.J.: Ablex.

"You've Read the Headlines" (1991). *Extra!*, 4,3:8.

Zeitlin, Maurice (1974). "Corporate Ownership and Control: The Large Corporations and the Capitalist Class." *American Journal of Sociology*, 79:1074-1083.

Zoglin, Richard (1991). "Live from the Middle East!" *Time*, January 28.

Zoglin, Richard (1991). "Just Whose Side Are They On?" *Time*, February 25.

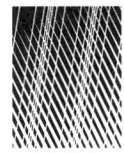

An Occidental Construction of the Orient: Media, Madness, and the Muslim World

Mashoed Bailie and David A. Frank

So saturated with meanings, so overdetermined by history, religion, and politics are labels like "Arab" or "Muslim" as subdivisions of "The Orient" that no one today can use them without some attention to the formidable polemical mediations that screen the objects, if they exist at all, that the labels designate.

– Edward Said, Orientalism

URING THE 1991 WAR in the Persian Gulf, images of the Middle East and its peoples saturated the U.S. media. These contemporary, mediated constructions of the Middle East and the people who live there are rooted in a historical racism, a racism that Edward Said has called "Orientalism." Mediated images of the peoples, customs, and cultures of the Orient were uncritically constructed and disseminated by the mainstream media and unquestioningly consumed by the general public, revealing the all-pervasive nature of this form of racism.

While members of the U.S. media claimed that limited access to information prevented a more complete coverage of the Gulf War, the major U.S. television networks uncritically followed the Pentagon script in their news reports. Indeed, we doubt that the depiction of the Arab world would have been altered significantly even if the media had gained access to the information necessary for a thorough accounting of the war.

It has been argued that institutions of knowledge production and distribution in the United States serve as societal cement, reproducing dominant ideologies and framing accounts that continually reconstruct Western hegemony (Altheide, 1976; Epstein, 1974; Gitlin, 1980; Schiller, 1969). Furthermore, the relationships between media and the state often lead to specific patterns of coverage based on implicit or explicit "frames" and "codes" (Altheide, 1976; Gitlin, 1980; Glasgow Media Group, 1980).

The codes and frames of reference, as we apply them to our analysis of the media coverage of the war in the Gulf, are interestingly developed by Edward Said (1979) and consist of a series of assumptions that Western scholars and others hold about the Orient and the Arab Orient in particular. This deeply ingrained ideology helps to explain why the mainstream press covered the war in a manner that abstracted, diminished, and distorted the reality of the Arab world. Until this ideology is revealed and demystified, the mainstream press will continue to "Orientalize" these various and variegated cultures.

Orientalism

Orientalism stems from a history of Western expansionism and exploitation of the Middle East. Said notes that the discovery of oil and the development of travel routes, combined with a mythology of "the mysterious East," produced a body of knowledge from which a Western elite, including scholars, artists, and journalists, reconstructed the Arab and the Arab world. The Orientalist, then, is one who teaches, writes, or reports on the Orient. These "experts" tend to assume a position of superiority and authority; they typically frame and describe the Arab world as inferior to the West in technology, religion, and culture:

Orient	*Occident*
Islam	Christianity
Revenge	Forgiveness
Passion	Intellect
Heart	Mind
Old World	New World
Violent	Peaceful

These values shape the methods used by Orientalists and dictate the categories that describe what is perceived to be the essence of the Arab world.

The Colonial Impulse

The contemporary Orientalist notions of the Arab world are historical, rooted in an ideology of Western superiority and colonial expansionism. Moreover, Orientalists assume the role of spokespersons while Arabs provide the background for this Western knowledge product. The diverse nature of the Middle East is rarely recognized, as the Orientalist abstracts the complexities into a series of clichés, turning to "classic" texts rather than to modern poetry and literature for evidence of Arab beliefs and worldviews. One tendency is to feature an individual Arab and assert that her/his behaviour provides indisputable proof of the beliefs and behaviours of the entire Arab world. Or, on occasion, the Orientalist will seek out Arab "mobs" and then abstract conclusions about Islam on the basis of those images.

The primary conclusions Orientalists reach and continually verify with their research is that Arabs and Muslims are the same everywhere. Malek (1963) notes that Orientalists "adopt an essentialist conception of the countries, nations and people under study, a conception which expresses itself through a characterized ethnist typology" and which manifests itself in racism. This view of the Orient reduces and eliminates all differences exhibited by individual Arabs, Islamic religious movements, and Arab cultures.

Orientalist Categories

This essentialist conception of the Middle East has produced invariable categories with which the Occident constructs the Orient – categories used whenever the Orientalist must compare the Western world with the Middle East, or when there is a need to interpret the motives and lifestyles of the Arab people.

A. *Technological Superiority*

The Orientalist, assuming that the logic, science, and technology of Western culture are inherently superior to the emotional and religious tendencies of the Arab world, sees technology as the product of a superior Western mind. From this vantage point, the tools of technology – and in particular those of war – demonstrate how much further evolved the Occident is than the Orient.

The full force of Western Orientalism was unleashed upon the North American public during the war in the Persian Gulf. The "technological discourse" provided by the networks contrasted U.S. superiority in telecommunications, use of satellite coverage, graphics, and high-tech production techniques with the Orient's inferior technology, religious blinders, and passion.

ABC's Ted Koppel spent many hours developing the paradigm of U.S. and Iraqi technology which, in light of the surrounding material concerning the backward nature of the warlike Arab world, reinforced Orientalist notions:

Koppel: [Close up on Koppel's deadpan face.] One more quick question Pierre [Salinger], and then I want to go to our Pentagon correspondent Bob Zelnick. When you talk about Iraqis telling their friends ... a few months ago it would have been so simple to say "of course they can tell their friends." [But now] How? Can they do it by phone? Can they do it by homing pigeon?

We watch Koppel grapple with the concept of Iraqis communicating with each other, and we understand why. Western technology is superior to Oriental "homing pigeons." ABC, which in the normal course of events has news crews in Baghdad, Tel Aviv, and Saudi Arabia, is everywhere, seeing the world via satellite, interpreting events by the minutes. We empathize with Koppel; it's hard to understand how these "other" people live in such backward conditions.

Peter Jennings took the control seat at "ABC World News" during the first few hours after the initial bombing raids into Iraq. The following example clearly reveals the celebration of the superior U.S. technology:

Jennings: We have a brief report now from ABC's Dennis Trout on just how difficult it is for American pilots to fight under these conditions.

Trout: [His voice is played over images of daylight movements of U.S. tanks in desert.] On a clear day anyone can see forever in the desert. But on a clear night? [Insert of a cameo-lit U.S. soldier against a pitch-black background. The soldier says: "Oh, we own the night. We own the night.] On a clear night special night-time vision equipment means that U.S. forces can see forever then too ... or almost forever. [Images of U.S. soldiers and heavy weapons moving, searching through the darkness.] U.S. forces are expected to have advantage against Iraq. That's because new technology [here images of silhouetted aircraft are inserted] allows Americans to do much of the fighting at night, when they can see and, presumably, the Iraqis cannot.

The slick visual inserts of high-tech radar and aircraft reinforces the power of the U.S. military. Technology not only overcomes a human enemy but also the enemy space, time, and distance. U.S. media were on the offensive with graphic inserts, live satellite coverage, military "correspondents," and battle-plan maps complete with up-to-the-minute results of search-and-destroy missions. North American audiences were left with little doubt that Western "science" and, by extension, the Western way of life were incongruous with the world of "the Arabs." By using retired military officials as "correspondents" the networks guaranteed Orientalist interpretations of the Middle East. Going beyond mere celebration of military technology, one past chairman of the Joint Chiefs of Staff seemed to suggest that the war offered an opportunity to test Western progress in technological warfare against the more "primitive" weapons systems of the Iraqis:

Past Chairman, JCS: Well you always want to know if it will work, in the real world. And from a professional viewpoint we're going to see some really interesting systems used for the first time in anger, and we will be extremely curious to see if they perform as advertised. What you're really looking for, of course, is some of the countermeasures that are taken by the enemy. You find sometimes in sophisticated weapons systems that some very primitive defences prove effective. We'll look to see if the Iraqis have developed any of those.

While the United States develops "sophisticated weapons systems," the major concern is that the Iraqis may have developed an effective "primitive defence."

CNN coverage during the first few hours of the air attack on Baghdad provides a further example of the Orientalist nature of U.S. coverage of the war. CNN correspondents were reporting live from Baghdad as bombs were dropping nearby. The image of anchorman Bernard Shaw is inserted over a map of Iraq that highlights Baghdad. The audience listens as Shaw and John Hilliman exchange small talk in a Baghdad hotel:

Shaw: John, it occurs to me that this attack is going to just shake the psyches of the Baghdadies here. This is unprecedented, and I'm really anxious for daybreak to come so that we can get out and see what has been wrought here.

Hilliman: I'll tell you, in my conversations Bernie, with the people of Baghdad, they've always said "Uh, we've had all these rockets coming in during the Iran and Iraq war." And I kept telling the people I spoke with ... well, you know the Americans and the coalition forces have bombs much stronger than the ones that came during the Iran-Iraq war. "Oh no, we'll be alright," they said. I have a feeling that when dawn breaks here in Baghdad, the Iraqis are going to have a whole different level of feeling of potential respect for the Allied forces.

That the people of Iraq are going to have a potential "respect" for U.S. bombing raids on Baghdad fits perfectly well with the concept of Orientalism. While the Occidental view that "Arabs" are an inferior, degenerate people would be reinforced if such an attack took place on Washington, it is in keeping with an Orientalist position that brute force is the way to illicit respect from war-like Arab nations.

Ted Koppel, in conversation with Sam Donaldson of ABC, struggled to uncover the reason for the U.S. military's early success against the Iraqi forces. It did not take long for Donaldson to explain:

Koppel: Did U.S. military exaggerate the amount of opposition they would find?
Donaldson: No ... just surprised how early Iraqi defenders folded up, but I think there are four reasons: Schwartzkopf talked about two of them [merciless air bombardments and tactical manoeuvres around Iraqi ditches filled with oil]. Thirdly, equipment. Ted, our equipment is simply better than theirs. And, if I may say, finally, the morale and the training of U.S. forces is simply superior. These are war weary Iranian troops, they fought ... Iraqi troops rather ...

These slips – calling Iraqi troops Iranian – happen often enough to provide an image of interchangeability between the various national origins in the Middle East. The enemy could just as easily be Iranians, Arabians, Syrians, or Jordanians. In all events, our equipment is simply better than theirs.

This interconnectedness between various ethnic groups in the Gulf region was represented most powerfully through images. During a typical NBC report from the Gulf, viewers watched as U.S. soldiers received a warning about possible nerve-gas attacks. It ran as follows:

Reporter: Many [soldiers] said they knew something was up when they were ordered to take pills to prevent nerve-agent poisoning. [The video shows U.S. soldiers in a cafeteria taking pills.] The Saudi pilots sought a different agent for their protection. [A wide-angle shot of uniform rows of Saudi pilots seen kneeling down to pray with their backsides pointed up towards the camera.]

This excerpt is interesting partly because of the contrast between East and West: Orient and Occident. We use modern science while they use "Old Testament" prayer. What becomes more revealing is the way in which the word "agent" is used to connect the threat to U.S. troops and the "cure" for Saudi pilots. While

U.S. pilots use Western science to protect them from the Iraqi "agent," the Saudis simply use another "agent." The United States is represented as caught between two "Oriental" groups who both call upon "foreign agents" to protect them.

Above and beyond the content of the visuals is the image itself. North American audiences were privy to a front-row seat at the war in the Gulf via the development and celebration of technology. While viewers saw little, if any, actual fighting on the screen, they were taken to the Middle East, saw American correspondents reporting live from areas that were being bombed – by Americans. The war in the Gulf was mediated not only via the media but also through the interpretations of "guest analysts" in the form of retired military generals or government officials. The technology of television lent itself to the technology of war. For a moment they became one – in action and resolve.

Following the end of the current episode in the Gulf War, a *Sixty Minutes* story aired on the plight of the Kurdish people. The story angle was, once again, from the point of view of U.S. superiority over the backward, unorganized masses of Kurds. Even after an explanation that many of the homeless were doctors, lawyers, and teachers, the story took up the following narration:

> The morning we arrived there was a near riot when the food trucks came. The strongest men grabbing and hoarding. That afternoon a group of U.S. military met with a group of elders to try and establish some order. By the very next day an orderly food distribution system was working. The camp had been divided into seven sectors each with a leader, no more bread wars. On our first day, everyone was using dirty water for cooking, but the next day, after the Americans organized the laying of pipes to carry clean water to one part of the camp, women stood politely in line.

The story ended with this commentary:

> It's tough not to get caught up in the emotion of a story like this and you try hard not to. But you do come away hoping that cousin Mohammad and all his Kurdish cousins grow up under the watchful eye of someone other than Saddam Hussein.

Whose "watchful eye," we might wonder, could the commentators be thinking of?

Here again the visual images provided viewers with the "mob" mentality of the Orient as U.S. reporters, clean and well dressed, walked among the hungry, homeless, Kurdish refugees. Images of young men removing food from trucks are reproduced with a voice-over that suggests the need for "U.S. intervention" even here. A group of Kurdish people are shown sitting with U.S. soldiers followed by a long shot of happy women standing in "polite lines" waiting for water. The pictures tell all: The United States can provide the education needed by the Kurdish people to bring a sense of civilization to their otherwise "backward" lives.

B. Cultural Superiority

The modern mass media often depict the Arab as a bloodthirsty, violent animal. Indeed, several studies have revealed the prevalent tendency in American movies and books to portray the Arab as a savage beast. It is the message of the senseless use of violence and force that found itself repeated time and again on network television. One representative example is provided by Ted Koppel during his interview with ABC's "military correspondent," Retired General Bernard Trainor. Trainor had served as a Marine Corp. General and military writer for *The New York Times:*

Koppel: How do you analyze, General, the destruction [by the Iraqis] of some of the public buildings in Kuwait City? The destruction of the oil wells and oil fields. Just sheer meanness, or does it actually have some military significance or worth?

Trainor: ... It's relatively insignificant in a military sense, so one must say it's out of pure meanness that they're doing this.

Koppel and Trainor sit in medium close-up, sharing a split screen. Koppel's background reveals rows of monitors on which, presumably, the affairs of the world are being played out. Trainor hides a map of the Middle East behind him (the same map used as his background throughout ABC's coverage of the Gulf War). Both men look out towards the audience as they speak, and they are surrounded by a map of the world upon which is written: ABC NEWS: THE GULF WAR. Through the use of sophisticated broadcast technology, viewers are moved between Washington and Boston and then to the split image, which places them in two places at once. Amidst the display of this advanced technological superiority, the idea of Iraqi "meanness" takes on an immature, childlike quality. There is almost a sense that these men are talking about children who need to be reprimanded, punished for bad behaviour.

On January 16th, some sixteen hours following the outbreak of war, Tom Brokaw interviewed "Middle East expert" Edward Peck, who had served at the U.S. Embassy in Baghdad, on *NBC Nightly News*":

Peck: One of the things that I'm thinking about in this connection is that if, and that's a big word, if Saddam Hussein has actually been de-fanged strategically, and is about to be de-clawed tactically, by what the Americans and the others are going to do to him, then I'm not sure you need a major massive force because the Iraqis are going to lose, if they haven't already, a major portion of their capability in the military sphere.

Thus, the image of feral Arabs is ingrained in the consciousness of the West, and deceit and violence are seen as central to their nature. Given this cultural stereotype of Arabs as essentially barbaric, it does not take much to demonize an Arab leader.

In these narratives, the point is often made that the United States must play a

paternalistic role in the "New World Order," and that the "sibling rivalry" between Middle Eastern countries must end. Dan Rather of CBS illicited this point
from Rep. Robert Torricelli of the Foreign Affairs Committee, who had voted in
favour of the Bush proposal to go to war with Iraq.

Torricelli: I think, Dan, the President has made the case that indeed that Saddam
  Hussein is such a unique danger ... having gone the extra mile, having tried
  everything to resolve this peacefully, he has no choice.... I suppose, Dan, after
  everything else, after forty years of a Cold War and endless international conflict, that finally the world has come together and said enough. That in the post
  Cold War period it's going to be different. International law is going to reign
  and what is happening in Iraq is not simply the suppression of Saddam
  Hussein and all the madness that he represents. That these kinds of wars simply are not going to be tolerated anymore.

This interview took place in the CBS studio. The camera cuts back and forth between Torricelli and Rather as they speak. Torricelli is lit with high-key lighting,
separating him from the out-of-focus background map of the Middle East. Then,
surprisingly, the camera cuts to an over-the-shoulder two-shot of Rather and
Torricelli from Torricelli's point of view, revealing eighteen television screens behind Dan Rather. Both men sit at a bright, white table, upon which can be seen
the dark squares of the Teleprompter screens. While the war goes on in Iraq, these
men, surrounded by Western technological superiority, sit comfortably considering how the United States will bring the "madness" that Hussein represents into
line in time to join the West's vision of a new world order. The Orientalist notion
is further reinforced in the discourse. Torricelli's invocation of the Christian edict
to "go the extra mile" provides an Occidental frame within which to contrast the
Arab World.

Shortly following the bombing raids on Baghdad, Walter Cronkite bandied
words with Dan Rather on a CBS special report. The following statements, one
from Cronkite and two from Rather, took place within thirty minutes of each
other, but the contradiction was never reconciled for viewers:

Cronkite: Baghdad's suggestion that there are "wave after wave" of American bombers overhead suggests a rather typical Iraqi, eh, overstatement. We don't attack in
  "wave and waves" of bombers anymore, that goes back to World War II.
Rather: [Minutes later.] ... We know that a tremendous air attack has been
  launched against Iraq and Iraqi forces in Kuwait.
Rather: [Later still.] Allan Fissey in Baghdad reports on what he's been able to
  see; that damage in downtown Baghdad, right in the centre, has not been
  much. He points out that it may not have been the intent of the wave after
  wave of air strikes to inflict heavy damage, since it is a civilian population.

Cronkite's role in this particular news report seems minor. Even the little that he
does contribute is contradicted shortly after. Indeed, not long after the above ex-

change took place, Dan Rather reported, "Now, from Baghdad, eyewitness reports of wave after wave of Allied war planes, principally those of the United States." But Cronkite's comment that "wave after wave" applied only to World War II delegitimized reports coming directly from Iraq, even though they were to be confirmed later by Western sources.

C. Religious Superiority

The Orientalist juxtaposes the Judeo-Christian West with the Orient and finds the former superior. Islam is seen as a static, warlike, anti-intellectual (or anti-science) religion. On NBC Tom Brokaw continues his analysis of the war with NBC's "expert," Edward Peck:

Brokaw: The streets of Jordan are relatively quiet today. That is the most volatile spot caught between Israel and Iraq, in that very heavily and very passionate Palestinian population. But so far, given these initial reports of success, there's been no report of an uprising against the United States or Operation Desert Storm. Edward Peck is in our studio. He's an expert on that area having served in the United States Embassy in Baghdad itself. Would you find that encouraging Mr. Peck?

Peck: The one thing I keep thinking about as this unfolds is that America, without putting too heavy a religious connotation on it, is a country of the New Testament, Tom. We believe in letting bygones be bygones, turning the other cheek and forgiving and forgetting. Whereas the people of the Middle East, both Arabs and Israelis, there again not from a religious perspective, are people of the Old Testament. They don't forgive and forget. There, the passions smolder deep for long periods of time.

Peck sits in medium close-up, centre screen, under high-key lighting that offers us an opportunity to explore Peck's benevolent features; he's a man with nothing to hide. Behind him, screen left, is the official seal of the State Department, and behind that are what appears to be the bars of a cage that separates Peck from the out-of-focus activity going on in the (official) distance. The image says: Here is an official representative of the U.S. government separated (by bars in background) from his official function so he can share "expert insider information" with the public as a (for the moment) representative of (the objective) NBC news team.

When Peck says "not from a religious perspective," we wonder from what perspective we should understand his description of those who live in the Middle East. If not religious, then what? Is their unforgiving nature something inherent in the people of this region of the world? Is it something "natural?" Perhaps something that even a strong dose of Christianity could not temper? Then there are the countries of the "New Testament," as Peck calls them – countries, one presumes, like Northern Ireland, that are naturally prone to forgiving and forgetting, unlike their Oriental counterpart?

No attempt is made to account for the various movements within the tradition, ǫr for the many strands of Islam. In addition, an inordinate amount of attention is paid to the purported "warlike" nature of Islam. The Jihad, which is perceived by Muslims as a war in defence of faith, is transformed by the Orientalist into the primary foundation of Islam.

Brokaw: Ed Peck, let's go back to the mind of Saddam Hussein ... they believe they can take two waves of attack from the United States, emerge from their bunkers and claim victory, is that viable?

Peck: I would tend to think that one of the things that he's going to do first, when he comes out of his bunker, is call on the Arab world to rise up and support him, and call on Muslims everywhere to do the same thing. I'm certain that Saddam Hussein can count on a very strong and very violent reaction from Muslims virtually everywhere.

Brokaw: And what are the prospects of that succeeding with the Arab masses, to say nothing of the other marginal leaders there?

Peck: I think it's going to succeed very well, well fairly well. And that's not something that pleases me of course ... I think there's going to be a very strong emotional reaction on the part of all Arabs ... when they know the United States has struck co-religionists, co-Arabs, co-ethnists, if you will.

"Bunkers," "masses," "emotions," "Arabs rising": These words, taken together, portray the Orientalist position on the Middle East. Brokaw and Peck represent the war as a threat to America from "Arabs everywhere." Americans are not safe from any "co-religionist," "co-Arab," or "co-ethnist." By extension, to be a Muslim is to be a threat to the "Christian West." What of Christian Arabs or non-Arabic Muslim converts? These complexities cannot be dealt with by Orientalists; for them the Orient is not complex, it is a single whole that must be dominated and controlled.

Dan Rather spent much of the Gulf War in monologue with himself before millions of U.S. viewers. One representative example of Rather's self-righteous representations of Arabs and the Arab world happens to include this concept of Jihad:

Rather: It is worth perhaps pausing when we say: well, we've gone into Israel fairly often, we've talked about the state of emergency in Israel. But Saddam Hussein in his interview with us when we were in Baghdad and interviewed him, made it very clear that while attention was focused on the Persian Gulf, that his dream – his long-range strategic mission – is to lead a triumphant Arab army into Jerusalem, the only true democracy in the region and the United States' ally. The other thing they emphasized was that they intended to make the world a battlefield with terrorism.

Rather sits close-up, centre screen. His face is full of sincerity and perhaps a little strained. Each word, each phrase, is developing right before the viewer's eyes; it is an intensely personal experience, this "sharing" with Rather: He's thinking, considering, and then carefully expressing profound thoughts based on, he tells us, his unique three-hour interview with "the mind" of Saddam Hussein.

These images, presented continuously by the mainstream press throughout the Gulf War, are consistent with the concept of Orientalism. Clearly the picture emerges that the Orient and the Occident are, by nature, enemies. Only through some form of "Western control" can stability be assured.

PBS aired what could only be called an Orientalist interview between David Frost and Norman Schwartzkopf in March 1991. References were made and comparisons drawn between Islam and Christianity and technological and cultural superiority. The interview is laced with examples of the contradictions between the Orient and the Occident, similar to those reproduced below:

N.S.: Someone once asked me what is the difference between me and Saddam Hussein. The answer is I have a conscience and he doesn't.

D.F.: And a man with no conscience is another way of saying that you really regard him as evil in a way.

N.S.: Oh, I think there's no question about it, in my mind his ... he's ... he is an evil man.

D.F.: Did you feel that God was on your side during this war?

N.S.: He had to be. Uhm ... I don't ... I don't ... the results show that he had to be ...

D.F.: You had the Bible, I keep reading, beside your bed.

N.S.: Yeah.

D.F.: You had ... did you have a favourite text?

N.S.: There is a prayer attributed to St. Francis, you know, that starts off ... "Dear Lord, make us instruments of your peace." And that's my, you know, the one I read the most.

D.F.: Absolutely.

Throughout the interview between Frost and Schwartzkopf the camera and the narrative developed a comradeship between the two and a decidedly Orientalist view of the Arab world and its people. Time and time again, the narrative of Western might and technological superiority is claimed as proof of Middle Eastern backwardness and inferiority. The Arab world remains unexplored. Worse yet, the underlying assumptions that the military complex, corporate America, and mainstream media use to analyze and report on events in the Middle East go unquestioned.

Conclusions

Although there are many other categories that the Orientalist uses to describe the Arab world, these three categories – technological, cultural, and religious superiority – provide a way to identify orientalist assumptions and discourses in the coverage of the Gulf War.

The implications for a democratic society whose citizens depend upon information provided by increasingly concentrated centres of knowledge production are vast indeed. Unless these unquestioned assumptions about the "Other" are relentlessly critiqued, and until the "Other" is acknowledged as a legitimate source of knowledge production and distribution in an increasingly global information age, we can expect continued depictions of the Arab world that reinforce Orientalist notions.

While the United States celebrates victory over the Arab world and sets about defining its future interests and role in the Gulf region, the Orientalist roots from which U.S. interests spring must be tirelessly and conscientiously critiqued. Through the development of new information technologies and weapons of mass destruction, the Occident and the Orient are brought ever closer together. How we view each other in this new information environment will depend to a great extent on how quickly we can explode these mythic notions – to reveal the human face of a people too long exploited by the Orientalist notions of the West.

References
Altheide, D.L. (1976). *Creating Reality: How TV News Distorts Events*. Beverly Hills: Sage.
Epstein, E.J. (1974). *News from Nowhere*. New York: Vintage.
Gitlin, T. (1980). *The Whole World is Watching*. Berkeley: University of California Press.
Glasgow Media Group (1976). *Bad News*. Vol.1. London: Routledge.
Malek, A.A. (1963). "Orientalism in crisis," *Diogenes*, 44 (Winter):107-108.
Said, E.W. (1979). *Orientalism*. New York: Random House.
Schiller, H.I. (1969). *Mass Communication and the American Empire*. New York: Augustus.

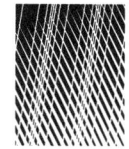

Privacy and Secrecy:
Social Control and the Prospects for
Democracy in the Information System

Giovanni Cesareo

I. "THOU SHALT NOT COVET THY NEIGHBOUR'S DATABASE." This new and peculiar Biblical commandment appeared in 1984 on the cover of the August issue of *The Futurist*. Inside the magazine it was quoted in the review of *Computer Ethics: A Guide for the New Age*, a book written by the Rev. Douglas W. Johnson, director of the Institute for Church Development Inc. The commandment and the book as a whole tend to assert that in the "New Age" it is necessary to elaborate new ethics: the "computer ethics," that's it.

That commandment, which substitutes the "neighbour's database" for the "neighbour's wife," is a hint of a new kind of neighbourhood and new concepts of interpersonal relationships and privacy. A general reference may be made to "social control," variously practised – from the top or from the bottom – in any community and in every social formation, but loaded with new meanings and problems in the present "Information Age."

As a matter of fact, the topic of "social control" has been long present in the core of the political debate and is strongly discussed among jurists, experts of informatic technologies, and sociologists and psychologists. Since the beginning of the 1970s the legislation of many countries throughout the world and some CEE (European Community Council) documents have referred to it.

This debate and the laws as well, though, are affected by a contradiction – or, at least, by a partition – that concerns the very concept of social control and runs the risk of breeding some misunderstandings.

By social control some scholars or critics refer only to control by the state or the public authorities, or by public and private corporations as well, over "privacy," which means the personal daily life of citizens. Others refer to social control, on the contrary, when they want to bring up the influence that citizens or the "masses" or the grassroots organizations might or should exert over social institutions or (but less often) private corporations. Of course, the partition is not always so strict, but it has existed and been reproduced for a long time, and it can be traced not only in the liberal but also in the socialist tradition.

Typical, for instance, was the presence of this partition (which often became a strong contradiction) in the fierce anti-authoritarian battle conducted by the '68 movements: The first meaning – of control by the state or public authorities – was used to refer to the pervasive drift of "capital" (and was then regarded as a trend that had to be defeated); the second meaning, on the contrary, evoked "Grassroots Democracy" (which in this case was considered an aim to achieve).

It is not an odd case, then, that this partition marks also the debate about the new technologies and the so-called "information society." In this debate and in the laws introduced in many countries the emphasis has so far been on the "defence of privacy," often exclusively. The approach has been negative or at least protectionist. And yet the same debate does not lack general and often generic (or taken for granted) scenarios in which the new technologies are presented as a decisive tool for an active democracy based upon people's intervention in public affairs.

Very few critics try to interlace these prospects or seem to perceive the contradictions that stem from the partition.

In the first place, to bring up only the problems connected with the defence of privacy means to conceive of social control as an intervention that can come only "from the top" and that is aimed mainly at regulating and restraining "private" liberties.

On the one hand, the very meaning of privacy is ambiguous: "Private" is what concerns the personal sphere, but it also always goes with property and, last but not least, it is usually the opposite of "public." That is why the philosophy of deregulation grows exactly here.

As a matter of fact, the defence of privacy may be easily misused to restrict public initiative, thus making very difficult the defence of the personal sphere itself, a defence that cannot be pursued, of course, on a private or an individual basis only, particularly in this technological age. This presents a subtle contradiction that resembles a boomerang.

On the other hand, the appeal to the mere defence of privacy may legitimate the protection – which means the concealment, in many circumstances – of all the information items "owned" by private enterprises or sank in the bureaucratic well of public administration. It is not by chance that through appealing to defence of privacy the debaters and the legislators mostly neglect to focus on the problems connected with the sources' *behaviour*, with the spreading *strategies of secrecy*, and, consequently, with the vital topic of the citizen's right *to be informed, to exchange information, and to intervene in decision-making processes.*

No one can deny, though, that the problems connected with the defence of the personal sphere are very serious and complicated, nowadays. What seems to be essential is to do away with that partition and to widen the outlook, altering the global perspective in theory and practice.

2. In this matter of the defence of privacy, the debate and the consequent law-making initiatives have been mostly connected with problems at the individual and domestic level, with property rights and the topic of individual consent for use of "private" information items. This starting point was probably induced by Western tradition in the field of civil rights and by the steady tendency to consider individual benefit above all – as well as by the abuses that have been discovered in the behaviour of public and private institutions entitled to collect, store, and distribute data concerning citizens' lives.

In more recent times the "right to access" has been added to defence of privacy and data protection. This new topic has brought a different perspective onto the scene: people have discovered the possibility (and then soon the necessity) of exerting, from the bottom, an active influence over institutions. The "right of access" implies that every person is entitled to get information about his or her own personal data as collected and stored by public or private institutions; and to eventually correct the data or even to have them erased.

In this perspective the problem of "transparence" has come up: not only the transparence of archives and data banks but also the transparence of the collecting processes and of the distribution strategies.

Lately the debate on the "right of access" has tended to include also *non*-personal data; and it has been suggested that representative agencies and democratic social organizations should be entitled to intervene. A special care has been dedicated to *data transfer* (Rodotà, 1984).

Thus, at last, the general topic of the "circulation of information" begins to impose itself also in this area. But the debate still takes into consideration *only the data that are usually collected and stored in the archives (the public archives, in particular)*. It seldom concerns the information items that could (and should, eventually) be collected and stored and distributed and are not at present. And in fact what is invoked is just the right of access – the right of request, we could say – and never the *duty of supply, the duty of reply*, the duty of collecting, storing, and, above all, distributing information that might be precious in view of people's control over institutions and of people's initiative within the democratic processes.

In this regard it is clear that not only the data stored by the governmental authorities, the police, the public institutions but also those "owned" by private corporations and commercial and industrial enterprises must be taken into consideration. It cannot be ignored that the strategies and the activities of corporations and private enterprises heavily influence social processes and people's daily lives (should we call it "privacy"?): To be informed about these topics may be very useful to people just so they better understand economic and social issues, environmental risks, and community prospects.

This recalls a basic question suggested by the Organization for Economic Co-operation and Development (OECD): "Whether it is better to consider information as a good which may be taken possession of, or a community source" (OECD, 1986).

3. A further starting point, considering the actual trends of the information system, could be the topic of secrecy. If privacy must be defended to prevent abuses "from the top," secrecy must be attacked and defeated to support interventions "from the bottom" in social and decision-making processes. The interlacement between these two pressing claims may break the old partition between the two faces of social control. Yet it can be asserted that while the defence of privacy does not affect secrecy (except to make it thicker, perhaps), the defeat of secrecy can surely help to protect personal life and privacy too.

In the overwhelming flood of information that is typical of our time, two different kinds of items are processed and circulated. Information may be produced to give "consumers" the data and items that sources and entrepreneurs want them to get; or it may be produced and circulated to give people what they need and/or wish to obtain in different times and circumstances. The two kinds of information items may correspond and they may not. People's needs and wishes are not easily traced and made out; entrepreneurs' and sources' will and aims are of course clearer and somewhat more compelling. Besides, there may be something that sources do not want to be circulated, at least out of the "dedicated" circuits.

This is not a simple hypothesis. Paradoxically, secrecy is spreading more and more over the information society. Nowadays we run across so-called "state security," and, under it, military secrets, and, more, we run across scientific secrets, industrial and commercial secrets, and so on. Some trends are quite new. Scientific secrecy, for instance, is getting more and more firmly established exactly in those countries where the prophets of the "electronic democracy" say that science and technology will soon bring about a high level of mass knowledge.

The problems concerning secrecy are heavy and subtle. First of all, secrecy does not only conceal information items. Nay, if secret data and information items were kept quite out of circulation and not used by anybody but the "owners," we could not even talk of "information," since information does not exist in default of an exchange process.

But here the picture is different. Secret information items serve the "owners" who possess and process them just because they are intended to be destined to *some* people in *some* circumstances for *some* purposes only. That is why I find it more correct to speak of "productive secrecy" (Cesareo, 1981), in that secrecy produces its effects exactly in relation to the restraints it imposes on the circulation and the use of specific information items. And that is why the analysis of "productive secrecy" must start from sources and take into account the processes of production as well as the processes of distribution and consumption.

"Sources" is a topic that is seldom brought up in the debate on the information system, at least at this level. And yet data banks and media collect, process, store, and distribute just information items (raw information items) that come from different sources, which release these items directly or through information providers. The sources, then, are the starting point and they are not information producers in the first place.

When we consider the sources, we must distinguish between the "active" and "passive" ones: The active ones are those that mostly release information on their own initiative; the passive ones are those that offer information items only when and if consulted. The "central" sources (big political and economic institutions, military officials, big industrial and commercial enterprises, scientific institutions, and big research centres) are always "active" and exactly being so they can employ the strategy of "productive secrecy." The "passive" sources (which are usually peripheral) may be reticent when consulted, but their reticence obeys a different logic and is mainly originated by their distrust of the information collectors and media.

The "productive secrecy" consists in: a) putting into circulation only the information items the owners hold to be profitable for them; b) releasing information items only *when* and *how* it is convenient for the owners (and rejecting, as far as possible, "extra" requests by data banks, media, information operators, even public authorities); c) selecting the "dedicated" circuits for each information item and controlling as far as possible the circulation processes (also by directly owning the distribution channels); d) hindering everybody from checking how the information items were originated and from verifying their truth, accuracy, and completeness. Here we realize that "productive secrecy" can be put into being only on account of the right of property that also includes information. In fact, any investigation from outside the source may be considered a "violation," even a sort of "robbery" that can be punished eventually by law.

Thus the secrecy produces its effects: a) making it difficult for anybody to acquire – and even to know about – information items that are considered risky or dangerous or directly/indirectly harmful to the interests of the source-owner; b) emphasizing every information item that is put into circulation by the source; c) giving every information item released by the source the mark of "genuineness" because it will be presented as true, accurate, and complete just because it has been put into circulation (and this is what makes it easy to brand as "rumours," on the contrary, all the information items that have not been put into circulation on the source's own initiative). This does not mean, of course, that it is impossible to test or to contest an information item coming out from the "productive secrecy." But it will surely be hard to do so, although it will always be done in return. So the autonomous queries and investigations eventually inspired by people's demands and by social needs become more and more difficult. Journalists and information operators are discouraged from searching and get accustomed more and more to wait for the source's offers, helped by new technologies that thus turn out to be the means of restraining instead of enlarging the circulation of information items.

Let us consider data banks. It is widely discussed how to make easier and cheaper the access to the information they store, but it is a discussion that deals with the present logic, still. Central sources and information providers are the subjects who lead the game: Access may be exerted only within the range of the information items they make available on their own and exclusive decision.

This leads also to the topic of the "passive" and peripheral sources. Many data and information items that could turn out to be precious with a view to understanding and control "from the bottom" of the social processes and, in particular, of the local situations do not circulate because they have not been collected or searched for. Still they exist and could be found out through the "passive" sources (the places where common people undergo their social experience, first of all).

The promotion of information requires, then, that "productive secrecy" be defeated, in the first place: It requires strategic interventions aimed to change the behaviour of the central sources, of the information providers, of the data banks, and of the media – and to claim the transparence of public and private enterprises. Otherwise we run the risk of finding ourselves, sooner or later, "in a society of secrecy which will question even the public use of telephone directories" (OECD, 1986).

But what is needed also is a vigorous spur to extend as much as possible investigations and the collection of information items out from the "passive" sources. This implies that these so often neglected sources be trained and enabled to draw information from their own experience and communicate it through the distribution circuits.

4. A generic reference to "communications democracy," as we very often find in the debates, is only demagogic, then. The first obstacles we run across in pursuing new communications patterns are the thick economic interests that thrive in this field too and influence the production as well as the distribution of information.

It is not only by chance, for instance, that there are strict rules for the collection and circulation of economic and financial information within "highly dedicated" circuits. These kinds of information items must be correct, complete, verifiable, and easily available. They must also be circulated regularly and with the maximum of efficiency at this "proper" level. In fact, it is rightly assumed that such warranties can only enable economic subjects to operate as being protected from ruinous mistakes and from deceit. There is always someone who can try to break the rules, of course, but violations – that can stem from the will to conceal useful information and not from the efforts to find it out, as happens in the "normal" circuits – may be strongly persecuted.

Out of "dedicated circuits" and far from the selected subjects everything changes: The "protection" rules go against free circulation and consumers may be deceived at any time.

What must be faced, then, are the motivations of secrecy and the specific interests that "productive secrecy" tends to protect (and the word "protection" has completely different meanings within different contexts). It is essential to ascertain which are the interests at stake and which ones should prevail in the different "information games."

In the case of industrial and commercial enterprises, for instance, "productive secrecy" is exerted, on the one hand, to protect business interests against competitors, and, on the other, to eventually promote the best business image on the market. These are at first glance legitimate interests; but the trouble is that these interests are often protected by holding back data and information items whose public circulation could help protect community interests and democratic control "from the bottom" or put in a proper perspective social (mainly local) processes. Let us only think of health topics, of the defence of the environment and of the thousands of chemical substances and toxicants that are employed in different production processes: A large amount of information in this field is still concealed not only from common people but also from researchers and public authorities just because of the concept of "information property." Or the information is circulated only in accordance with the logic of "productive secrecy."

Another big obstacle to the circulation of data and information items consists in the trend to use new technologies to entirely entrust the productions and distribution of information "goods" to the present market logic.

The worshippers of the "total market" often assert that the play of demand and supply is the best way to prevent censorship and to enforce the "right to be informed." But, apart from the heavy effects of "productive secrecy" (which is strictly connected with market logic), if the collection and distribution of information are regulated only by the logic of marketing, it becomes unavoidable that some data and information items will never be put into circulation or collected and processed because the "owners" or the information operators will believe they are not sufficiently marketable or profitable. There are also many data that should be collected, processed, and distributed because of their social relevance even if it is not profitable to do so. But the potential consumers of many socially valuable information items haven't got the purchasing power or the cultural background that may induce them to request those items on the market. And, last but not least, it is very difficult to find out and interpret the demand, especially in this field.

This leads to a number of questions. Is it possible to attain a socially inspired definition like "public utility information"? Is it possible to find out "public utility information items" by investigating sources at different levels? Is it possible to establish, and enforce by law, the duty to collect and store, to release, and to distribute the "public utility information items"? Is it possible to consider an offense or a crime the act of concealing or neglecting this kind of information item and the behaviour of the source that restrains it from distribution? Is it possible to build proper circuits at different levels to make sure that the public utility information items reach the concerned people?

These questions lead us also to the matter of "when" the information should be collected and distributed. Who is entitled to decide this matter and by what criteria? The strategy of "productive secrecy" implies that the "when" is mostly up to the source. But if democracy and participation must be pursued, it is necessary to change the rules, once more. For instance, to be correctly and opportunely informed about decision-making processes, concerned people should get the necessary information *before* the possible alternatives are determined, even before all the interests at stake and the involved problems are singled out. To be enabled to intervene, citizens should have the information *in progress*. Besides, people should also be enabled to urge sources and public authorities and operators to search for, collect, and circulate this or that information item in relation to collective interests and developing needs. Sources and operators and public authorities should meet these requests following the "public utility information" logic.

Does this mean that the already overwhelming flood of data and information items should be increased? This increase cannot be taken for granted. Once more, it must be emphasized that the exponential development of distributed information has been accompanied by the progressive extension of secrecy, so that in the nebulae of the information society the very core of events and processes is often obscured. The "public utility information" rules, then, should not necessarily bring about a larger quantity of information items, but it surely should lighten that core, the rest being, so to say, optional.

5. Pursuing "communications democracy" we should take into careful consideration the production, distribution, and consumption processes of information, distinguishing the different levels but not disconnecting them. Here we meet problems concerning the processing of information items, the general "information culture," and what could be defined as the "consumer's competence."

It has been said that to use information to the best advantage, individuals and groups need at same time to *know, to be able, to be willing* (FAST, 1985). To know and to be able, it was added, depend mostly or totally on the social and cultural context; to be willing is up to the subject. But, as a matter of fact, the "subjective" will is also influenced by cultural background and social environment: That is why it has been said that in the information society the "poor" include ethnic minorities as well as women. To promote a proper "information culture" may therefore be one of the first steps towards communications democracy.

Here also the "user's competence" comes in. To get the proper information items the user must in the first place be able to search for them and find them. This takes time and requires an adequate know-how, especially if new technologies are involved. In fact, new technologies may be vital to improved information hunting, but they undeniably require skill (and not only on the technical side); otherwise they may, on the contrary, discourage any "subjective will."

Furthermore, an information item becomes really useful only if it is connected and compared to other pieces of information, only if it is placed or replaced in its proper context (Cesareo, 1984). But the sources that produce and release information and data are – apart from "productive secrecy" – scattered and separate; they operate at different levels, each one in its own interest. Thus the alternatives are: to entirely trust highly processed information and the syntheses produced by the "active" sources, by some information providers, and by media; or to search for different information items and work them out by connecting them and finishing them.

When we consider that "social control" and initiative from the bottom take place mostly in a partial and local dimension and therefore need specific and aimed information items, we easily conclude that skilled work is requested from the users, unless everything is once more delegated to the "experts" or the "representative" (at which level, however?). This work – even if it were to be carried on by social groups rather than by individuals – requires that problems be faced at the production and distribution levels.

First, speed and quantity, beyond a certain degree, may definitely complicate the task: That is why the information flows should be regulated according to the users' logic (the "public utility" logic) rather than according to the sources' and entrepreneurs' interests, as now happens.

Secondly, "public utility information" should be collected, processed, and stored so as to bear the mark of its origin and the necessary reference to other information items connected to it. Professional operators could be trained to process information so as to give "public utility" items transparence and to improve the comparability of these items.

Thirdly, "public utility information" could be produced, on the one side, through a continuous investigation into the sources by the operators and, on the other, through a continuous dealing between operators and protagonists in the different social processes. This collective work could produce "collective discourses" that could connect and bring together different areas and experience – which means that information could at last be built and interpreted in relation to the different, specific social processes and situations, problems, and needs without losing its exchangeability.

This approach could also make distribution more correct and easier. Nowadays the multiplication of channels and distribution circuits makes it much more difficult for users to orientate themselves and to search out the proper items (that is why the central sources' and entrepreneurs' strategies and suggestions turn out to be more compelling than ever).

On the other hand, just starting from this difficulty, sources and entrepreneurs tend more and more to distribute only "aimed" information, so that audiences and user groups are selected in advance according to the market logic rather than to users' homogeneous interests and social needs.

"Public utility information" could rather be distributed through flexible circuits programmed in relation to different social needs and processes. A clear map of these circuits could be made available to the users. Moreover, "public information operators" could be trained to constantly help users search for, find out, and finish all the information items they need. Such a system of "public utility information" networks could be aimed at serving social groups rather than individuals and at fitting dynamically different social situations. Some projects of this kind are taken into consideration by the Green movement in Europe and appear to be an alternative to corporate or basically professional or leisure networking.

The global prospects of "public utility information," then, imply a qualitative development of the information system, whose main features should be the strong connection between "circulation" and "transformation." It is necessary to distinguish once more in this prospect two different kinds of information items: the ones produced, collected, processed, and distributed primarily to create general or local consent to the initiative and decisions of specific sources or for specific political proposals; and the others produced, searched for, collected, processed, and distributed to enable concerned groups to appraise problems and participate in the decision-making processes.

The second kind of information item must not only be programmed but also produced and distributed in collaboration with social protagonists in the different situations. This also requires some large and specific investments: New technologies, for instance, should be developed and diffused for these purposes. As a matter of fact, new technologies might help very much to produce and properly distribute "public utility information," thanks to their flexibility and increasing capability to collect, store, put together, and compare huge quantities of different information items. But this will never come about spontaneously and automatically as part of the development of the present information system: Without specific financial and cultural investments, without research and planned initiatives, the potential of the new technologies to help defeat the strategy of "productive secrecy" and improve participation can easily be wasted.

6. "Information is power": This is almost a cliché, by now. And, consequently, only too often it is said that the development of the information system will bring about the redistribution of power and a new democracy. Some take this for granted, while others think of it as a useful utopia.

But the equation itself must be questioned. The maximum of information availability, the maximum of transparence, may produce the biggest show. Decision-making processes may be performed in a glass house; but if the people who are enabled to look into the house cannot go through the door, participation remains only a form of peeping.

Sure enough, information is a founding factor of power, now more than ever. But it does not provide power by itself. The position any one person occupies in the power structure is determined by many factors and is decisive. People in positions of authority may better exert their power if they are well informed, but those who are only well informed (and "productive secrecy" restricts access to information for those who cannot use the privileged circuits) are not enabled, just because of this, to decide and exert power.

Although "authority tends to be decentralized, residing in individuals with pertinent information rather than in those who occupy assigned positions" (McInnis, 1984), this tendency cannot be taken for granted. It is more likely that those who occupy assigned positions will get pertinent information than the contrary. We can only be sure that information increases power and that power enables people to get pertinent information and to use it. For the rest, a deep transformation – not only of the information system but also of the power system – is needed to produce a factual participatory democracy.

This does not mean that efforts towards "communications democracy" – as, for instance, the struggle to defeat secrecy or the theoretical and practical work to elaborate and organize "public utility information" networks – are useless in the push to attain a better democracy. But there are no automatic "byproducts" in this field. Communications networks and power structures cannot be identified. And even if it can be said that, nowadays, the power structure is polycentric, nothing entitles us to assert that different positions in relation to different centres of power may be modified only through a better or wider distribution of information.

It is true, though, that what in Europe is called "governability" (that is, the actual possibility of planning and governing social processes) depends more and more on the real capability of different social subjects to participate in the selection of problems, in the elaboration of solutions, and in the decision-making processes, rather than on a broader consent to strategies and solutions eventually worked out and decided at central level. Conflicts and solutions must be managed day by day at the bottom level; and the different social subjects will not be able to manage them or engage in managing them if they are not involved from the beginning, not properly informed, and not enabled to exert power.

The complexity of the "postindustrial" or "postmodern" societies surely requires this complete engagement. But we should be fully aware that a new, suitable form of democracy – one that would produce a circular social control springing from the bottom and, at the same time, would be capable of ruling social processes at the bottom level – is still only flickering in front of us.

References

Cesareo, G. (1981) *Fa notizia: fonti, processi, tecnologie e soggetti nella macchina dell'infomazione.* Roma: Editori Riuniti.

Cesareo, G. (1984). "Towards an Electronic Democracy?" In V. Mosco and J. Wasko, eds., *Changing Patterns of Communication Control.* Norwood, N.J.: Ablex Publishing.

Eurosocial (1985). "Welfare State Developments and The New Technologies." *Report,* No.26. Vienna.

FAST (1985). "Europe 1995: mutations technologiques & enjeux sociaux." Doc. No. Eur 8936 IT, CEE, CECA, CEEA, Bruxelles.

Joinet, L. (1983). "Etudes des principes directeurs concernent de recours a des fichiers de personnes informatises." ONU, Doc. E/CN4/Sub2/18.

Maccacaro, G.A., ed. (1976). "Seveso: un crimine di pace," Sapere (Bari, Italy), New Series, No.976,4-158.

McInnis N. (1984). "Networking. A Way To Manage Our Changing World?" *The Futurist,* June 6.

Organization for Economic Co-operation and Development (OECD) (1986). Report on "Lafraude liée à l'informatique: analyse de politiques juridiques."

Rodotà, S. (1984). "'1984' and After: The Societal Challenge of Information Technologies." Report of position speaker at the international conference organized by the government of FRG in co-operation with the OECD, Berlin, November.

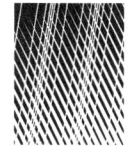

Part III

New Technologies and Oppositional Cultural Practice

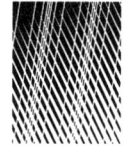

Public-Access Television and the Struggle for Democracy

Douglas Kellner

A community will evolve only when a people control their own communications.
— *Frantz Fanon*

GENUINE DEMOCRACY requires the participation of individuals in matters of concern to their common social and political life. During an era in which mass media of communication arbitrate political and social reality and wield tremendous power over how individuals see the world and live their lives, the democratization of the media becomes an issue of paramount importance. Democratic media require media that further democracy and allow individuals access to their fellow citizens. Genuine democracy requires individuals who, minimally, are informed about the political issues and processes in their country and, maximally, participate in public debate and decision-making. One could argue that in the United States today, neither of these preconditions is met and that this country is thus suffering from a crisis of democracy (Kellner, 1990).

In this chapter, drawing on over ten years of experience as an activist in public-access television, I will argue that public-access television provides not only one of the few existing possibilities for alternative television but also the best possibility for using the broadcast media to serve the interests of popular democracy.[1]

Public-Access Television

The rapid expansion of public-access television in recent years provides new possibilities for progressives to counter the conservative programming that dominates mainstream television. Innovative access programming is now being cablecast regularly in New York, Los Angeles, Boston, Chicago, Atlanta, Madison, Austin, and perhaps as many as twelve hundred other towns or regions throughout the country.

When cable television was widely introduced in the early 1970s, the Federal Communications Commission mandated that: "Beginning in 1972, new cable systems [and after 1977, all cable systems] in the 100 largest television markets be required to provide channels for government, for educational purposes, and most importantly, for public access." This mandate suggested that cable systems should make available three public-access channels for state and local government, education, and community use. "Public access" was construed to mean that the cable company should make equipment and air time available so that any people who wanted to could make non-commercial use of the access channel to say or do anything that they wished on a first-come, first-serve basis, subject only to obscenity and libel laws. Creating an access channel required, in many cases, setting up a local organization to manage the access system, though in other cases the cable company itself managed the access centre, providing the equipment and personnel to make access programming.

In the beginning, few, if any, cable systems made as many as three channels available. Some systems began offering one or two in the early to mid-1970s. For the most part, the availability of access channels depended on the political clout of local governments and committed, often unpaid, local groups to convince the cable companies – almost all privately owned – to make the channels available. In Austin, Texas, for example, a small group involved in video production formed Austin Community Television (ACTV) in 1973 and began cablecasting with their own equipment through the cable system. Eventually ACTV received foundation and CETA government grants to support their activities, buy equipment, and pay salaries to regular employees. A new cable contract signed in the early 1980s called for the cable company to provide $500,000 a year for access, and after a difficult political struggle the access system was able to get at least $300,000 to $400,000 a year to support Austin Community Television activities.

In 1979, however, a Supreme Court decision struck down the 1972 FCC ruling on the grounds that the agency didn't have the authority to mandate access – an authority that supposedly belongs to the U.S. Congress (*FCC vs. Midwest Video Cor.*, *440 U.S. 689*, discussed in Koenig, 1979). Nonetheless, cable was expanding so rapidly and becoming such a high-growth, competitive industry that city governments considering cable systems were besieged by companies making lucrative offers of twenty- to eighty-channel cable systems; in such an atmosphere, city governments were able to negotiate access channels and financial support for a public-access system. Consequently, public access grew significantly during the 1980s.

Where there are operative public-access systems, individuals have promising, though not sufficiently explored, possibilities to produce and broadcast their own television programs. In Austin, for example, there have been weekly anti-nuclear programs, black and chicano series, gay programs, countercultural and anarchist programs, an atheist program, feminist and labour programs, and a weekly progressive news magazine, *Alternative Views*, which since 1978 has produced over five hundred hour-long programs on a wide variety of topics, providing a conduit for "alternative views" usually excluded from the broadcasting spectrum.

Alternative Views

Although the producers of *Alternative Views* had little television experience and no resources, we immediately began doing a weekly program by using video equipment and tapes at the University of Texas as well as the broadcast and editing facilities of Austin Community Television. In fact, a group wishing to make access programming does not need technical experience or even financial resources to begin producing access programming where there is an access system in place that will make available equipment, technical personnel, and video-tapes. A few systems charge money for use of facilities, or a fee for use of air time, but due to competitive bidding between cable systems in the 1980s for the most lucrative franchises, many cable companies offer free use of their facilities; occasionally they even provide free video-tapes. Many public-access systems also offer training programs, if groups or individuals want to make their own programs from original conception through final editing. The costs of equipment have also been rapidly declining, so it is possible for some groups to purchase their own video equipment.

From the beginning, those of us involved in *Alternative Views* were convinced that our programs would prove of interest to the community, and indeed we gained a large and loyal audience.[2] On our first program, in October 1978, our guest was an Iranian student who discussed opposition to the Shah and the possibility of his overthrow; we also had a detailed discussion of how the Sandinista movement was struggling to overthrow Somoza. This was weeks before the national broadcast media discovered these movements. We then had two programs on nuclear energy and energy alternatives. Among the guests was Ray Reece of Austin, whose book *The Sun Betrayed* (South End Press, 1980) later became a definitive text on corporate control and suppression of solar energy. On early shows we had long interviews with former Senator Ralph Yarborough, a Texas progressive responsible for legislation like the National Defense Education Act, and we learned that he had never before been interviewed in depth for television. We had an electrifying two-hour, two-part interview with former CIA official John Stockwell, who told how he had been recruited into the CIA at the University of Texas. Stockwell discussed CIA recruitment, indoctrination and other activities, and his own experiences in Africa, Vietnam, and Angola, experiences that led him to quit the CIA and write his book *In Search of Enemies*, which exposed the Angola operation he had been in charge of. Stockwell presented a thorough history of CIA abuses and provided arguments as to why he thought the CIA should be shut down and a new intelligence service developed.

Other exciting interviews included discussions with U.S. Atheist founder Madalyn Murray O'Hair, who gave her views on religions and told how she had successfully produced lawsuits to eliminate prayer from schools, thus preserving the constitutional separation between church and state; with Benjamin Spock, who discussed the evolution of his theories of childrearing, his political radicalization, and his adventures in the 1960s as an anti-war activist; with the former Stokley Carmichael (now Kwame Ture), who discussed his 1960s militancy and theories of black power, his experiences in Africa, and his perspectives on world revolution; and with Nobel Prize winner George Wald, former Attorney General Ramsey Clark, anti-nuclear activist Helen Caldicott, and many other well-known intellectuals, activists, and social critics.

As our connections grew, we began receiving documentaries from various filmmakers and began to mix together the documentary and talk-show formats. We also presented a regular news section that utilized material from mostly non-mainstream news sources to provide stories ignored by establishment media or interpretations of events different from the mainstream. We received very positive responses to our show and began regularly taping interviews with people who visited Austin as well as with local activists involved in various struggles. We began varying our format, using documentary films, slide shows, raw video footage, and other visual material to enhance the visual aspect of our program. In addition, one of our members, Frank Morrow, became skilled at editing and developed impressive montages of documentary and interview material to illustrate topics discussed.

Once the project got under way we had little difficulty finding subjects, people, or resources. We discovered that almost anyone we wanted to interview was happy to come to our program, and after we began gaining recognition, local groups and individuals called us regularly to provide topics, speakers, films, or other video material. We encouraged local groups to make their own weekly shows, and a variety of peace, countercultural, gay, anti-nuke, chicano, anti-klan, women's, and other groups have done so. Indeed, we have continued to serve as an umbrella organization for over one hundred local groups, using their speakers and film or video materials to produce our programs.

Aside from the hour-long interviews with nationally known guests, other feminists, gays, union activists, and representatives of local progressive groups have appeared on our show. We have also done in-depth interviews with officials from the Soviet Union, Nicaragua, Allende's former government in Chile, the Democratic Front in El Salvador, and many other Third World countries and revolutionary movements. In addition to the documentaries and films that various filmmakers and groups have provided for us, we have made some video documentaries ourselves, on a variety of topics. We received raw video footage of the bombing of Lebanon and the aftermath of the massacres at Sabra and Shatilla, of the assassinations of five communist labour organizers by the Klu Klux Klan in Greensboro, North Carolina, of daily life in the liberated zones of El Salvador, and of counterrevolutionary activity in Nicaragua.

Most of this material would not have been shown on network television, or if shown would have been severely cut and censored. Consequently, at present it seems that the best existing possibility for producing alternative television is through public-access/cable television. Obviously, progressive groups who want to carry through access projects need to develop a sustained commitment to radical media politics and explore local possibilities for intervention. We began our work with a small group, mostly graduate students, and – given the high degree of turnover in a university community – only two of us, Frank Morrow and I, have been active throughout the entire project. Over the years several other people have worked with us regularly, helping us with production, fundraising, publicity, and other projects. The first few years we had some internal conflicts concerning topics, format, or organization, but we worked through these problems and during the last few years have functioned smoothly in our internal politics. Nevertheless, external problems have emerged, both here in Austin and elsewhere in the United States.

Public-Access Television: Problems and Challenges

Once progressive public-access television became more widespread and popular in Austin it also became subject to political counterattacks. The establishment daily monopoly newspaper, *The Austin American-Statesman*, published frequent denunciations of public-access television, claiming that the medium was controlled by the "lunatic" fringe of "socialists, atheists, and radicals" and was not representative of the community as a whole – an interesting charge since many conservative church groups, business groups, and political groups were also making use of access. The newspaper attacked community television for the "irresponsibility" of many of its programs as well as its allegedly poor technical quality (in fact, technical quality has constantly improved). In 1983 these criticisms were repeated in editorials and articles in the more liberal monthly magazines *Texas Monthly* and *Third Coast*. It seems that representatives of these publications wanted to get part of the access pie themselves and thus attacked the group currently in control – as did some members of the local public broadcasting system.

The criticisms became a tangible threat when Austin Community Television had to apply for a five-year renewal of its contract as access manager. Certain interests in the community were attempting to eliminate ACTV and substitute another access manager and system controlled by city government and local media interests. After an intense political struggle, the city cable commission and city council approved the renewal of the ACTV access management and the community remained in control of the access system, which is open to whoever wants to use it on either a regular or occasional basis. Since then the Austin system of access has been nationally recognized as a model for other communities. In 1986 the National Association of Local Cable Programmers presented ACTV with an award as the best cable access system and recognized *Alternative Views* as the best public-affairs access program in the United States. In 1989, for contributions to access television Frank Morrow and I won the Stoney Prize – a yearly award presented in honour of George Stoney, a New York University communications professor often considered the father of public-access television.

Other U.S. cities have not been so fortunate.[3] The cable company in San Diego reportedly took over the access centre after gaining a long-term renewal of its contract; a company recently bought out the San Antonio cable company and threatened to deny the terms of a previous contract that had mandated several access channels; Warner Communications in Dallas threatened to renege on earlier contract obligations and then sold the franchise, creating an uncertain access situation; Tulsa shut down its access system completely; and many cable companies have never provided access channels while others rigidly control the access channels and tend to not permit programs like *Alternative Views* to be cablecast. In addition, cable companies have taken over access and leased the time to commercial interests rather than make time available to community groups.

But still, many cities *do* have relatively open access channels, and where possible progressives should start using this vehicle of political communication with an eye towards developing a national public-access network in which tapes can be exchanged and circulated. Various groups have already made beginnings in this direction. The Austin organization, for instance, has developed a national access network, which began in spring 1984 with the distribution of *Alternative Views* program tapes to access TV contacts in Dallas and San Antonio. In the fall of 1984 we added Fayetteville, Atlanta, Minneapolis, Pittsburgh, and Urbana to our evolving network. We then made contact with access systems and groups in other cities around the United States and as a result our tapes have been shown in New York, Boston, Portland, San Diego, Marin Country (California), Fairfax and Arlington counties (Virginia), Cincinnati, San Francisco, Columbus, Chicago, New Haven, Durham, and many other cities.

The project began with the contacting of local groups or members of the access centre who might be interested in sponsoring our program on a regular weekly basis. Then we duplicate and send packages of five tapes to access systems in these cities. Frank Morrow of Austin has managed to provide as many as fifty access centres with our tapes and keep track of what programs have been distributed to the various centres to avoid duplication and provide variety. [Groups or individuals who would be interested in sponsoring our program in their areas are invited to write us at the address given in note 3, and we would also like to hear from individuals or groups with programs that could be included in our series or with ideas about a possible progressive access network.]

At the Union for Democratic Communications conference in Washington in October 1984, several access groups explored the possibility of leasing weekly satellite time so that progressive access programming could be beamed all over the country. This would·mean that the millions of people with home satellite receivers could watch progressive public-access programming. Preliminary inquiries suggest that renting satellite time for access programming is not prohibitively expensive, so that a grant of around $100,000 or $150,000 a year might yet make it possible for hundreds of thousands of people all over the country to receive progressive television in their homes.

During 1985-86, Paper Tiger Television, a New York-based access project founded by DeeDee Halleck, received grants that made possible a ten-week satellite access project, Deep Dish TV, which broadcast via satellite ten programs on such topics as militarism, agriculture, racism, Central America, and children's TV to access systems and private dishes all over the country. This effort could eventually lead to a left satellite channel able to compete with the multitude of religious, business, and other satellite outlets that tend to present the ideologies and agendas of the right. In addition, however, existing access centres must be persuaded to carry progressive access programming; this has indeed proved possible, for Paper Tiger says that over three hundred systems carried its Deep Dish TV series. Paper Tiger followed up with a second and third season of Deep-Dish television, showing a new series of programs on selected topics produced by various access groups around the country from material submitted.

How to Produce Local Access Programming

To begin the process of making use of public-access television, individuals and groups must first explore the availability of an access channel and approach the people in charge of it. The individuals and group should make clear what type of programming they want to produce and make inquiries about the availability of equipment, training, and tapes in the access centre. Next, group members must decide if they wish only to produce occasional programs or develop a regular weekly, bi-weekly, or monthly series. *Alternative Views* began by immediately producing weekly one-hour programs, and we developed our programming organization, philosophy, and projects as we went on. In some cases, however, it might be better to have more fully developed projects outlined before beginning.

In many ways it is preferable to undertake a weekly program, aired at the same day and time every week, to help build up an audience. A talk-show format is usually the easiest approach and more imaginative uses of video can be developed as experience and expertise expand. Paper Tiger Television in New York, for example, combines media critics talking about various types of corporate media with imaginative sets, visuals, and editing. In Pittsburgh, a labour-oriented program, *The Mill Hunk News*, combined news reports of labour issues with documentary interviews with workers, music-videos, and other creative visuals.

An alternative television project can also draw on the many progressive films and videos already available. Many groups and individuals are happy to provide copies of their films and video-cassettes for broadcast on public access, and if the films and duplicating equipment are available, this is a good way to begin. Then, as the project progresses, the group may want to begin developing its own documentaries and perhaps mix documentary, film, and discussion formats by editing in titles, slides, and other images to make fuller use of the video format.

Once the project gets under way, the group should consider incorporating as a non-profit corporation and applying for tax-exempt status from the IRS. This helps in fundraising activities because donations become tax-deductible; it also makes possible the purchase of non-profit bulk-mailing permits, which can be useful for fundraising and communicating with audiences by mail. An access project can also be funded through regular benefits, solicitation of contributions, or various local and national foundation grants. A few access systems actually pay for programming but this is, unfortunately, a rare exception. Indeed, developing progressive access systems will eventually involve struggling for funding from the access system and the city government so that members of access groups could be paid for their activity and have proper budgets to purchase cassettes of films and video programming from independent producers. In this way both public-access television and independent film and video could be established on a more financially secure foundation.

Public-access television is not a substitute for political organization and struggle but is rather a vehicle for participants and local political groups to provide information about their activities and to involve people in their efforts. Almost all of the more than one hundred groups that have appeared on *Alternative Views* programs report that they have subsequently received many phone calls and letters and that appearing on public-access television was a useful organizing and recruiting tool. Public-access videotapes can also be made available to high schools, the university campus, churches, and other local groups. Our tapes on Central America, for instance, have been frequently shown in churches and elsewhere as part of educational and organizing efforts, and we make our tapes available to groups who want to use them for organizing and educational purposes. We also make ourselves and those who appear on our program available to groups to discuss specific issues, programs, or public-access television itself. We regularly appear as well on panels at conferences all over the country to discuss public access. Thus we see public-access programming as a useful tool for political education and organizing that goes beyond regular broadcasting by reaching into community politics and organizing.

While public-access television is still in a relatively early stage of development here in the United States and is just beginning in Europe, it contains the promise of providing a different type of alternative television. Despite obstacles to its use, public access provides the one opening in the commercial and state broadcasting systems that is at least potentially open to progressive intervention. It is self-defeating simply to dismiss broadcast media as tools of manipulation and to think that the print media are the only tools of communication and political education open to progressives. Surveys have shown that audiences take individuals, groups, and politics that appear on TV more seriously, and the community use of television will thus help progressive movements and struggles gain legitimacy and force in the shifting and contradictory field of U.S. politics. The right has been making effective use of the new technologies and media of communication, and a state of aloofness is a luxury that the left can no longer afford. The possible breakup of the conservative hegemony of the 1980s confronts us with both new challenges and dangers. But if the left is to produce a genuine alternative to the right, we must increase our mass base and circulate our struggles to more segments of the population. After all, most people get their news and information from television, and the broadcast media arguably play a decisive role in defining political realities, shaping public opinion, and determining what is or what is not to be taken seriously. If progressives want to play a role in U.S. political life, they must come to terms with the realities of electronic communication and develop strategies to make use of new technologies and possibilities for intervention.

There is the risk that time and energies spent in other projects may be lost in the occasionally frustrating politics of media. But these risks must be taken if progressives want to intervene more effectively in the changing technological and political environment of the future. To ensure that we get the full free flow of information that an informed democratic citizenry needs to participate intelligently in the political process, we need an expanded system of public-access television, which could be funded from revenues received from cable systems (as is currently the case in Austin and elsewhere in the country). In fact, even more spectacular alternatives exist in the new satellite television technology and other new information technologies that contain the potential for a greatly expanded democratic communication system.

Satellite Television and Some Utopian Proposals

During the mid-1980s there was a rapid growth of the satellite television industry. In 1986, however, the satellite networks began scrambling programs, forcing people to buy decoders and pay monthly subscription rates. While this development significantly slowed down the growth of the satellite television industry, there are still more than two and a half million satellite dishes operative in the United States, and satellite television continues to provide a technological foundation for a national system of alternative television – for a democratic, innovative, and diverse television system. A combination of cable and satellite technologies would make possible the creation of a truly excellent system of communications. But this requires an immediate halt to satellite scrambling and a free flow of information and entertainment to satellite dishes. While the U.S. government has consistently followed a communications policy in the field of international communications based on the "free flow of information," the government has not allowed a free flow to its own citizens by sanctioning scrambling. The scrambling process has gone so far that even most PBS channels have been scrambled, along with the American Arms Forces Services television, and some CBS transponders. Why the government would want to scramble its own services makes no sense whatsoever, nor is it clear how it is in the "public interest" to allow the scrambling of network television, or for that matter any television channels. Once again, commercial interests ride roughshod over the public interest, with the FCC and Congress sanctioning the process or sitting by and allowing the most powerful corporate interests to control the communications spectrum.

A reversal of this process and an unscrambled satellite system would make possible a truly diverse and plural system of broadcasting. And so here is my proposal: In an age of cable and satellite television, with over 60 per cent of the nation wired for cable and over two and a half million homes with satellite dishes, why not make a satellite transponder available to various groups that want to broadcast political views and information. There could be a public-interest satellite channel – provided to representative groups free of charge – so Democrats, Republicans, labour, blacks, hispanics, women, gays, and any number of other groups could present their political views and programs every day. Once all representative groups with a specified number of members or supporters had an opportunity to use the satellite channel, time could be allotted according to the number of members in the group applying for access. This national political channel could then be picked up by every cable system in the country and people could be assured of getting real debate over issues of public concern.

Since I am not a free marketer, I would imagine that to be effective – to ensure its maximum distribution – such a channel would have to be legislated as a required channel for cable systems to broadcast. This would be easy to implement and relatively inexpensive to maintain, because every cable company in the country has satellite reception dishes and most have satellite transmission dishes that could be used by the various groups of the public-interest satellite channel free of charge. Eventually the channel could be expanded to make possible a genuine public-interest system of democratic communications. The government could dedicate an entire satellite to public broadcasting and make available the twenty-four transponders currently on each satellite to the various groups that would constitute the public broadcasting system. This would require that individuals had home satellite dishes, but this too will be viable as prices inevitably fall. Such a revitalized and democratized public broadcasting system could greatly expand the current spectrum of ideas and information and would allow voices so far excluded from the media to discuss issues of interest and importance.

There are a number of steps, then, needed to transform our broadcast system:
1) expand and democratize the current public broadcasting system;
2) expand and strengthen the public-access system;
3) use cable and satellite television to produce new public-broadcasting channels open to groups currently excluded from national communication; and
4) develop an entire satellite and cable system of broadcasting that will allow every group, alternative voice, and political opinion to be broadcast.[4]

Steps 1 and 2 could be undertaken immediately and steps 3 and 4 are both technologically and financially feasible. Yet the act of developing such an alternative democratic communications system requires educating the public and government about the real possibilities for democratic communication inherent in cable and satellite television.

If we do not radically transform our media system, things will only get worse. The rule of the slick, the manipulators, and the handlers will continue, and our democracy will be further imperilled. In the words of Max Weber:

The question is: how are freedom and democracy in the long run possible at all under the domination of highly developed capitalism? Freedom and democracy are only possible where the resolute will of a nation not to allow itself to be ruled like sheep is permanently alive. We are "individualists" and partisans of "democratic" institutions "against the stream" of material constellations. (Weber, 1946:71)

Indeed, the very future of democracy is at stake. To be revitalized and even survive, democracy requires the development of an open-access communications system. If radical transformation of the system of communications and broadcasting is not undertaken immediately, democracy in the United States will become even more imperilled and segments of the society are going to be condemned to a Third World information order, lacking access to information, communications, and social power. Indeed, empowering individuals to participate in society must be an important part of a democratic communications system.

Other possibilities for expanding a system of democratic communications reside in new computer and information technologies. It is possible that there will be a merger of entertainment and information centres in the homes of the future, with all possible print media information accessible by computer and all visual media entertainment and information resources available for home computer/entertainment-centre access. But the threat – and likelihood – is that this information and entertainment material will be thoroughly commodified, available only to those who can afford to pay. Consequently, it is necessary to begin devising public alternatives to these private/corporate information/entertainment systems of the future.

Given the growing importance of computers and information in the emerging technocapitalist society, new information networks and systems must therefore be an essential ingredient of a progressive communications system. The computerization of North America is well under way and possibilities are growing for new information networks and computer communication systems. These technologies make possible, as I suggested earlier, computerized polling and voting in elections and referenda that would give citizens much more input into the formation of public opinion and decision-making than they currently have.

New public-information networks and centres are also necessary so that citizens of the future can have access to the information needed to intelligently participate in a democratic society. Already vast amounts of information are computerized, but much of this information is commodified and accessible only to those who can purchase it. Thus every community needs a Community Information Centre, much like the libraries of the past, where a public institution will subscribe to all of these information services and make them available to the public free of charge. Such a Community Information Centre could also provide free computer training classes so that all individuals could attain the requisite computer skills and literacy for the new information age. The Community Information Centre could also provide a community bulletin board and information system so that individuals with home modem devices could tap into the new information systems and receive needed information free of charge.

National information networks could also be established via modem where individuals and groups could communicate with other groups and individuals via national bulletin boards and information systems. Many cities now have a diversity of computer bulletin boards, and many national groups and the services like Peacenet that link them are already setting up information distribution systems. Such systems should be expanded, democratized, and open to all.

The information and communications revolutions pose both threats and promises to U.S. democracy. So far in its history, capitalism has been the major threat to democracy (Wolfe, 1973 and 1977; Cohen and Rogers, 1983; Bowles and Gintis, 1986), and some of the major struggles of recent decades have been between property rights and democratic rights, the rights of capital versus the rights of the people. This contradiction is at the centre of our communications system as well, and so far capitalism has prevailed over democracy – to an alarming degree in the past decade – so that the United States has really never had a democratic system of mass communications, by the people, for the people, and of the people. Instead, television and other mainstream media have been used by the capitalist class to maintain its hegemony.

Ultimately, the struggle for a democratic communications system is therefore the struggle for a democratic society. The technologies and possibilities are there. It is a matter of imagination, will, and struggle to realize the democratic potential that still exists in a system organized for the hegemony of capital in an era of conservative political rule. Yet liberation from the yoke of capital remains possible, as does the possibility of imagining how a truly democratic society could be organized. Such a vision remains utopian, but in the words of Bertolt Brecht: "If you think this is utopia, then I would please like you to reflect on why it is utopian" (1967:130).

Notes

***This article is excerpted from my book *Television and the Crisis of Democracy* (1990). I am grateful to Steve Bronner for discussions of issues in the book and to Frank Morrow for more than ten years of discussion on and participation in the issues raised here.

1. For an earlier discussion of the need for a radical media politics and intervention in the broadcast media, see Kellner, 1979; Downing, 1984; and Mattelart and Siegelaub, 1979 and 1983. The Mattelart/Siegelaub collections contain a vast amount of material on left media politics and projects; unfortunately, there is no interventionist consideration of the potential progressive uses of public-access television, though a third volume on *Liberation and Socialism* will contain studies addressing this issue. On the early history of access in the United States, see Shapiro, 1976. On the history of alternative media, see Armstrong, 1981. On attempts by the broadcast industries and government to suppress access, and for liberal proposals for a more democratic communications system, see Johnson, 1970. The National Federation of Local Cable Programmers indicates that there are over twelve hundred access facilities operative in the United States. Some of these

systems, however, are limited to a channel that presents teletype of time, weather, and announcements of local activities. Thus it is difficult to ascertain how many full-blown access centres are operative; it is clear, however, that the number is growing.

2. A survey by the ELRA group of East Lansing, Michigan, indicates that access is rated the fifth most popular category of television programming (ahead of sports, women's, children's, and religious programs); and that 63 per cent of those surveyed had an interest in access programming. Local surveys in Austin have confirmed that access programs have a potentially large audience. Two surveys, one undertaken by the cable company and another commissioned by it, indicate that from twenty thousand to thirty thousand Austin viewers watch our show each week, and that public-access programming in general receives about 4.7 per cent of the audience; a recent cable company survey indicated that the viewership of access was on a par with the local PBS station. National surveys of viewer preferences for cable programs also indicate that public access is a high priority for many viewers. Thus there is definitely a receptive and growing audience for public-access television, and the possibility of progressives making alternative television programs should be a much higher priority for radical media politics.

3. It is difficult to get up-to-date information on the state of local access projects. Journals such as *Access, The Independent, Alternative Media, Community Television Review*, and newsletters like those published by the National Federation of Local Cable Programmers and other local access groups have some material, but overviews are scarce. Material on ten access projects in the mid-1970s is surveyed in Anderson, 1975, which also has suggestions on how to develop grassroots video projects. Material on early access projects can be found in issues of *Radical Software* (1970-1975), in Shamberg, 1971, and Frederiksen, 1972; a good review and critique of these projects are found in Jacobson, 1974. Suggestions on how to set up an access system and provide quality community programming are found in Price and Wicklein, 1972; Zelmer, 1979, has information on setting up a community media centre; and a booklet by Ianacone, n.d., provides "A Citizens Guide to Forming a Media Access Group," though it does not really focus on how to develop a public-access program. The National Federation of Local Cable Programmers also provides guides concerning how to produce access television, as do some other sources. We would appreciate receiving copies of such guides, because frequently people write us asking for material on how to set up an access centre or how to produce an access program, and we are forced to refer to material that might not be up to date or directly relevant to their interests.

    The Alternative Information Network has been amassing material concerning radical media politics and progressive use of public-access television and other new media of communication for production or a future book on these topics. Readers who have material on these topics or who would like to correspond with us can write: Alternative Information Network, PO Box 7279, Austin, Texas 78713.

4. On my proposals for a reinvigorated public-broadcasting system, see Kellner, 1990.

References

Anderson, Chuck (1975). *Video Power*. New York: Praeger.

Armstrong, David (1981). *A Trumpet to Arms: Alternative Media in America*. Boston: Houghton Mifflin; reprinted by South End Press.

Bowles, Samuel and Herbert Gintis (1986). *Democracy and Capitalism*. New York: Basic Books.

Brecht, Bertolt (1967). "De Rundfunk als Kommunkiationspparat," *Gesammelte Werke*, 18. Frankfurt: Suhrkamp.

Cohen, Joshua and Joel Rogers (1983). *On Democracy*. London and Baltimore: Penguin Books.

Downing, John (1984). *Radical Media*. Boston: South End Press.

ELRA Group (1982). Survey compiled in 1982, East Lansing, Michigan, and discussed in *CableVision*, April 26.

Frederiksen, H. Allan (1972). *Community Access Video*. Menlo Park: Nowells Publications.

Ianacone, Evonne (n.d.). *Changing More Than the Channel*.

Jacobson, Bob (1974). "Video at the Crossroads," *Jump Cut*, 1 (May-June).

Johnson, Nicholas (1970). *How To Talk Back to Your Television Set*. Boston: Little, Brown and Company.

Kellner, Douglas (1979). "TV, Ideology, and Emancipatory Popular Culture," *Socialist Review*, 45 (November-December).

Kellner, Douglas (1990). *Television and the Crisis of Democracy*. Boulder, Col.: Westview Press.

Koenig, Josh (1979). "Court Strikes Down FCC Access Rules," *Community Television Review*, Spring.

Mattelart, Armand and Seth Siegelaub, eds. (1979). *Communication and Class Struggle*, Vol. 1, *Capitalism, Imperialism*. Paris: International General.

Mattelart, Armand and Seth Siegelaub, eds. (1983). *Communication and Class Struggle*, Vol 2, *Liberation, Socialism*. Paris: International General.

Price, Monroe and John Wicklein (1972). *Cable Television: A Guide for Citizen Action*. Philadelphia: Pilgrim Press.

Radical Software (1970-1975).

Shamberg, Michael (1971). *Guerrilla Television*. New York: Holt, Rinehart and Winston.

Shapiro, Michael (1976). *Media Access*. Boston: Little, Brown and Company, 1976.

Weber, Max (1946). In Hans Herth and C. Wright Mills, eds., *From Max Weber*. New York: Oxford University Press.

Wolfe, Alan (1973). *The Seamy Side of Democracy*. New York: McKay.

Wolfe, Alan (1977). *The Limits of Legitimacy*. New York: Free Press.

Zelmer, A.C. Lynn (1979). *Community Media Handbook*. Metuchen, N.J.: The Scarecrow Press.

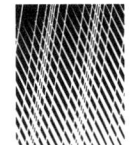

Of the People?
The Case of Popular Music

Deanna Campbell Robinson

Rock 'n' roll, as I see it, is the ultimate populist art form, democracy in action, because it's true: anybody can do it...

For performing rock'n' roll, or punk rock, or call it any damn thing you please, there's only one thing you need: NERVE.

– Lester Bangs, 1980

THE DEFINITION of "popular" has travelled from the early Latin *popularis* (of the people) to the American Heritage Dictionary's now primary definition of "widely liked or appreciated," a numerical or public-opinion definition. This journey corresponds, in Seth Siegelaub's words, to "the history of an open active marketplace of multiple small producers/citizens – at least for propertied white men – and its evolution to a closed monopolized marketplace" (1983:11).[1]

Today five major recording companies – WEA (U.S.), RCA (German), EMI (British), CBS (Japanese), and Polygram (Dutch-German) – control anywhere from 33 (the lowest estimate, in Laing, 1986) to 70 per cent (Shore, 1983) of international music production and distribution. This world concentration is fed by the very hand that challenges it. The recording industry's constant appetite for innovative material is fuelled by the work of millions of local bands spread throughout the world. Furthermore, in complete contradiction to the formulation of the international core industry, the same technologies developed by that industry to serve its expansion purposes are now being used to introduce an entirely new mode of production – self-production – that musicians can use to circumvent core industry production and distribution.

In 1987 Bright and Geyer argued:

The world has moved apart even as it has been pulled together, as efforts to convert domination into order have engendered evasion, resistance and struggles to regain autonomy. This struggle for autonomy – the assertion of local and particular claims over global and general ones – does not involve opting out of the world or resorting to autarky. It is rather an effort to establish the terms for self-determining and self-controlled participation in the processes of global integration and the struggle for planetary order. (1987:69-70)

This chapter discusses the struggle between global concentration and local determination in the context of popular music production.

The Evolution of the Popular Music Core Industry

The definition of popular music as the commercial product of a centralized industry is well supported by the evolution of the transnational music corporations (TNCs). This evolution is closely tied to the development of technology and advanced capitalism, especially within the context of the United States, whose music still dominates the international recording industry's repertoire.

Before the introduction of the phonograph in the late nineteenth century, all music was transmitted through live performance or printed notation and stored in the minds of individuals or symbolically on paper. Recorded music technology gave birth to centralized music production and profoundly influenced both the nature and experience of music.

Industry-produced music became increasingly standardized and reached ever larger audiences as people's ears acclimated themselves to recorded music. The social nature of the musical environment changed as people listened to recorded music individually rather than live music collectively. The nature of non-recorded, live music also changed when consumers and musicians began comparing local music with centrally produced and distributed music. As recorded music production became more complex, a professional class of musicians developed whose competencies were determined to a great extent by the requirements of the industry. The introduction of radio in the 1920s further widened the audience for centralized music production. Local musical diversity dwindled as radio stations sought ever larger audiences.

Ownership diversity decreased as smaller recording companies went out of business or were bought up by larger companies. Vertical accompanied horizontal integration as RCA bought Victor Talking Machine and CBS acquired American Record and Columbia Gramophone. From just before the turn of the century to the middle 1940s, the musical production of local and small independent companies dwindled. The centralized industry assumed increasingly greater control.

Peripheral music activity blossomed again after World War II, when increased buying power and renewed social activity – especially the courtship activities of returning soldiers – encouraged both live performances and record purchases. New demand opened the record industry to new artists and the relocation of people around the country increased the audience for alternative kinds of music. For-

merly rural blacks and whites who had moved to the cities during the war remained there and influenced the kinds of music played on radio and recorded by
the industry. Conversely, their musical tastes were influenced by new living conditions and exposure to each other's and mainstream music.

As television took over general programming from radio in the 1950s, the older
medium had to find a new function and new programming to fill those empty
hours. At the same time the postwar babies became teenagers and, because the
1950s were relatively prosperous years, teenagers with money in their pockets.
Popular music became the answer for radio stations and the leitmotif of youth.
The merging music of blacks and formerly rural (now largely urban) poor whites
in the United States blasted out as rock 'n' roll, and music production took off.
The tremendous demand gave rise to many small independent record companies
that took on innovative material in the hopes of finding the golden hits that would
make them rich (see Gillett, 1970).

At first the largest record companies stayed with tried and true "recombinant"
music (see Gitlin, 1983) for adult listeners. They began to regain control towards
the end of the 1950s when they grasped the lucrative potential of the new music.
A few years later eight out of forty U.S. recording companies controlled half the
sales.

In the 1960s, U.S. and British popular music became world music. The Beatles
toured the globe; Beatles' recorded music filled the airwaves everywhere; transis-
tor radio sets accompanied people, whomever they were and wherever they went.
Individuals around the world could live their lives with music – to a great degree,
the same music. Sequential modifications of rock styles reinforced the political
identifications of a whole series of dissatisfied, alienated British and North American youth groups and popular music became the rallying point for huge social
movements. Stokes (1977) sees this internationalization of what came to be called
"rock" as one reason why large U.S. companies eventually achieved world dominance in popular music production and distribution.

The large companies expanded their areas of operation and solidified their industry positions through both horizontal and vertical integration. The vertical integration proved especially important as these companies acquired primary control of popular music distribution. Gillett (1970) defines majors, the term commonly used to signify the largest recording companies, as companies with their
own distribution systems. These majors could make sure their records reached
retailers in every market. The independent distributors who served smaller, "independent" companies profited according to volume of units sold. They had little interest in the costly task of pushing a few units recorded by an unknown artist
who might make it big when, in the same time span, they could sell many units
by a recognized star. Majors also acquired retail outlets and music publishing
houses. Publishing music enabled them to profit from, rather than pay out, copy-
right fees.

Another factor that helped the majors achieve their position of unparalleled market power was the development of long-play recordings and, subsequently, albums. Small companies could not risk putting all their capital into production of one costly album. They continued to hope for success with the much less lucrative singles. Stokes (1977) estimates that by 1974 a handful of majors accounted for 90 to 95 per cent of the U.S. domestic popular music market; according to Shore's 1983 data the majors accounted for at least 50 per cent – in some nations over 90 per cent – of foreign markets.

International productive dominance by a few corporations, however, does not necessarily dictate worldwide musical homogenization. Unlike television programs and films, only a small percentage of recordings are produced in one country and shipped to others. Most records are pressed in the countries where they will be sold. This means that whatever is popular in a specific country can theoretically be produced there by the TNCs, their licensees, or their subsidiaries. If nationally originated music is what sells, that is what TNCs will produce.

The catch is that nationally originated music has to sell more units than internationally originated music, for two reasons. First, a new master tape has to be made; and second, that master tape may not be reusable in other countries where the music is not popular. Therefore, a company will not press records that will sell in only one country unless the national market for them is very large. In Greece, for example, national music has to sell fifty thousand units to be regarded as a success and international music only ten thousand (Papageourgiou, 1984).

The Evolution of a New Production Mode
In the 1970s the potential profit from corporate innovation tapered off along with the supply of new teenagers in most countries that had been involved in World War II. Recession in the early 1970s led to intense market research in hopes of maximizing the audience as much as possible. Walter Yetnikoff, President of the CBS Recording Group, observed:

> Things are considerably different than a few years ago, when the philosophy was to throw a lot of products against the wall and see what sticks. That approach is too expensive today. Now, every album that goes out has a complete marketing plan, with full details on advertising, displays, discounts for the trade, personal appearances by the artists, sales targets and national and regional breakdowns. (Quoted in Blaukopf, 1982:17)

U.S. radio stations also emphasized market research. In all but the largest cities, a few standardized formats played the same tired music over and over again. The 1979 recession cut back on record sales and further increased industry conservatism. Companies reduced the vinyl in records and cut tape quality, thus reducing the desirability of these products for audiences.

Most importantly, these years were marked by the growing up of the baby boomers. At the end of the 1970s, twenty-five- to thirty-five-year-olds were the largest population group in the United States and they formed a group whose musical tastes had been largely set. Population changes have a profound effect on popular music production, which thrives on successive crops of teenagers. Each "new wave" of young people demands music to call its own. Thus, unlike television and film, popular music must constantly change to stay afloat in its largest, eternally fluid constituency.

The majors had set the stage for the stagnant situation by buying up the independents during the 1960s. Independent companies are traditionally the productive avant garde, the places that "throw the products against the wall." Musical "products" are mined from the raw material of local production. Television and film have no parallel local productive level, with the possible exception of community-access cable television, a service that most frequently removes the "mass" from electronic communication. Television programs and films are expensive and difficult to make, and locally produced products can be expected to command the attention of only a few friends or other very special-interest people. Unlike theatre and music, film and television cannot be performed "live."

Curiously, despite these adverse changes at the national and international levels of recording production, local production of music increasingly flourished during the 1970s and 1980s (see Robinson, Buck, Cuthbert et al., 1991). Perhaps this is partly because the baby boomers reached drinking age in the 1970s and could go to bars, where live local music is most commonly played. Or perhaps it is because many of these people were musicians themselves in the 1960s when almost every teenager seemed to belong to a local band.

Another impetus to widespread participation in popular music-making was the passing of new industry-developed technology down to the common folk. Electronic instruments enabled everyone to sound good enough to get up on a stage. As Bangs (1980) said, all it took was nerve. Less expensive, smaller-scale, multitrack recording equipment made it possible for even poverty-line local musicians to scrape together basement recording equipment and for small regional companies to set up professional-standard recording studios that musicians could afford to rent.

As with the problem of saying all popular music is produced by the dominant corporations, saying all popular music is commercialized is too simplistic. Local music production, even in a capitalist context, can be accomplished without commercial mediation between musician and audience, with the goal of profit but without the aspect of wage labour. Musicians may simply play their music live before an audience or make their own recordings and sell them directly to fans. Because of advances in recording technology, master tapes that are quite acceptable to the average fan's ears can now be made on local equipment owned by local recording studios or, in some cases, on equipment owned by local musicians themselves.

In the United States, master tapes can be made for less than $6,000, sent out for pressing, packaged in contracted covers designed by the musicians or hired artists, and distributed by local independent distributors or the musicians themselves. A group in the sparsely settled state of Oregon sold more than forty-thousand albums this way. In Latin America, Nueva Cancione (New Song Movement) groups have been able to record music locally and sell up to forty thousand copies of their work outside the central recording industry. These recordings are still commodities – but commodities in the sense of artifacts produced by craftsworkers rather than centralized, wage-labour-dependent manufacturers.

The Interface Between Core and Peripheral Self-Production

Self-production cannot be seen as denying centralized influence upon locally interacting musicians and fans, all of whom necessarily are part of a world musical environment dominated by concentrated international capitalist production. Within this capitalist environment, local musicians compete with centrally produced music – both they and their fans have been conditioned to respond to this music. In addition, many local musicians hope to join the centralized industry by acquiring a large independent or major recording company contract. Some musicians compose music and formulate presentation styles to meet a commercial formula in order to sign a contract and acquire a large number of fans.

Other musicians refuse to do this and struggle for a new sound or (much more rarely now) political relevance. Still others incorporate, and thus maintain, traditional sounds within their own contemporary compositions. If the music that results from these cultural struggles is appreciated by a large enough group of people, the centralized industry may pick it up through exploitation of local musicians, as in the case of Jamaican reggae, or by creating stars, as in the case of Robert Cray, who resurrected rhythm and blues in Portland, Oregon. A central question then becomes how the nature of the music is altered by this change in mode of production. Lewis (1982) remarks that even if a musician begins with truly alternative music, as a star "he"

> tends to be culturally trapped by his own success. He has painted this sort of thing and gets $5,000 a throw and there is demand for "his" style. As a leader of fashion he is himself subject to fashion. Moreover, his success as a star depends upon his "playing with the market": he is not in any educative interplay with publics that support his environment. By virtue of his success, the star too becomes a marketeer. (35)

Most research done on popular music production so far concentrates on the capitalist mode of production, ignoring both the type of local production and the formerly socialist mode of production.[2] Within socialist economic systems such as the former German Democratic Republic, the state subsidized the creative production of musicians, and national recording companies produced records on a largely non-commercial basis. Again, however, even though no direct or formal commercialization was present in the GDR's immediate economic system, East German musicians necessarily operated within the international capitalist environment.

Core-produced popular music crosses all national boundaries. Hence, even if GDR musicians did not have to conform their music directly to any profit-making standards, they did have to compete for fans with internationalized commercially produced music. Furthermore, they had to compete with each other for both recording contracts and fans. We might presume that at least in some socialist environments, recording companies have followed dominant tastes in the awarding of record contracts, although this is not necessarily the case (see Szemere, 1984).

The influence of dominant taste can be quite subtle. Robert White, speaking of the work of Stuart Hall, comments, "Even when cultural production is in the hands of nationals, the formats of popular entertainment, news, and other forms of media have been introduced by North Atlantic nations and, specifically, by the United States" (1983:292).

This is true in popular music production to some extent but not completely. "East German" rock music has a classical sound; its lyrics often address serious themes and the songs are often longer than the norm on Western top-40 radio stations. The former nation's musical tradition and, perhaps, the length of German words (which present a challenge to lyricists working with rock beats) may be responsible for the unique sound of this music, despite the obvious international rock elements it incorporates (see Robinson, Wicke and Banks, 1987).

Reddi (1985) notes that internationalized rock music has similarly had a strong effect on Indian popular music. Yet despite this influence Indian music retains its cultural distinctiveness. Over 80 per cent of Indian music fans prefer Indian film music that incorporates Western musical elements and instruments into a basically Indian format (Reddi, 1985:376). The result is a unique fusion of Western and Indian elements. Reddi sees this "borrowing from the international music industry while not being a victim of its domination" as a positive sign (1985:379).

The Role of the Audience

Adorno not only decried what he saw as popular music's complete lack of aesthetic appeal but also believed that such music led to the industrialization of the mind, the development of "commodity listening," a listening whose idea it is to dispense as far as possible with any effort on the part of the recipient" (1946:211). Mass communication theorists have long abandoned the old hypodermic needle model upon which this notion of passive reception of mass-mediated messages depends.

Current theories about communicative meaning question the very use of the term "receiver." Rather than being passive receivers, people interact with cultural products in the context of the overall social environment. In this sense the nature of the interaction creates the ultimate meaning. The meaning that exists in the mind of an audience member is not necessarily the same as the social meaning of that interaction, because it may not concur with the incorporation of the interaction into everyday life. Grossberg (1986) expresses this perspective: "The significance of the music is not in the music, nor in the fan. For example, the meaning may be found outside the text, in the way it marks our history" (52). Popular music is not only produced by the social context but is also a force within that context. This view permits Grossberg to define rock and roll "as a mode of functioning" (50).

At least three modes of functioning open up the possibility for cultural struggle within the terrain of popular music. One of them is local production of music that always affords the *opportunity* to reflect the values, traditions, and thinking of the musicians and fans who live in a certain time and place, whether they grasp this opportunity or not. The two others involve recontextualization of non-local music.

Interaction with externally produced music imported into a different social context is one possibility. Indigenous musicians may incorporate foreign musical elements into their own local production. Indigenous fans may use foreign music to establish an identity separate from the mainstream of the area they live in. For example, recent immigrants may import music from their homeland to maintain a feeling of separate ethnicity. A recent study by Wallis and Lull (1987) of the Vietnamese community in San Jose, California, establishes that these newcomers to the United States do indeed import music from their former country. The irony of this process is that the imported music often comprises Vietnamized versions of music popular in Western countries several years earlier. Nevertheless, despite its origins this music functions in everyday life as a force for ethnic coherence.

A third possibility for cultural struggle, manifested brilliantly by punks, comprises the reinterpretation and co-optation of core-produced music or other cultural artifacts as material for alternative modes of functioning. Either fans (as in the case of punks) or musicians (as in the case of jazz variations on established themes) may reinterpret core music and make it conform to their own cultural needs. An interesting twist on the usual core exploitation of local musicians and their music occurs when local musicians take core music and localize it. An example is the Jamaican rendition of John Denver's "Country Road."

A More Radical Interpretation
Enumeration of these possible methods of cultural struggle does not obviate the tremendous influence that the core popular music industry continues to have on everyday life. The international popular music industry supports world hegemony by its encouragement of a market mentality. It promotes a whole range of commodities from dress to food to other media products. It pushes buying and the establishment of individual and group identities through consumer-based styles rather than through accomplishments or inheritance. The groups of youth so aptly described by Hebdidge (1979) based their lives on styles created from "things." Granted, they used these commercial items very creatively, in ways different from the original intentions, but they still literally bought into the consumer ethic.

We can place this contradiction inside the cultural-political economist debate. A limited cultural perspective ignores how increasing vertical and horizontal integration within the core industry has constrained musical choice and how ever-more sophisticated marketing techniques have created consumer needs. This perspective neglects consideration of how hearing particular kinds of music over and over on the radio has tuned listeners' ears to specific sounds. On the other hand, a strict political-economic orientation leaves out the equally obvious ability of audience members to individualize musical meanings.

Garofalo (1987) puts these two views together in support of an argument advanced by Rick Dutka, a music industry executive who was one of the organizers of the Sun City project. Dutka sees musical "arenas of struggle" as embedded in three relationships: those between creators and record companies, creators and their music, and creators and their fans. Garofalo adds a fourth relationship: between the music and its fans.

No doubt these sites of conflict will continue to exist, but they will exist within a new context. Jacques Attali (1985) posited four states in the evolution of music, and he saw the onset of each of these stages as heralding a new social order and as having socially different functions. In the age of ritual and sacrifice, music served to divert people's attention from the violence and uncertainty present in society. In the age of reproduction, the rules surrounding composition and performance of music served to convince people of the harmonious character of their society. In the age of repetition, that of the centralized recording industry, mass production silenced those who opposed bureaucratic power – in other words, it kept them entertained and oblivious.

A fourth stage may be in the offing: the age of composition in which "a new music is on the rise, one that can neither be expressed nor understood using the old tools, a music produced elsewhere and otherwise" (133). Attali is speaking not about "a *new music, but a new way of making music* (134, emphasis in original). Despite what seems to be excessive idealism on Attali's part, he has hit upon the element others seem to have left out of their popular music analyses to date. *A different mode of production has emerged.*

Jet planes, new communications technologies, and the operations of TNCs in creating a world marketplace have shrunk the world to the point where musicians from all regions of the world can get access to and appreciate the music of others without relying on the musical products of the core recording industry. Self-produced recordings, alternative radio signals, and people cross national boundaries without industry interpolation. Just as people in far-flung locations now enjoy Chinese, Mexican, French, Californian, or whatever cuisines, a new innovative spirit and tolerance for the unknown have become commonplace in musical production and consumption.

The situation gives new meaning to Grossberg's comment (1986) that the power of music can be found in the "affective alliances" it sets up between musicians and their audiences. Music can now set up alliances among people who live in many parts of the world. Musicians and audiences can set themselves apart or bring themselves together through musical exchange on a global scale. And they can do this by completely individualized modes of production and consumption.

The recording industry in the late 1960s and early 1970s seemed to have devised a system for beating the "crap shoot" of popularity. It reduced risks by conducting intricate market research, claiming as many consumers for as few products as possible and varying subsequent products only a tiny bit from the tried and true. But in an age of composition, where anyone anywhere can make whatever music he or she can conceive, where inexpensive musical alternatives abound in the local and international contexts, where fans can choose from myriad alternatives right in their musical backyards, the crap shoot has become dicey indeed. Worldwide local music activities may not guarantee what Attali (1985:148) foresees as "the inevitable victory of the aleatory and the unfinished," but they certainly contradict any monolithic image of global popular music production.

Notes

1. See Robinson, Buck and Cuthbert et al. (1991), especially Chapter 1, for an expanded definition of "popular."
2. Since the fall of the wall in Berlin, few socialist production environments exist, at least not the type that formerly existed within the Eastern Bloc.

References

Adorno, T. (1946). "A Social Critique of Radio Music," *Kenyon Review*, 2:208-217.

Attali, J. (1985). *Noise: The Political Economy of Music*. Translated by Brian Massumi. Minneapolis: University of Minnesota Press.

Bangs, L. (1980). *Blondie*. New York: Simon & Schuster.

Bennett, T. (1986). "The Politics of 'The Popular' and Popular Culture." In T. Bennett, C. Mercer and J. Woollacott, eds., *Popular Culture and Social Relations*. Philadelphia: Open University Press.

Blaukopf, K. (1982). *The Strategies of the Record Industries*. Vienna: Mediacult Institute.

Bright, C. and Geyer, M. (1987). "For a Unified History of the World in the Twentieth Century," *Radical History Review*, 39:69-91.

Cutler, C. (1985). *File Under Popular: Theoretical and Critical Writings on Music*. London: November Books.

Garnham, N. (1981). "Contribution to a Political Economy of Mass Communication." In G. Wilhoit and H. de Bock, eds., *Mass Communication Review Yearbook*. Beverly Hills, Cal.: Sage Publications.

Garnham, N. (1983). "Toward a Theory of Cultural Materialism," *Journal of Communication*, 33:314-329.

Garofalo, R. (1987). "How Autonomous is Relative: Popular Music, the Social Formation and Cultural Struggle," *Popular Music*, 6:77-92.

Gillett, C. (1970). *The Sound of the City: The Rise of Rock and Roll*. New York: Outerbridge and Dienstfrey.

Gitlin, T. (1983). *Inside Prime Time*. New York: Pantheon Books.

Grossberg, L. (1986). "Is There Rock after Punk?" *Critical Studies in Mass Communication*, 3:50-74.

Hebdidge, D. (1979). *Subculture: The Meaning of Style*. London: Methuen.

Laing, Dave (1986). "The Music Industry and the 'Cultural Imperialism' Thesis," *Media, Culture and Society*, 8:331-341.

Lewis, G. (1982). "Positive Deviance: A Labelling Approach to the Star Syndrome in Popular Music," *Popular Music and Society*, 8.

Lull, J. (1985). "On the Communicative Properties of Music," *Communication Research*, 12:363-372.

Matta, F. Reyes (1982). "Canto popular, discos y alternativas," *Media Development*, 1:22-25.

Murdock, G. and P. Golding (1979). "Capitalism, Communication and Class Relations." In J. Curran, M. Gurevitch and J. Woollacott, eds., *Mass Communication and Society*. Beverly Hills, Cal.: Sage Publications.

Papageourgiou, F. (1984). "The Music Industry in Greece." Paper presented to the International Association for Mass Communication Research, Prague, Czechoslovakia.

Reddi, U. (1985). "An Indian Perspective on Youth Culture," *Communication Research*, 12:373-380.

Robinson, D. (1986). "Youth and Popular Music: A Theoretical Rationale for an International Study," *Gazette*, 37:33-50.

Robinson, D., E. Buck, M. Cuthbert et al. (1991). *Music at the Margins: Popular Music and Global Cultural Diversity*. Newbury Park, Cal.: Sage Publications.

Robinson, D., P. Wicke and J. Banks (1987). "Popular Music as the People's Expression: A Comparative Study of Socialist and Capitalist Cultural Production." Paper presented to the International Communication Association, Montreal, Quebec.

Rosenberg, B. (1957). "Mass Culture in America." In B. Rosenberg and D. White, eds., *Mass Culture: The Popular Arts in America*. New York: The Free Press.

Shore, L (1983). "The Crossroads of Business and Music: A Study of the Music Industry in the United States and Internationally." Doctoral dissertation, Stanford University, California.

Siegelaub, S. (1983). "Working Notes on Social Relations in Communication and Culture." In A. Mattelart and S. Siegelaub, eds., *Communication and Class Struggle*, Vol.2, *Liberation, Socialism*. New York: International General.

Stokes, G. (1977). *Starmaking Machinery: Inside the Business of Rock and Roll*. New York: Vintage Books.

Szemere, A. (1984). "Basic Structures and Processes in the Hungarian Pop Music Field." Paper presented to the International Association for Mass Communication Research, Prague, Czechoslovakia.

Tagg, P. (1982). "Analysing Popular Music: Theory, Method and Practice," *Popular Music*, 2:37-67.

White, R. (1983). "Mass Communication and Culture: Transition to a New Paradigm," *Journal of Communication*, 33:279-301.

Wicke, P. (1987). "Rock Music and Everyday Culture in the GDR." Paper presented to the Department of Speech and the School of Music, University of Oregon.

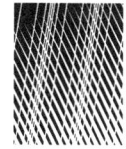

Working with Unions II:
A Photo Essay

Fred Lonidier

I

MY WORK ADDRESSES the growing inability of the U.S. labour movement to *protect* its interests. My work attempts to point towards the unnameable socialist program that can *advance* the working class to its full political potential. I have to say "attempts" because since 1975 I have been carrying on this slow, uneven, thin, difficult task with just enough support, encouragement, and "success" to keep going. This is not a complaint but an acknowledgement that this goal, for all of us committed to it, demands the tenacious resolve of the long run. I must also say that when I began making artwork about and for the labour movement I had hoped – no, expected – things would move much faster.[1] I especially hoped that the unions and their federation, the AFL-CIO, would embrace my first project, "The Health and Safety Game" (H&SG), and commit resources to its wide distribution. I also feared that the way I chose to work would not go at all. I have been working in this way long enough now to evaluate what has happened and point to future directions.

II

The artworks I am discussing here – "The Health and Safety Game" (1976),[2] "L.A. Public Workers Point to Some Problems" (1973),[3] "I Like Everything Nothing But Union" (1984)[4] – have a dual social role, one in the art world and another in the unions, but tend to play one or the other depending on the place shown.

This art originates from and continues to be a part of the avant garde high-art world, and it remains there to challenge and contradict a sacrosanct bourgeois cultural institution. Along with other radical artists who have the requisite credentials, I work to prevent high culture from entirely going on with its business and hypocrisies (art for business sake) without having to occasionally answer (and sometime even concede) to criticism. We rally those artists, students, and critics who are inside the art world but share in few of its benefits and who can potentially be encouraged to view their alienation and discontent as related to problems of the society at large.

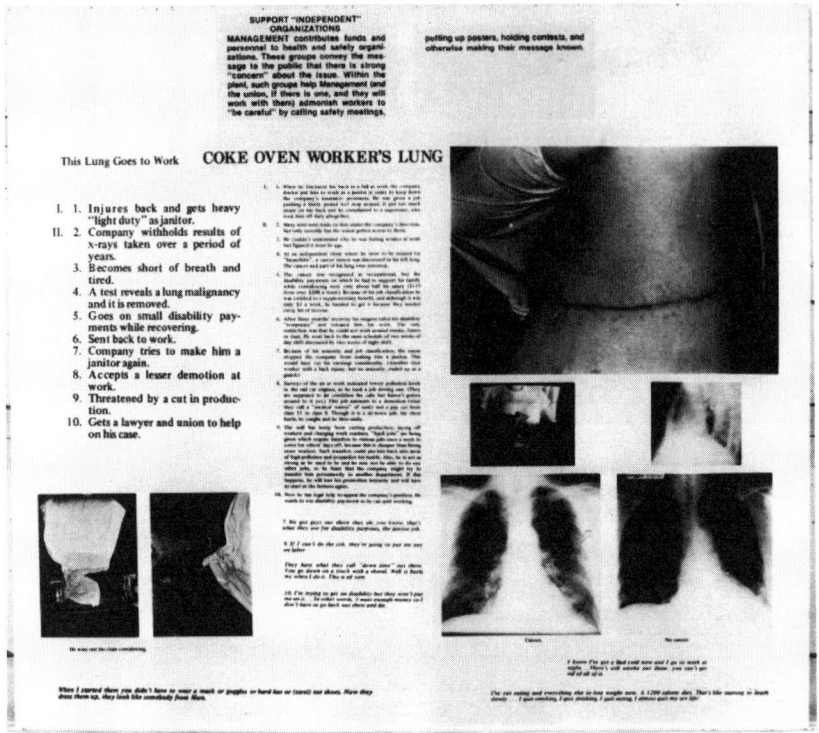

The Health and Safety Game: I

Legitimacy in the art world has been traditionally claimed by the theoretical contribution any given work makes to the cultural-formal questions raised. In the art world's terms: What is the nature and boundary of art? In spite of the degeneration of modernism's own theory and practice, there is still some knee-jerk acceptance of serious attempts at this. And "political art" often looks very serious to those still concerned about upholding art's intellectual respectability.

In the labour unions, the work is legitimized by its "artness" as well as by the seriousness of the social issues involved. Because organized labour and its concerns have been relatively marginalized – in spite of an overall membership that makes the art world look like a game of solitaire in comparison – unions may welcome an outsider (or in my case, a member of the American Federation of Teachers) who speaks on their behalf to a public audience within the prestigious social institutions. As for my work, it doesn't look like anything they'd usually consider art except that they know modern art often takes unusual forms. This is not a satisfactory understanding of what I do, but it allows me to develop my photo-text pieces until both the workers and I can afford the time and energy needed to discuss all manner of cultural issues. If there is any other legitimate justification for separating art of this

The Health and Safety Game: II

nature into high or low categories, it is not on the basis of status but in the acceptance of a vanguard role in the experimental sense. In the same way political
economy must continuously reassess and test its theory and practice, so must any
subarena such as cultural work. I have the greatest affinity, then, with those who see
their work as offering something fundamentally new to the long traditions of
oppositional cultural practice. I hope this does not sound pretentious and stuffy. I
genuinely believe there is a need for a theoretical distinction in our activities even if
we have not yet worked out completely non-elitist ways of using them.

Photo-text documentary has evolved as an answer to humanist photography's
commitment to singular, dramatic images. I am not arguing that the issue is one of
style, but that an artwork needs to be more ambitious in representing the issues
and in keeping an audience's attention fixed on the camera's subject rather than
on the heroism and virtuosity of the photographer (Sekula, 1984). I support a self-
reflexive mode that reveals the documentarian and the tools for scrutiny as long
as the balance is maintained between looking inward and outward. Also, the dependence of photographs on context for their meaning makes a demand upon
those of us who want to say what we think needs to be said – and not something
else – to control as much of the viewing environment as possible. As in film, where
it is now unthinkable that the images and sound/text would not be shaped to create a whole "statement," the documentary photographer produces a complete
thing. I am talking about autonomous, self-contained artworks and am not, of
course, ruling out other more limited or dependent uses of the medium (such as
illustration).[5] There is so much labour history lost to union people now and so

Public Workers Point to Some Problems: I

much reorientation necessary that I resort to rather lengthy texts. There are always interviews with workers that tell what is experienced, seen, thought, and felt about the situation from their perspectives. This commentary runs the full range from the specifics of their experience to the long-run historical context, but for the most part the specifics dominate. The big picture is not well developed, for political reasons, among the U.S. rank-and-file.

Because of this I provide an overview that is historically derived and more global in reach. "How has this issue developed through time? What does it look like in other places?" Usually I also provide some kind of outline for the text, to make it more accessible. This gives the reader an opportunity to assess what any given panel of the artwork may be about so choices can be made as to which one(s) to pursue in depth at the moment.

I am frequently asked if union members in particular read the entirety of my pieces. (This is often said in response to the widely known rise in illiteracy among us; I don't know why people who bemoan this fact encourage it by arguing for less literature.) Based on the experiences I now have, it is clear that people will make an effort to get through something if the following conditions prevail:

First, and most important, is the choice of subject matter. I always look for the submerged, missed, or forgotten labour issue – or for an issue that is about to emerge. In hand with this choice is the particular way the issue is treated, the point of view. I look to the absences, inadequacies, or invisibilities of the *available discourse*. In fact, much of what I have to say is already known and discussed – or suspected – by workers themselves. It may only be a question of legitimizing or distilling and organizing certain ideas rather than teaching in the one-way sense.

Public Workers Point to Some Problems: II
Anna Acosta: Tenant Relations Assistant AFSCME 143, Los Angeles, California
"Everyone comes in, you know, on emergency basis. 'I don't have anywhere to go,' and been put on the street or the landlord sold the house ... or the rent has gone up and they can't afford it, or they don't want kids.... But we don't have anywhere to put 'em. Our places are packed and our people don't move.... But for each apartment we have vacant we have maybe 200 to 300 applications waiting for them....

In the position where I'm in, if you don't have a person that's really capable and good and knows what they're doing your Manager's going to work hard. In fact, a lot of weak Managers are carried by people in my position."

Second, the language must be visually well organized and widely understandable.

Third, the artwork should be installed in a place frequented by workers for lengthy periods of time. If possible, parts of the work should be reproduced in the union's or labour council's literature. It must be publicized. This third require-ment causes the most problems for works like mine, because so often it is just not possible for one reason or another.

One other major issue I will only touch on is the active/passive role of the docu-mentation. I do not believe that any phenomenon *necessarily* speaks for itself well. In my editorial choices I give emphasis to the more conscious expressions out of pro-portion to their occurrence among U.S. workers. I am concerned with what *is* in or-der to move my audience to consider what *ought* to be. To represent things "as they are" without indicating *why* they are this way – that is, how they came about – is to reify causation and reinforce the contention that the status quo is immutable. My own contributions to the pieces (such as the "Management" section of the "Health and Safety Game" or the "Crises of Western Capital" in "L.A. Public

I Like Everything Nothing but Union: I

Workers") are efforts to intervene in the discourse of the trade unions (and art world) and insert that which is needed but absent.

Anti-communism is still a prevailing sanction against the explicit expressions of certain political ideas within U.S. unions and the working class itself, although socialism has become a little less threatening as a few major and visible unionists have come out as socialists in recent years.[6] This raises a problem faced by all leftists working with the unions today and especially with their leadership. Some groups in the 1970s and early 1980s thought they could go directly to the rank-and-file with revolutionary politics and unite with them to replace the centrist labour officials. All of those groups, at least the ones that I know of, now find themselves on the margins of the unions or out altogether. The only alternatives remaining for those who favour a socialist program is to enter through the muddy waters of reformism or dual unionism. Many of my choices of issue and of perspective, then, are attempts to push at the limits of discourse (liberalism) in order to open the way towards a new working-class politic in this country.

A final consideration of cultural work in the unions is that there are few outlets for these artworks. However, there is great potential because the unions already have members, spaces, and newspapers. (Cable TV opens up possibilities I can only touch upon here.)[7] The problem is to get some of these resources committed and adapted to cultural work. Just because a union has a hall does not necessarily mean that there is a reasonable space inside for exhibits. Unions also sometimes have money. Direct funding for projects is always a possibility, and each year unions and federations support a number of varied things (mostly films, slide shows, pamphlets, posters, calendars, and occasionally theatre and art exhibits). Naturally, it usually takes a lot of time/energy to get an allocation of scarce funds, especially from a movement that is under attack.[8] The issue of patronage control enters here too. Personally, because of my art world/university base, I have been able to draw support from outside labour through a few grants. I have also used a lot of my university salary for this work (and can take tax deductions for this as a research/education expense). However, labour's political clout must be used to expand government support for the arts as aid for cultural work. In the English-speaking world, the United States has the smallest per capita *public* art endow-

I Like Everything Nothing but Union: II
Ola Hosley: International Association of Bridge, Structural and Ornamental Ironworkers
Shopmen's Local 627, SanDiego, California

ment; art here is privately owned or controlled, a consequence of political factors.[9]

One way to work with limited resources is to form a group to divide up the efforts. People engaged in film and video production are accustomed to collective modes of working. Eventually I want to work with my fellow unionists from start to finish, but now they participate only as the objects of consideration and have minimal input in the artworks as a whole. Poetry, music, literature, and murals once flowed from the labour temples. Our goal has to be to revive, and renew, the cultural side of the labour movement. In short, a lot of work is yet to be done to create a broad viable support system.

III

"The Health and Safety Game: fictions based on fact": Really about the political economy of occupational health, the H&SG was my first photo-text artwork for and about the labour movement. It puts a number of photo-narrative "case histories" into the context of the winning political strategies and tactics of "management" (capital). I include, but downplay, the significance of technical-medical answers to the horrendous slaughter in the workplace because, although these remedies are in many cases already available, the political unity of the workers needed to force their implementation is not. When this piece has been exhibited for a sufficient time, I think it has proved effective in its intent to provoke a higher level of discussion about labour's strategies and tactics.

"L.A. Public Workers Point To Some Problems: sketches of the present for some point to the future for all?" was produced for the Social Works show at the Los Angeles Institute for Contemporary Art. I used this piece as the hub of an expanded exhibition idea. Since it is very difficult to get labour to come to galleries, editions of the artwork were hung simultaneously in the unions involved and in the L.A. County Federation of Labor. The "public worker" issue was selected, with the help of the Federation, because of the timely impact of Proposition 13.[10] Speaking from the perspective of city and county workers about the consequences of this widely supported initiative, this piece addresses several questions:

• Was there "fat" in government? (Some.)
• Did the new law cut the fat? (No, fat is in administration, which can protect itself.)
• What about government services? (Declining.)
• And working conditions? (Good and bad to worse.)

Another major change from "The Health and Safety Game" was to place the fiscal crises of Los Angeles into international, national, and then regional contexts by outlining certain facts (surplus industrial capacity has produced a glut of many commodities on world markets, causing a drop in overall profits and a consequent shrinking of the tax base) and quoting contradictory authorities from the business press. Formally, this work was less successful than the H&SG. The images are more interesting, I think, but less shocking than scars and burns. More significantly, I gave a lot of space to an outline that was too long to work as such, and I tended to overload each panel with type. I received generally favourable feedback from the unions at that time but virtually no response from the art establishment reviewers. I don't think a single one of these critics went to any of the unions to see how the project might look and work there or to talk to local officers and members.

"I Like Everything Nothing But Union": This work was requested by the head of my own San Diego-Imperial Counties Labor Council (AFL-CIO) and, after two years of photographing and interviewing, was installed in the Labor Council's Executive Board office. Additional editions have travelled locally and nationally. The artwork sums up two broad but critical questions for organized labour today: Who are we and where should we go from here? We begin with the point that the crises of occupational health and the public sector are symptomatic of deeper issues and that the labour movement will have to thoroughly examine itself before it can move ahead. The primary role of the photos is to present the diversity of occupations, ethnic background, and gender that have to be unified. Lengthy quotations address the issues as rank-and-file workers see them. The Council's interest in the project springs from a desire to raise these concerns both within the unions and the public at large. This is a significant first step away from the Cold War years (under George Meany), when public silence was maintained on a lot of big questions about the role of unions in society by containing them within the top levels of the unions and our federation, the AFL-CIO.[11]

Afterword A

There are enormous limitations on an anthology like this,[12] limitations that are primarily a result of the marginal terrain most radical art occupies. This in turn results from the marginal position of radicals in society, especially in non-Latin North America, and the consequent lack of resources to compete in the major arenas of the mass media and high art (which has to a great extent been commercialized on a large scale). Radical art is a small-shop home industry, then, taking on the multinational conglomerate for the allegiance of the masses. The outcome of this marginalization is that most oppositional cultural practice is largely invisible even to those of us who are obsessed with it. By necessity, if not by choice, we work fairly locally and it takes almost all we've got to do what we're doing. There is a major role yet to be played by non-artists (radical curators) to help get this work in front of a public.[13] (There is especially a lack of outlets for things that hang on walls.)[14] But this collection of essays and reproductions is only a step towards a real discourse presenting real choices to the reader. Choice in this case – if most readers weren't already predisposed to certain ideas, practices, and forms – is probably overwhelming without some critical evaluation that is informed enough and has a clear perspective for presenting a case. Choice, which should be based upon the judgement, description, discussion, and illustration of our often complex, socially specific, and extensive works, is rarely adequate to the task. What we need more and more, as oppositional work achieves wider dissemination, is writing that itself compares and contrasts and interrogates our works. When we are invited to group shows and anthologies, the host must see to it that the political and formal issues are laid out in some way; otherwise we have lettuce and tomatoes but no salad. This is no small problem. It can only be solved by those who can take the time to actually observe our works in the contexts in which they are intended and do (or don't) work. Furthermore, the apprehending mind must have some ideas about what things work and which don't, about which jobs need to be done and for whom. However successful any of us are in our own contexts with what we do, we are floundering as a movement of cultural contenders and have much less of a meaningful contention with each other than the political left has within itself.

On the positive side, though, is the surfacing awareness – on national and international levels – of the vitality and viability of oppositional cultural practice. There are now fledgling networks that transcend our localization, and many artists are aware of the need to connect left intellectuals with our burgeoning practice.[15] These writers are largely trained and located in academia (when a job can be found) and, until recently, heavily steeped in the traditions of critical theory. They are preoccupied with the postmodern. By and large they have remained aloof from contemporary art-in-struggle unless they are discovering the past (the 1920s and 1930s especially) or unless the work is being done in the Third World or, to a small extent, by ethnic minorities (see Huyssens, 1986).

Afterword B

Afterword A indicates the level of the theoretical/critical crises I see in the "art for social change" arena in the United States. When I turn to the "communications for social change" field (in which I am not nearly so embedded), there is plenty of attention to theory but I don't see much interest in art. Perhaps some of the other chapters in this book will be concerned with art in some sense of the meaning to some extent, but I see little hint of this in their titles. I would guess that my contribution was accepted because of its emphasis on labour rather than art. In the United States, with the exception of film and video and to a lesser extent theatre, art lies way above the plane of "democratic communications" in the estimations of left social scientists. And oppositional art is not prominent in the mass media. Art's democratic credentials are in question and without mass distribution are of dubious significance anyway.

So, in the "information age," where is oppositional art and where is it going? Some of it is making use of the new informational technologies, especially computers and cable TV via video. The PC publishers have been unleashed, "Deep Dish" spreads Paper Tiger around the globe. And all of this is what we've been waiting for; it's no longer a question of where you are but whether or not you are on line. But (before you quote that) consider that democracy without place is problematic.[16] In fact, millions of people, while electronically connected, are still very rooted somewhere or *wish* they were. Working-class culture in particular is both fascinated with sound and picture gadgets *and* is attached to locality. Work, family, or hobbies/recreation make use of amateur state-of-the-art technologies to preserve an essentially provincial outlook. Of course corporate media exploit this, shaping consciousness towards the conservative and consumerist. On the production end, lots of artists committed to social critique and change are going to continue to work in forms of media that predate the new information age: painting and drawing and sculpting and writing poems and songs, by hand even. Side-stepping here the issue of how effective that work is as "art" (or whether it should not be art or really isn't art anyway), do the new technologies of electronic reproduction render this work irrelevant? Are the new technologies a kind of flashy convention for all public messages; to be heard one must speak in its language?

In the new information age, I am going to make a democratic argument for place.[17] Feedback on the spot, in fact, is one of the virtues of placement. The effectiveness of whatever goes onto a given wall or floor is to be judged by paying attention to what happens to it. But even the reception of a lot of film and video today is now difficult to assess as audiences retreat into their homes (cable TV, VCRs) and away from collective forms of viewing in theatres or bars. Keep in mind that we are sometimes talking about messages that will not be easy for the intended audience to accept and that I am assuming messages that have rhetorical power but do not attempt to persuade by appeals to mystery or by "mystification."

Notes

1. After all, I was getting respectable attention in the art world, including a one-person installation in the film and video space of the Whitney Museum of American Art.
2. *Red-Herring*, No.2, *Praxis*, No.6, and *Proceedings of the Marxist Caucus of the College Art Association*, 1980.
3. *Obscura*, Vol.2, No.5, *Art & Ideology*, New Museum Catalog, 1983.
4. "Working With Unions," in Kahn and Neumaier (1985).
5. This is one use of photography that has very widespread use and thereby distribution. Publications can now very cheaply reproduce photos rather well and this creates

a big demand. Occasionally my pictures appear in this manner and I have no strong objection to this vernacular use. The photos you see here are of this order as "details" from their artworks. That is, they belong as images to the specifics of a particular work where they are rooted or "anchored" (Barthes), as *all* photos are in their taking. They are uprooted when used as universal icons as is the practice in many "photo essays" and most photojournalism. So I am referring here to the myriad left newspapers, magazines, and journals as well as leaflets, posters, and the like.

6. This means primarily those people who are in the Democratic Socialists of America (DSA). It is a well-kept secret from the general public that much of the top leadership of the AFL-CIO belongs to the Social Democrats U.S.A. (SDUSA), which, along with DSA, is a member of the Socialist International. On foreign policy, SDUSA is very much to the right of the rest of the SI.

7. Since Lane Kirkland replaced George Meany as head of the AFL-CIO, there has been a growing interest in media in the trade unions. The Labor Institute Of Public Affairs produces programming for public television and promotes the use of video and cable TV locally. Between two and three dozen U.S. cities now have some kind of labour cable-TV programming or have it in the works (in San Diego Labor Link TVB has a monthly program on three cable stations). See Glass, "Notes Toward a Morphology of Labor Video," *Afterimage*, September 1989; and *MediActive*, Vol.II, No.2.

8. There is a recent development of significance; the AFL-CIO has formally established a relationship with the Labour Heritage Foundation. This is the outcome of efforts by labour musicians who began holding festivals hosted by the George Meany Center. Joe Glazer is the most prominent name among the organizers. Most recent festivals have had workshops devoted to oral histories, photography, and video in addition to signing and songwriting, and it is their wish to expand to all the arts as interest is demonstrated and resources found. Labour Heritage Festivals are now held yearly in the west, northwest, and midwest regions. I should also mention that the Workers Cultural School at the University of Michigan (Ann Arbor) has started annual spring workshops across several disciplines: "Art From, By and For the Workplace." Also see *Talkin' Union*, Bx 5349, Tacoma Park, MD 20912.

9. I briefly want to mention one place abroad where art and labour are more tightly connected than here. There art has been greatly socialized (state-owned, state-funded, and state-exhibited): a legacy of social democracy. The Australian Council of Trade Unions formally adopted an arts policy "in the late 1960s." But not until the early 1980s was there a formal link between the Australian Council for the Arts and the ACTU through the Community Arts Boards. The outcome has been government funding for the "Arts and Working Life Program" that augments support from the unions and the ACTU. Because Canada too has a relatively high public funding for the arts, there is movement there in the trade unions and their federations to follow the Australian example (Beveridge, 1985).

10. This California ballot initiative was successfully promoted as a property tax reform in 1978, at a time when these taxes for residential property were doubling and nearly tripling within a few years due to real-estate speculation. The actual outcomes were significant relief from residential taxes, a tremendous windfall tax break for commercial property owners (the initiative's unstated purpose), and a substantial reduction of the tax base for local public services.

11. In February 1985 the AFL-CIO Committee on the Evolution of Work produced "The Changing Situation of Workers and their Unions," which was adopted as policy for the Federation. When promoting this artwork to the labour movement, I stress its dovetail with this critical document (though I have much more affinity

with the militancy of "The Inside Game: Winning with Workplace Strategies," AFL-CIO Industrial Unions Dept. 1986).

12. Afterword A is the Prologue of my article "Working With Unions," published in *Cultures In Contention* (Kahn and Neumaier, 1985), a collection of essays and reproductions. That article is reprinted here as an updated, reorganized, and expanded version.

13. Film and now video have had a much more developed system of distribution and criticism than other left media. The collective nature of filmmaking has more naturally evolved branches devoted to brochures and networks of distribution. From the early 1970s, Newsreel and New Day Films have successfully got their works moving around in substantial circuits of screenings. Organizations, colleges/universities, and cable TV provided many outlets. Later, Media Network (NYC) set itself up as a clearing house for film and video. "Media" clearly has a following out of which a few people come forward to encourage the outreach. In recent years, groups like New York Political Art Documentation and Distribution (NYPADD has a publication, *Upfront*) and Group Material have organized large group shows. A couple of years running, PADD became national with multi-site exhibitions and performances in various cities around the theme of non-intervention in Central America. Art Against Apartheid is another example. However, these efforts come and go: There is nothing that approaches a regular circuit of exhibitions for floor/wall artworks. Screens are in and walls are out.

14. Shipping and hanging things (sometimes big and/or many things) is difficult with small budgets. Space has to be commandeered and supervised for at least a few weeks to allow a show to reach enough people to justify the effort and expense.

15. In *Praxis*, No.6, I expand on the thesis that the theoretical and formal underdevelopment of much of our work is partly a result of the left intelligentsia's neglect. However, we need to go beyond the scope of the critical community that is available for left filmmakers. The problem is that critics write largely to each other and for the *viewers*; it is not very evident that the critical circle is closed with the *makers* of films. It is a full-circle ideal that I point towards for all our work. Many artists are not really open to criticism nor do many read theoretical work.

16. Of course person-to-person communication on site is not unmediated, but when contemplating the conference call as the alternative (even with videophones) we must be startled at any naive acceptance. Electronic communication attenuates mediation under a guise of directness.

17. It is also an argument that in the real world of contention between working-class and corporate culture, for example, it should be expected there will be a co-existence of old and new technologies. There is no implication here that work should not be done with the electronic media. To some extent our limited access to it leaves no choice but other means of communication for the foreseeable future.

References

Beveridge, Karl (1985). "Report on the Art and Working Life Program in Australia." Toronto.

Glass, Fred (1989). "Notes Towards a Morphology of Labor Video," *Afterimage*, September.

Huyssens, Andreas (1986). *After the Great Divide: Modernism, Mass Culture, Postmodernism.* Bloomington, Ill.: University of Indiana Press.

Kahn, Douglas and Diane Neumaier, eds. (1985). *Cultures in Contention.* Seattle: The Real Comet Press.

Lonidier, Fred (1985). "Working with Unions." In Kahn and Neumaier (1985).

Sekula, Allan (1984). "Dismantling Modernism, Reinventing Documentary (Notes on the Politics of Representation)." In *Photography Against The Grain: Essays and Photo Works 1973-1983*. Halifax, N.S.: Press of the Nova Scotia College of Art and Design.

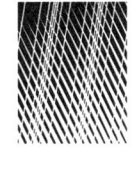

Part IV

Social Movements and Media Strategies

Discursive Movements and Social Movements: The Active Negotiation of Constraints

Peter A. Bruck

The Inscription of Democratic Models in Critical Scholarship

Among North American communication scholars it is critical theorists and cultural analysts who like to distinguish their work from the academic deeds of positivists, empiricists, good liberals, or bad conservatives, arguing that critical work does more than describe and analyze. As well, critical writing and scholarship try to explain and to provide a normative context (see also Wellmer, 1970). Put differently, critical work separates phenomena in the world into what they appear to be and what they "really" are, and it relates them to what possibly should be. Critical work has a theoretical-explanatory as well as a normative-prescriptive dimension. These characteristics do not per se imply that critical theorists have to stand by Hegelian notions of essence and appearance, but it does mean that critical theorists undertake to place their analytical categories in relation to and out of interest in the organization of the social totality.

The theoretical-explanatory effort is undertaken with a transcendental intention. This intention is not necessarily linked to a utopian vision. It can as easily mean a program of negative engagement or resistance. But the effort of analysis and explanation is directed towards an intervention into the political-social reality and the incumbent pragmatics of wilful action.[1]

However, the theoretical-explanatory effort as well as the normative-prescriptive intent of much North American critical research into the news media are tied to a politics and a conception of democracy that disempower activists in social movements and are counterproductive to active engagement in alternative and oppositional work.

138

I shall first argue this on a theoretical plane, then extend this argument to press the point that most critical media theories are also inadequate in their treatment of empirical developments; namely, by failing to account for the often contradictory operation of the news media. The evidence for this comes in an analysis of the coverage of disarmament, peace, and security issues in thirteen Canadian daily newspapers over a period of six months. I will conclude with some observations on the relationship between critical analysis and political practice.

Capitalism, Industry, and Bureaucracy: The Untold Form of the Media System

Those analysts who can rightly be called critical share a number of assumptions about the empirical operation of the news media – although they may accord these assumptions different theoretical status or analytical priority in any given study.

The news media have to be understood as being capitalistically organized, that is, they are commercial enterprises governed by the logic of capital rentability and profit accumulation. As a result, audience maximization overrides most other operating factors, most of the time. Even if the media enterprise is not privately owned, but is a public service, the pressures of audience maximization persist and become reconstructed in the imperatives that justify and legitimate programming, corporate plans, and resource allocation choices.

The news media have to be, furthermore, understood as industrially organized with an elaborate division of labour and the continuous mass production of texts. Production labour is divided between reporters on the scene, desk personnel, assignment and copy editors, editorial writers, columnists, managers, and publishers. The news media employ complex systems of machinery, and the labour of news workers becomes productive only in interaction with these mechanical systems.

The separation of intellectual powers of production from manual execution has not progressed – and possibly cannot progress – as far in the news industry as in other industrial sectors. However, the decisiveness of capital's interest in rearranging the entire production organization of news media has found vivid demonstrations in the flight of the British press entrepreneurs from Fleet Street in 1983-86, dramatic shutdowns of a number of Canadian newspapers in the last decade, or the restructuring of U.S. network news operations by the accountants of their new owners in the late 1980s.

The news media are bureaucratically organized. Journalists are directly dependent on a stock of regular sources. They habitually scan and check those institutional sites that are organized parts of their beats, and they depend on the information subsidies and documentary practices of their sources; that is, they depend on sources that can make available and efficiently supply "facts," documentation, or proof. News workers construct their work practices around offices and organizational hierarchies, their hours and places of operation, their divisions of labour. News work routinizes textual production in substance and in form, in terms of what is made to be known and how it is to be known, that is, how it is to be produced or written up.

Wire services and press conferences are thus pragmatically connected to the practice of attribution – the ritualistic use of quotes in news texts and the persistent attempts to find no less and preferably no more than two sides to any issue.

The bureaucratic organization of news work ties journalistic practice and media operation to the operational modes and agendas of the management apparatuses of the state and the economy. Having on first sight a proclivity for the sensational, and therefore the unbureaucratic, the news media on closer examination are an integral part of present-day social administration and control.

If Democracy Is a Goal and Not a Fact, What Are the Questions about News Media?
The identification of the news media as part of the dominant system, as a key element in the processes of reproduction and legitimation, can only mark a starting point of analysis.

Two points in particular need further consideration. To begin with, the dominant system does not "reproduce" itself in an uncontradictory or conflict-free fashion, and the news media – daily press, television, and radio – do not do their reproductive labour in a uniform and unitary way. The question, then, is: How does the system leak?

Secondly, given this first point, what then decides the success and/or failure of reproduction? More specifically, what options are there in the social system for people who oppose its main operating logic and mechanisms? Or to put it in another way, what room to manoeuvre do the established news media allow for non-establishment organizations and movements to become politically effective and "alter the course of history"?

Most critical research in the area of news analysis suggests that there is little or no room, that the media do their job in a consistent manner, that social movements are systematically and regularly excluded and rendered ineffective, and that the media are reproducing the dominant ideology largely without slip or hitch. All these assertions are empirical claims about what becomes textually available on a social scale from the established news media. The evidence shows that these texts are effective without much further effort.

I do not want to introduce here arguments about the tenuousness of this assertion. The question of the politics of reading and the possibilities of alternative or oppositional strategies need to be addressed separately, and there is no need here to include the problematics of reader-response or audience labour. Rather, I want to make my point regarding the political practice of critical communication scholars and Marxist culture critics, including myself. I would argue that much of our analytical focus can be said to be directed towards the study of ideological closure. This goes back as far as Lazarsfeld and Merton (1949).

In recent years critical scholars have produced a number of significant studies that have come to occupy centre stage in the field of news research (Gans, 1979; Clark and Taylor, 1981; Knight, 1982; Tuchman, 1978; Hall et al., 1980; Gitlin, 1979; GUMG, 1976, 1980, 1982). By explicitly stating that the media produce/impose a dominant ideology, these studies have successfully established this point as an orthodoxy within critical media and culture studies, if not for most of the field of mass communication (see also Bruck, 1989).

These studies, however, have yet to address a number of problems, not the least of which is an epistemological one. Most of the studies are textual examinations that consider *ex post facto* the outcome of what is often a contradictory accomplishment. Considerable analytical problems arise here regarding the distinction between success and domination.

Any interpretation is arbitrary in the way that almost all signs are arbitrary (Eco, 1976). Interpretations can be thought of as competing in the process of producing an account about a happening in the world. The fact that an interpretation has been successful, inasmuch as it is used in the media to report an event, is textually not readily distinguishable from what interpretation or set of interpretations is dominant. The analytical effort to determine solely from textual data the existence of a "dominant ideology" tends to produce a formalist, ahistorical, and in the end theoreticist tendency, and thus to obfuscate..concrete historical changes, struggles, and, most importantly, action alternatives.

In more practical terms, this position has led to difficulties for social movements, minority groups, and non-establishment organizations attempting to assess the chances for, and measures of, effective work through the mass media. Often these social actors find themselves in the ambiguous situation of depending on the establishment media for the dissemination of their messages, while knowing that these messages will be considerably altered along the way. The conclusions of critical media research offer little help in these situations.

System Control and Hegemony

This discussion, then, suggests the need to reexamine the strategic basis of hegemonic analysis in any consideration of democratic action alternatives in the social here and now. Given the capitalistic, industrial, and bureaucratic structure of the news media's operation, the finding that the media reproduce the dominant ideology does not come as a surprise. Rather, it means that the news media do perform their functional job. What is of interest, then, is how the media accomplish their reproductive labour, when they fail to do this, what alters this operational functioning, what opportunities for change exist, how these opportunities are differentially distributed, and what conclusions can be drawn for alternative or oppositional practices and movements.

It is important to allow in our analysis for the fact that news media do their work in differing ways at different times depending – among others – on topic, political circumstance, and, I would argue, the alternative social and discursive pressures exerted at a given time.

Writers such as Todd Gitlin articulate well the general point of view of critical communication scholars and activist media critics (Gitlin, 1980, 1987). Given this, we need to reexamine some of our general conclusions about the operation of the news media, and we have to avoid being entirely preoccupied with the dynamics of closure. We have to avoid what I would call the fallacies of systemicism.

Problems of Systemicism I: The Hegemonic Homogeneity or the Historicity and Hetero-Discursivity of News

The media do speak in their own particular ways about the world. They produce particularly structured accounts – their own discourses – and employ reporting dynamics that textually characterize coverage but are organizationally routed (Fishman, 1980; Bruck, 1984). The media have networks of authorities, of people who are to be interviewed and accessed, people they pay attention to and listen to. And the media have their specific ways of presenting events, making their stories work, seeking their audiences' assent. They have their own regimen of intelligibility, and so forth.[2]

In doing all this work the media employ their own well-described codes and conventions – their modes of speaking and editing, of contracting voices and stories. The discursive material they work with, however, is not their own. Rather, the media build their accounts of what happens in the world on the accounts of other people, for example, eyewitnesses, police officers, experts, lobbyists, politicians, or business leaders.

What these people have to say enters into the media accounts either as unacknowledged background information or as acknowledged and attributed sources. Either way, what these people have to say and how they say it influence to varying degrees the angle of the news story, the emphases placed in it, or the structure and the flow of the report. This influence extends as well to what is said in documents and texts, and all the other material the media work with.

In this sense we can speak of the media as *reprocessing* the discourses provided by their sources; they *reassemble* the information, *rearrange* the different parts, and thus create their own particular way of telling the stories of events in the world. Reprocessing is a well-structured, professional (skilfully done, according to specific codes) activity in which the media appropriate other discourses and reproduce the social and political order of the day. In news analysis, we need to make the analytical separation between the discourses the media produce and the discourses they use as material to build on, to process and deliver. We need to be interested in the structures of transformation.

The media fate of social movements is thus not decided in a transhistorical context, and challenges to the social order are not always thwarted in the same way. How news workers establish relationships of temporal stability between discourses, and between discourses and social relations, is part of the historical specificity of the treatment of social movements by the media.

For instance, when I analyzed six months' coverage of peace, disarmament, and security issues in Canadian newspapers I started out with the assumption that it is possible to distinguish five main discourses as circulated by the media apparatus: a) the bureaucratic-technical discourse; b) the discourse of the leaders of state; c) the diplomatic-scientific discourse; d) the discourse of victims; and e) the discourse of survival.

We sampled the press coverage from thirteen English-language dailies in all regions of Canada from November 1985 to April 1986, breaking news down into fourteen different stories (for further detail see Bruck et al., 1987). "Stories" are those issues and events covered over a lengthy period of time, which provide a thematic focus as well as a news-peg for individual reportorial items.

One of the major stories in our sample concerned the testing of the U.S. Air Force's cruise missiles over the Northwest Territories and Alberta. Since their inception the cruise missile tests have been vigorously opposed by Canadian peace and disarmament groups, and "Refuse the Cruise" became the rallying cause for a resurgence of mass demonstrations, public education, and political lobbying. Much of what Canadians look back on as the peace movement of the 1980s in this country was organized around the issue and in opposition to the cruise testing.

The Testing of the Cruise Missile in Canada as a Newspaper Story
The cruise missile story started in 1982 with the publication of the announcement of the testing agreement between Canada and the United States. The agreement was signed in 1983. News coverage of the story peaked in the periods of the demonstrations against the agreement and during the time of the first test flights in 1984 and 1985. During our sample period, the tests had become a continuing news story. A time-line of news events shows this more clearly:

- December 22, 1985: Military spokesman announces that two Canadian CF-18 fighters will participate in cruise missile (CM) tests in March.
- January 4, 1986: Department of National Defence (DND) announces it will give the public forty-eight hours' notice before each of the four CM tests to take place over Canada.
- January 20: CM test to take place this week. Greenpeace plans to protest at the CM test corridor.
- January 21: Test delayed twenty-four hours because of fuel-pump problem.
- January 22: Test on. Greenpeace protest at Cold Lake Canadian Forces (CF) Base. Twenty protesters at Edmonton Legislature. *Jane's Defence Weekly* prints stories re Soviet trained agents infiltrating Greenham Common peace camp.
- January 23: CM test ends five minutes early and lands without a parachute. Four Greenpeace protesters arrested. Officials say aborted test a "failure," not a "crash"; this is the first "failure" of a CM test in Canada, where four other CM tests have been successful.
- January 24: "Failure" of previous day delays second test. Remains of CM found in heavily wooded area. External Affairs Minister Joe Clark speech: Canada will continue to allow CM tests to show solidarity with the United States.
- February 24: U.S. Strategic Air Command and CF Information Officers at Cold Lake say: CM crashed because it ran out of fuel. Test no.6 scheduled for February 25.
- February 25: Peace activist states: "resignation" of peace movement explains the few protests over Test no.6. CM crashes into Beaufort Sea on launch due

to engine ignition failure.
- February 26: Tests stop until cause of accident determined.
- February 27: CM crash took place 180 kilometres from community of three thousand.
- March 1: CM debris sent to United States.
- March 7: NWT Legislative Assembly votes to halt CM testing and to urge federal government to reconsider test agreement with the United States.
- March 10: CM tests declared over for year, will resume in January 1987.
- April 3: Yukon legislature votes to urge relocation of CM tests. Cause of February crash: CM incorrectly rigged to wing of B-52 bomber.

Since the first test of the U.S. cruise missile over Canadian soil in early 1984, the cruise controversy had been popularly regarded as the preeminent peace issue in the country. The first reports in our sample, dating from December 22, 1985, lead off by quoting a military spokesperson and statements from peace groups, thereby recognizing both as established sources in the overall news story. The coverage in our sample period breaks down into two distinct time periods – January 20 to 24 and February 24 to 27 – each centred around a respective test.

Most if not all of the news coverage of the cruise testing assumed that members of the public shared a considerable background knowledge concerning what was at issue. The journalists took for granted that cruise missile testing was a continuing story. News leads did not explain the contestations and debates about the testing but treated it "naturally" as the object of considerable political dissent: "The controversial testing of the U.S. cruise missile over northwest Canada will resume tomorrow, Ottawa has announced." The full news accounts then revolved around a structured exchange between competing ways of framing the issue. This set up the knowledge terrain of the coverage and was augmented with a continuing reference to the already executed test flights. The "we have done it" was used as a rhetorical form, lending the quality of "fact" to the military's claims and a certain amount of non-contentiousness to the otherwise quite contentious issue. In this way, limits were set to the further conceptual development of the cruise missile as a security or disarmament issue for the peace groups. This was unlike the coverage during the original 1984 tests, which allowed for more oppositional voices. The above dynamic was further reinforced by the event-oriented coverage of the daily press, that is, the press's tendency to focus on the tests themselves at the expense of the larger social and political issues.

Ways of Speaking: The Military Bureaucrats Tell the World
When on January 22, 1986, the first of the four cruise missile tests ended with the missile crashing in heavy woods, miles short of its designated target on the Primrose Lake, Alberta, Air Weapons Test Range, it was the Canadian Forces (CF) spokespersons who primarily defined the first coverage. They told reporters what the test failure "meant," provided details about the functioning of the missile and its guidance systems, and supplied "expert analysis."

In the terms of our assumptions regarding the use of different discourses in the coverage of disarmament and security issues, the spokespeople used the bureaucratic-technical discourse to make the events intelligible and assign significance to the happening. As the single source of pertinent "facts," this discourse defined the "reality" of the test event and its consequences. It defined the terms in which the launch would have been a "success," that is, as a technical military task requiring precise execution. This notion of success was naturalized within the coverage as the military spokespeople were used as primary news actors and definers.

The bureaucratic-technical discourse creates its own realities. It never addresses the concrete realities outside its frame of reference, for example, the "little" wars in "off" places such as East Timor or Northern Brazil. Rather, it is hung up in the exhortations of the sterile sophistication of military tests and operational specifications, of ritualized and routinized negotiation, electronic precision and semantic fine-tuning. It is held up by an unbending will to power, hardly cognizant of its legitimation needs and quite terrified of any imaginable threat aimed at its diminution. A dull and bureaucratic version of shadow boxing, the voices of the spokespeople in this discourse have no power to speak for themselves or of themselves. They are mere auxiliaries for the voices of the state.

In our analysis of the coverage of the cruise missile story we distinguished between actor sources and institutional sources. We conceptualized actor sources to be those narrative characters who were not only accessed for quotation and reference but who were also portrayed as actively involved in the story action: Their activities were part of the material reported. Institutional sources are those sources that supplied story material by quotation or reference but were not portrayed as being among the main actors. Generally, people who are used as institutional sources are always identified in relationship to the organization they speak for.

The cruise missile story was dominated by institutional sources speaking the bureaucratic-technical discourse. Of the total of ninety story items, only 32.2 per cent had an actor in their lead topics. But 91.1 per cent had an institutional voice in their leads. Armed forces spokesmen were the lead source in 73.4 per cent of the items.

A tally of the total number of quotes and references further illustrates this point:

Institutional Sources	*Quoted*	*Referred*
1. Canadian Armed Forces spokesmen	202	27
2. U.S. Air Force officials	132	10
3. Greenpeace spokesperson	46	36
4. Government leader, NWT	15	8
5. Operation Dismantle spokesperson	11	2
6. Can. Centre for Arms Control & Disarmament	9	1
7. Assistant Mayor, Inuvik	8	0
8. Peace Association for Nuclear Awareness (Grande Prairie) president	8	0
9. U.S. Ambassador to Canada	6	1
10. Assembly of First Nations (chief)	6	0
11. Alberta Citizens Anti-Cruise	5	0
12. Cold Lake Town Council	4	0
13. Lakeland Coalition for Nuclear Awareness	4	1

14. Former advisor to George Shultz   3   1
15. Toronto Disarmament Network spokesperson   3   1
16. Women at Greenham Common   2   2
18. NORAD   1   5

These findings suggest the extent to which the bureaucratic-technical discourse spoken largely by military officers, diplomats, and other experts of state and governmental institutions dominated the coverage of the story. The discourse generally tends to feed on knowledge of international law, military strategies, and weapons technology, combined with ways of speaking on these matters, replete with acronyms and specialized vocabulary.

Sincere treaties and solemn declarations serve as standardized references, supplementing the categories of national security with concerns for state sovereignty and territorial integrity aiming at "international accords," "mutual efforts," and "deterrence." The process readily accesses questions of military hardware and emphasizes equipment capabilities and requirements.

This discourse assumes that security is the result of well-functioning weaponry. No concrete actors are named. History is decided by anonymous subjects like military strength or the arms race in general, and much is done to avoid identifying any other subjects of history.

When it comes to the question of disarmament, the discourse gets largely bogged down in its own maze of technical detail and administrative textualizations. It can only follow its course, but is unable to reverse itself. It is a discourse without a reflexive subject.

The news media tend to use but not to focus on this discourse. They often make it simply their own. The discourse's predictability makes it good material, stemming as it does from prescheduled events and producing hard news. Yet it is rarely used outside an event context. Institutions or institutional arrangements rather than persons are displayed as authors, and few if any visuals are provided.

The bureaucratic-technical discourse is evidently the dominant way in which the media reported on the cruise missile story during the sample period. But it does not go unchallenged nor is it without a need for support. Rather, it is to a considerable extent a discourse that derives its legitimation from another more authoritative way of representing the issues. This discourse is spoken by the leaders of the state.

Ways of Speaking: The Leaders of the State Claim the World
The Canadian Forces released a statement for publication on February 24 declaring that a sixth test of the cruise missile would be conducted the following day. Also at this time it was announced that the missile launched a month earlier had "run out of fuel because of stronger than forecast headwinds." Dropped from a U.S. B-52-G bomber flying at an altitude of 10,668 metres, the sixth missile plunged into the frozen Beaufort Sea. An immediate halt to all testing was ordered until the precise reason for the mishap could be determined.

Coverage of the second missile launch differed from the first test in that the primary source of the relevant information was the House of Commons, as opposed to military personnel. Associate Defence Minister Harvie Andre provided details of the incident before the House, where the subsequent interpretation was immediately subjected to rigorous debate amongst Members of Parliament. Defence critics for the New Democratic Party and the Liberals were quoted extensively to provide a "balanced" account of the second test, thereby fulfilling professional notions of objective reporting.

Excluded from the terrain upon which the formal parliamentary exchange was based were those individuals positioned outside the boundaries of political talk, its conventions, and its preferred subjects, values, and authorities. Thus the debate recorded in the House of Commons and reproduced in the daily press led to a news account that was limited by the characteristics of the political site itself. Contending ways of speaking the issue were reduced to those views articulated by members of the House – the institutionalized form of conflict resolution within the larger society. Having framed the issue in relation to this discourse, the press largely denied access to alternative interpretations, including those proffered by various peace and disarmament groups. Background information gathered from news periodicals confirms that organized demonstrations took place; thus their absence from the corpus is of significance.

The discourse of the leaders of states, and particularly the leaders of the nuclear nations and the superpowers, centres around categories such as national security, national greatness and the goodness-of-its-social-political-order, threat-from-outside, and need-to-prevail-through-heightened-defence-efforts; the category of détente originates from here; the sincerity of one side's commitment to peace and the unwillingness of the other side to reciprocate in kind through an equally strong commitment are repeatedly asserted.

This discourse works mostly in bipolar terms with the characteristic Manichaean split between the good side and the bad side – a split that serves as a discursive procedure structuring the different formations of the discourse. The discourse proceeds frequently by enumeration of the government's armament efforts; it works with abstract acontextual notions of history and statements of facts (Barthes, 1973:151-154).

Specific to the circumstances of the cruise missile tests and the geopolitical situation of Canada was the repeated insistence by government ministers that Canada had to choose sides, that Canada had to prove its allegiance to the United States, and that it was necessary to prepare and hone war-fighting skills.

This discourse is highly privileged in the media due to the status of its authors as news promoters (see Molotch and Lester, 1974, 1975). News bulletins take it as their main staple and the front pages and first sections of newspapers are filled with it. Most of what is typified as hard news (Tuchman, 1978:51-53) consists of, or echoes, this discourse. What is said is closely reported if not cited verbatim, and the presentation of state leaders provides for "good visuals" according to the dominant news judgement: speeches, getting on and off airplanes, walking through entrance doors, shaking hands.

Our analysis of the cruise missile story reveals that the state leaders are seen as the only actors in the entire news story; they are the only characters who are both quoted and referred to and described as doing things, as setting actions.

Actors	Quoted	Referred To
1. Harvie Andre, Ass. Minister of Defence	78	9
2. Ed Broadbent, NDP Leader	17	4
3. Jean Chrétien, Liberal Foreign Affairs critic	11	0
4. Pauline Jewett, NDP Foreign Affairs Critic	11	0
5. Joe Clark, Minister of External Affairs	7	3
6. Len Hopkins, Liberal Defence Critic	4	7
7. Erik Nielsen, Minister of Defence	0	1
8. Brian Mulroney, Prime Minister	0	10

It is part of the Canadian parliamentary system that statements from the government do not go unchallenged. Especially during times when the House of Commons is in session, the daily question period offers an institutional arena for contesting views of an issue.

The views advanced by the opposition are reported in the context of government announcements. They are covered as reactions to the statements in the official state discourse. For journalists the news value and intelligibility of these opposition views are thus not derived from propositional content or value as an alternative point of view but from an institutional location within the Canadian parliamentary system and its tradition of required party antagonism within the established order. This situation means that alternative conceptualizations must work from within the dominant discourse. The process suggests that the consensual system of a representative democracy offers sites for critique; but these sites are placed and contained within the larger institutions. The news media behave accordingly. They give the opposition their "due" space while at the same time allowing the reproduction of the government's legitimacy through its primary news acting position. Spokespersons for the parliamentary opposition thus have to accept more often than not the conceptual foundations of the government's presentation of the issues. Their challenges have to work around the legitimacy of the government's discourse, attempting to undermine it. Generally, they formulate challenges only to such an extent that their own legitimacy will not be threatened should they take power. This can be further demonstrated in a discussion of the dominant themes of the coverage; but first we have to examine the other main discourses in which the story was or could have been spoken.

Ways of Speaking: The Diplomats' Balm and the Victims' Cry
Closely related to the discourse of the leaders of the state and also to the bureaucratic-technical discourse is the way of speaking of the diplomats and scientific experts. Indeed, the diplomatic and scientific discourses build on each other,

share particular formations and/or elements, and serve each other as reinforcements.

In its formations the diplomatic-scientific discourse resembles the bureaucratic-technical discourse, from which it frequently takes its agenda. The diplomatic-scientific is the discourse of the disarmament experts, replete with data and well-equipped with technical vocabulary. Unlike the first two, this discourse depends not on bare claims or strict assertions but on the fine-tuning of negotiated language and on scientific-rational procedures of documentation and construction of evidence. It is a post-enlightenment discourse where power allegedly rests on the truth of the content and not on the status of the author. Analytical procedures thus dominate alongside constructions of rational grounds for stated arguments and proposed hypotheses.

This discourse has its own social spaces at conferences and roundtables, as well as in journals such as *Foreign Affairs, Arms Control, Defence Week*, and *Defense Monitor*. The media use this discourse to supplement the first two. More prestigious papers such as *The New York Times* or *The Globe and Mail* allow their op-ed space to be used for the discourse, thereby accomplishing "critical distance" and providing "challenging commentary." While this discourse cannot be allowed enough space to unfold in regular news reports on radio or TV, it is solicited in a calculated manner and in an interview format by current affairs programs such as CBC's *The Journal*, ABC's *Nightline*, CTV's *W5*, and radio programs such as "Sunday Morning" or "As it Happens." These shows depend on the availability of the diplomatic-scientific discourse for their operation.

In our analysis of coverage the diplomatic-scientific discourse is most dominant in clippings covering the story of the superpower arms negotiations. In the cruise missile story this discourse is submerged under the military-technical discourse.

As a fourth discourse we can distinguish the victims of war. Central elements of its formations are the short cries of death, the muffled expressions of horror whose codes the media do not care to decipher, the weeping spells of children unarticulated in any sense beyond the bodily production of tears. The victims' discourse is unelaborated, unsophisticated, and almost hostile to the logos that failed to rescue the physis (Japanese Broadcasting Corporation, 1981).

The barren quality of this discourse makes it unable to lie, to be mythical speech in the sense used by Roland Barthes. It is speech of the real (Barthes, 1973:148). Its imperfections make it closer to silence than to talk. This discourse goes largely unrecorded in the press but finds its place in the Western news media as TV-visuals of blood or death, of destruction and horror. TV and boulevard press and magazines use the images to sell their wares. Like other pornographic material the images produce excellent profits.

The discourse of the victims of war is restricted in the variety of its articulation. This limitation and repetitiveness does not make the material fit well with the news media. Its use of real time lends itself to editing only with difficulty.

As a discourse of the real it is essentially subversive in relation to the previous discourses. Its power does not lie with the status of its authors or the truth function of its content, but with its close links to non-reducible reality. In its face the other discourses are arrested, and they can move on only by circumventing this victims' discourse, ignoring it, denying it. The existence of this sparse discourse reminds us that the most prolific discourses on disarmament are produced by those who prevent disarmament from taking place. We hear most about ending wars from those authors who are most likely to be the agents of war-making. It is those authors who are recorded in detail. It is their words that fill the books of history and the films, tapes, and paper columns of today. This is no surprise, indeed, because recorded talking is as much an effect of the possession of power as the making of war. Having no power means not being able to wage war and also not having a distinct voice that can be recorded by the news media or heard in history.

Not restricting the victims' discourse would turn the news media over to the challengers of the authors of the previous discourses, to the challengers of the authorities. Indeed, the real opposition in the case of war, as well as of the arms race, is not between the enemies who fight the war but between the war-makers and the war victims. This might have been less clear in past history, but in the nuclear age, when entire populations are targeted for annihilation, this should be obvious. The victims' discourse is truly oppositional in relation to the first three discourses.

Ways of Speaking: Survival
When the fifth cruise missile test under the 1983 weapons testing agreement failed on January 25, 1986, the unexpected crash reopened for discussion the conceptual terrain of speaking the event. On the day following, the newspapers across Canada covered positions that represented alternatives to the military-technical discourse that had dominated the reporting. Three papers even carried a photograph of a Greenpeace protester challenging an officer of the Royal Canadian Mounted Police at the entrance gate to the cruise missile test site in Cold Lake.

Coverage included attempts to redefine the test's failure as a "victory" because "the incident showed the weapon's unreliability." More generally, the test's failure positioned the spokespeople of peace groups across the country as the "other side" in the story. Thus, the dynamic of routine coverage via quotation/reference to two contrasting views in the press provided alternative views with space to speak and articulate a different logic regarding the arms race.

The majority of the reports in our sample address this opposition at least once. The majority of themes presented in the ninety reports belong to the bureaucratic-technical discourse. More interesting, however, is the fact that the opposition to the cruise missile testing turns out to be the most frequently used theme over six months of coverage of the cruise missile story in the Canadian English Press.

Theme	*Frequency*
1. Opposition of peace groups against the military and government.	50
2. Necessary to prepare war-fighting skills.	29
3. The danger of relying too much on technology is too great (for example, the space shuttle).	20
4. Cancel 1983 Test Agreement with U.S. (effective until 1988).	16
5. Cancellation necessary to guarantee public safety. The flight path of the CM covers an area with a population of 100,000. Ottawa is gambling with the lives of innocent people.	15
6. The cruise is safe to test due to the advanced monitoring systems used during testing.	15
7. Canada provides landscapes similar to the Soviet Union.	10
9. Delay tests.	8
10. More tests needed to avoid crashes. Tests provide insurance for the CM, which is already deployed.	7
11. Flight corridor not a danger to public since it's largely uninhabited, carefully monitored.	7
12. CM test record "looks good": 8 failures out of 54 tests.	6
13. Necessary to prove allegiance to U.S.	4
14. Change flight corridor to less populated area.	2
13. Verification regarding arms testing.	2

This is not to avoid the fact that a good number of the challenges to the testing program also have to use elements of the bureaucratic-technical discourse, and that this discourse is the dominant way in which the press spoke of the entire issue. The conceptual terrain for the tests was relatively solid. It is important to recognize that oppositional views must often insert themselves within the established definition, and because they do so they also can offer ways of speaking that counter the bureaucratic-technical discourse.

Related to this point is the distinction of a fifth discourse, one produced by peace and disarmament groups: the discourse of survival. This discourse draws its formations from the experts' discourse as well as from the victims' discourse. It is torn between the two, and relative to the others it exhibits less cohesion and is internally replete with discontinuities and ruptures. It seeks richness in articulation to better make its point. It works to leave space for the victims' discourse and gain the elaborateness of the experts' discourse, in the hope of thereby increasing in effectiveness.

In assembling their reports the news media differentially process all of these discourses. Over the period of six months' coverage the sampled Canadian newspapers used these specific ways of speaking about events-in-the-world around questions of disarmament and peace in order to report and render intelligible the testing of a remote-controlled low-flying object. The changes in the press reports regarding how the test flights were constructed and explained constitute what I call *discursive movements*.

This use of the analytical concept of discursive movements is developed out of recent studies in discourse analysis of media texts (Schlesinger, Murdock and

Elliott, 1983; Bruck, 1984; Van Dijk, 1985). The concept's usefulness depends on the argument that discursive dominance is the result of continuing social and ideological struggles, and that it is never permanently established but requires constant maintenance and repair. This view has the advantage of circumventing some of the theoretical problems of hegemonic analysis (see also Newcomb, 1984; Becker, 1984).

The notion of discursive movements does not just imply that different discourses are being reprocessed and rearranged by the media over time. But the relatively open or closed discursive nature of the five discourses shifts according to the contextual pressures generated by the social actors struggling for dominance in society.

Problems of Systemicism II: The Seamlessness of Hegemony or the Discursive Variations in News Formats

In a systemicist framework the media are depicted as relatively seamlessly reproducing an apparatus that consistently serves the entrenched powers.[3] A synchronic seamlessness of hegemonic closure submerges the discursive openings, inconsistencies, and contradictions of media coverage.

But newspaper writing consists of various types of narratives and different formats. These different formats follow different rules and conventions of composition and subject treatment. For news workers a format determines, for instance, the shelf life of an article or event. The shelf life not only suggests when a report may be printed but also offers instructions on how much researching of possible alternative sources is possible, necessary, and permissible. Formats also determine how open or closed a news item will be to the use of alternative discourses.[4]

On a continuum of distance and proximity to the discourse of the established powers, the different formats of news reporting can be organized in the following way:

1. **News Briefs:** These one-paragraph bits of wire copy generally rely on a single source. Bureaucratic statements and official reports dominate. When not used for the sensationalistic or catastrophic, the items are used as daily updates on events around the news world. Their briefness and simple event-orientation link them directly to dominant discourses and establishment sources.

2. **News Reports:** The hard-news angle and the inverted-pyramid style of writing give a distinct advantage to the agenda of governments and officials as actors. Sources are selected and legitimated according to political, organizational, or professional hierarchies. The requirements of balance, fairness, and objectivity are used to neutralize oppositional views. Most often, news reports pick up the interpretative frames and phrase structures of administrative officials and political authorities (see Fishman, 1980). Besides news briefs, news reports are the formally most restricted and, in their use of news frames, most reductive format. News reports are the basic staple of press reporting. In our sample, 56 to 95 per cent of

coverage on any particular story consisted of news reports. More to the point of our argument, we found that the more contentious an issue is in terms of the dominant discourses and the interests of the established social and political powers, the lower the percentage of news reports in the general coverage. This indicates two things. First, ideological reproduction does not work uniformly. Rather, contentiousness and news format are related, that is, ideological challenge/reproduction requires different formal leeway, depending on the threat posed to established forms and ways. Second, the constraints of news writing work two ways. On the one hand they force the discursiveness of quantification, officialdom, visuals, and drama onto the activities of, for instance, the peace movement; on the other hand, ideological challenges cannot be handled sufficiently within the formal constraints, and other discursiveness is needed to contain them. The more an issue moves onto the public stage, the more highly structured it becomes; the more it becomes constrained by the existing meaning structures and the available resources of interpretative addenda and understanding, the more socially validated feelings, emotions, and attitudes are mobilized around it (Hall et al., 1978:130-138). We can discern the pressures of highly structured ways of speaking about the issue and these ways seem to move in more than one direction.

3. Editorials: The opinion pieces written by institutional players are the most explicit news format in terms of stating the boundaries of the dominant consensus and arguing its merits. Yet this dominant consensus does not necessarily coincide with the interests of the social and political authorities of the day. In our sample concerning the testing of U.S. cruise missiles in Canada, editorial writing in a number of papers openly contradicted the government. This does not happen only with single issues. For instance, the largest circulation daily in Canada, *The Toronto Star*, attacked the government explicitly and directly in regard to what is by many considered the most important domestic and foreign policy issue in Canada since World War II, namely the free trade agreement with the United States. This campaign by the Toronto paper exceeded the traditional oppositional posture of the fourth estate vis-à-vis government. The campaign did not deal with patronage, broken promises, and violation of rules or law, but it made an issue out of the ideological framework of the government's action. The *Star* has a past record of doing this. On the occasion of the United Nations' second special session on disarmament, the *Star* created a peace beat and assigned a senior member of its editorial staff to cover it. It is worth noting that the journalist was the former religion editor of the paper. At *The Ottawa Citizen* the religion and social affairs beat included coverage of the local peace movement. This suggests that the discursive space for alternative movements in Canada today may to a considerable extent depend on the critical potential of mainstream religion.

4. Features: Essay-style reports researched and written by journalists are used to place issues and events into context. The subject-matter might be the same as in news reports, but reports are given a soft-news angle. This typification as soft news allows the discursive accessing of, for instance, individual experiences, the contextual features of an event, the personal involvement of the reporter in the event, the use of news sources whose news authority depends less on organizational/ institutional status and more on personal or expert knowledge. Although features discursively resemble backgrounders they tend to reproduce the dominant consensus due to the fact that they are largely written by professional news workers.

5. Backgrounders: These essays are written by journalists and other writers considered experts on specific issues. This format shows considerable leeway in the reproduction of the dominant agenda and interpretive frames. The pieces often establish connections not necessarily made by news actors. While often relying on current events for their newsworthiness, these pieces use the authority of expert knowledge to publicize alternative and, in some cases, oppositional views. An example from our sample is a number of full-page articles on and by British social historian and peace activist E.P. Thompson concerning his views about the new Cold War and nuclear arms race.

6. Columns: The individually authored opinion piece that is printed at prescheduled intervals in the paper irrespective of events or breaking stories gives its writers considerable discursive space. This can be illustrated by a column on October 4, 1986, in *The Globe and Mail*, Canada's only daily with national circulation and politically the country's most influential newspaper. On page 2 New York columnist Michele Landsberg reviews the U.S. television networks' coverage of the Nicholas Daniloff and Andrej Zakharov cases. Daniloff, a U.S. reporter in Moscow, had been imprisoned and then expelled from the Soviet Union on spying charges. Zakharov was expelled from the United States on similar charges. Under a bold-face top-page headline, "Win-lose coverage makes U.S. media a 'voluntary Tass,'" the columnist struck straight at the core of the then dominant North American ideology. She disputed the Cold War claim that one of the key differences between the totalitarian and communist East and the free and democratic West was that the West had news media of a different kind: free, uncensored, not centrally controlled. Landsberg took on the U.S. president's dumb reliance on tough-guy movie clichés when dealing with the Soviet Union's release of the U.S. reporter, and she sharply critiqued *The New York Times* for its score-card approach to superpower relations and the U.S. television networks for their "bright-eyed, blowdried, mindless chauvinism in the coverage of the case."

7. Editorial Cartoons: These sketches or drawings illustrate, comment on, and caricature news events and actors and show the greatest divergence from the official discourse reproduced in the other news formats in the daily press.

8. Letters to the Editor: These short opinion pieces from people who are almost always outside of news organizations and do not receive any remuneration exhibit the most divergence of views in written content carried in the thirteen Canadian newspapers analyzed.

Differences in the discursive processing of happenings in the world, then, are related to formal elements in the construction of daily papers. In other words, the symbolic reproduction of the dominant structures has to take place through the specific logics of the field of media production – the logics of news formats. More precisely, the term "format" names these different logics.

The differences in formats suggest not only that the reproduction of ideology or hegemony is more complex and varying than previously assumed but also that the results of the reproduction are not and cannot be a seamless web. Rather, I would argue, we can detect considerable discursive movement. These discursive variations are due to a relatively small formal element in present-day newspaper production.

Problems of Systemicism III: Creating the Media as Vanguard or the Media as a Tool and a Site for Struggle

As I argued earlier, in communication studies critical work has both a theoretical-explanatory dimension and a normative-prescriptive dimension. But, in addition, many critical scholars normatively conceptualize the news media as a political avant-garde and vanguard: They have undertaken to theorize their analytical categories in relation to and out of interest in the transformation of the present social order; and they have directed this effort of analysis and explanation towards an intervention into the political-social reality.

The problem with this position is not just that it does not take into account the ownership structures that root the media subsystem into the political economy of late capitalism. The position is problematic also because it takes the proverbial ball out of the hands of activists outside of the media and passes it over to an analytical abstraction.

In Canada there is no shortage of specialized peace groups and organizations set up by professionals. Physicians for the Prevention of Nuclear War, Lawyers for Peace, Health Professionals for Nuclear Responsibility, Psychologists for Social Responsibility, Performing Artists for Nuclear Disarmament, Generals for Peace and Disarmament, and Educators for Social Responsibility are some of the more active ones (see Peringer, 1987). Yet, as far as I know, journalists have not formed a group or organization to fight within the media apparatus the kind of institutional battles fought by doctors and nurses within the medical apparatus, by educators and teachers within the educational apparatus, or by active and retired officers within the military apparatus.

The demand for the news media as a whole to play the political avant-garde on a social issue or the vanguard for the transformation of the contemporary social formation suggests a hope for *deus ex machina* solutions. It ignores the fact that social struggles have to be waged concretely both inside and around the media apparatus. It places news workers on one side of an abstract political dividing line. It suggests to social movements that they are continuously let down by someone else. This undermines outreach, organizing, and solidarity work across the perceived division of inside-outside the media.

Information retrieval and reporting is not work that necessarily privileges its practitioners with special insights, political courage, or an activist vision. It is routine labour that has to be done under constant duress in terms of time and resources.

We can view the media system as closed and as producing uniform results. We can do so on the economic and socio-organizational and on the ideological levels. But theoretical examination, empirical evidence, and political pragmatics suggest that this approach is unhelpful.

System Constraint and Political Practice

We should not, then, look at the structure of the material and symbolic production processes of the news media as unalterable conditions awaiting an ever distant revolutionary overthrow. We should not look upon the media system and its textual products as unitary. The news media do not recuperate and co-opt all social dissent with facility and ease outside of history. Social dissent is not unitary; it is articulated in discourses that are quite intriguingly related to more dominant forms of speaking an event.

The democratic opportunities for social movements depend not only on real social conditions but also on the adequacy of the social analysis that informs them. To view the media production process as constrained rather than controlled or determined is an important step. Capitalistic ownership, industrial organization, and bureaucratic proclivity do not determine the coverage of the news media. But they definitely constrain the work of journalists. These constraints limit the options for reporting at the same time as they serve as resources.

Ideology is part of the continuing negotiations and struggles between social actors or – in more structural terms – part of a continuing struggle between social forces with conflicting material and ideological interests. The news media – their relations and processes of production, their product-texts – are part of this lasting struggle.

Notes

***This chapter makes use of and builds on material contained in Peter A. Bruck, "Arms Control and Cruise Missiles: The Information Labour of the Canadian Press," in Bruck (1988:25-40); and Bruck et al. (1987).

1. Foucault's famous interview about political strategy and the role of the intellectual (Foucault, 1981) or Edward Thompson's (1982) key essay on exterminism can be used to demonstrate this point.
2. I have presented this argument in the context of discussing the notions of discourse and discursive variations in Bruck (1989).
3. Papers presented at the 1987 ICA conference session on "Discursive Practices of Information and News" are cases in point. Taking up a Foucaultian framework, the presentations by Thomas Streeter ("Soft News as a Discursive Practice: PM Magazine, the State, Capital, and the Domestic Sphere") and David Scholle ("The

Technique of Surveillance in News Practice: Journalism and the Circulation of Knowledge") argue each in their own way the seamlessness of the dominant social formation (Streeter) or the pervasiveness of the panoptic disciplinary function of the media.
4. A related point has been made in the context of television's treatment of terrorism. See Schlesinger, Murdock and Elliott (1983:31-33), who distinguish between tight and loose formats and open and closed types of programming. Open-closed refers here to the range of knowledge fields made accessible in the media discourse; tight-loose refers to the rhetorical property of achieving an argumentative closure through the specific structure of a statement.

References

Arkin, William and Peter Pringle (1983). "C31: Command Post for Armageddon," *The Nation*, April 9, 434-438.

Bakhtin, Mikhail M. (1981). *The Dialogic Imagination*. Austin: University of Texas Press.

Barthes, Roland (1973). *Mythologies*. Frogmore: Paladin.

Becker, Jörg (1983). "Methodological Problems of Dealing with Disarmament in the Press," *Current Research on Peace and Violence*, 1:29-51.

Becker, Samuel L. (1984). "Marxist Approaches to Media Studies: The British Experience," *Critical Studies in Mass Communication*, 1.

Bruck, Peter A. (1984). "Power Format Radio." Ph.D thesis, McGill University, Montreal.

Bruck, Peter A., R. Hargadon, J. Servage, J. Scott and S. Allan (1987). *CCCS Report: Arms Control and the Media*. Ottawa: Centre for Communication, Culture and Society.

Bruck, Peter A., ed. (1988). *A Proxy for Knowledge: Arms Control, Verification and the News Media*. Ottawa: Norman Paterson School of International Affairs.

Bruck, Peter A. (1989). "Strategies for Peace, Strategies for News Research," *Journal of Communication*, 39,1 (Winter):108-129.

Brunsdon, Charlotte and David Morley (1978). *Everyday Television: Nationwide*. London: British Film Institute.

Clarke, A. and I. Taylor (1981). "Inequality of Access to Political Television: The Case of the General Election 1979." Paper presented to the annual conference of the British Sociological Association, Aberystwyth, England, April 6-9.

Eco, Umberto (1976). *A Theory of Semiotics*. Bloomington, Ill.: Indiana University Press.

Fishman, Mark (1979). "Crime Waves as Ideology," *Social Problems*, 25:531-543.

Fishman, Mark (1980). *Manufacturing the News*. Austin: University of Texas Press.

Foucault, Michel (1981). *Power/Knowledge*. New York: Anchor Books.

Gans, Herbert (1979). *Deciding What's News*. New York: Pantheon.

Gitlin, Todd (1979). "Prime Time Ideology: The Hegemonic Process of TV Entertainment," *Social Problems*, 26,3:251-266.

Gitlin, Todd (1980). "Making Democracy Safe for America," *Columbia Journalism Review*, March-April:54-58.

Gitlin, Todd (1987). "The Greatest Story Never Told," *Mother Jones*, June/July:28-31,45-47.

Glasgow University Media Group (GUMG) (1976). *Bad News*. London: Routledge and Kegan Paul.

Glasgow University Media Group (GUMG) (1980). *More Bad News*. London: Routledge and Kegan Paul.

Glasgow University Media Group (GUMG) (1982). *Really Bad News*. London: Writers and Readers Publishing Cooperative Society.

Glasgow University Media Group (GUMG) (1985). *War and Peace News*. Milton Keynes: Open University Press.

Hall, Stuart et al. (1978). *Policing the Crisis: Mugging, the States, and Law and Order*. London: Macmillan Press.

Hall, Stuart et al. (1980). *Culture, Media, Language*. London: Hutchinson.

Hallin, D.C. and P. Mancini (1984). "Speaking of the President: Political Structure and Representational Form in U.S. and Italian Television News," *Theory and Society*, 13:829-850.

Jaffe, Susan (1982). "Why the Second Session Flopped," *The Nation*, September 4:174-176.

Japanese Broadcasting Corporation-NHK (1981). *Unforgettable Fire: Pictures Drawn By Atomic Bomb Survivors*. New York: Pantheon Books.

Knight, G. (1982). "Myth and Structure of News," *Journal of Communication*, 32,2:141-161.

Lazarsfeld Paul and Robert Merton (1949). "Mass Communication, Popular Taste and Organized Social Action." In W. Schramm ed., *Communications*. Urbana: Illinois University Press, 1960.

Molotch, Harvey and Marilyn Lester (1974). "News as Purposive Behavior: The Strategic Use of Routine Events, Accidents, and Scandals," *American Sociological Review*, 39:101-112.

Molotch, Harvey, and Marilyn Lester (1975). "Accidental News: The Great Oil Spill as Local Occurrence and National Event," *American Journal of Sociology*, 81:253-260.

Morley, David (1980). *The Nationwide Audience: Structure and Decoding*. London: British Film Institute.

Newcomb, H.M. (1984). "On the Dialogic Aspects of Mass Communication," *Critical Studies in Mass Communication*, 1 (March):34-50.

Parkin, F. (1972). *Class Inequality and Political Order*. London: Paladin.

Peringer, Christine (1987). *How We Work For Peace: Canadian Community Activities*. Dundas: Peace Research Institute.

Schlesinger, Philip, Graham Murdock and Philip Elliott (1983). *Televising Terrorism: Political Violence in Popular Culture*. London: Comedia.

Thompson, Edward P. (1982). "Notes on Exterminism, the Last Stage of Civilization." In New Left Review, eds., *Exterminism and Cold War*. London: Verso.

Tuchman, Gaye (1978). *Making News*. New York: The Free Press.

Van Dijk, T., ed. (1985). *Discourse and Communication: New Approaches to the Analysis of Mass Media Discourse and Communication*. Berlin: DeGruyter.

Wellmer, Albrecht (1970). "Empirico-Analytical and Critical Social Science," *Continuum*, 8,1 (Spring/Summer):12-26.

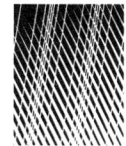

The Environment and the Media: Two Strategies for Challenging Hegemony

Sean Cassidy

Deep ecology is a process of ever-deeper questioning of ourselves, the assumptions of the dominant world view in our culture, and the meaning and truth of our reality. We cannot change consciousness by only listening to others, we must involve ourselves. We must take direct action.

– Bill Devall and George Sessions, 1985

FEW SOCIAL MOVEMENTS in the United States have managed to seize the attention of the mass media more effectively than the eclectic coalition of organizations that comprise the environmental/ecology movement. Born in the social upheaval of the 1960s, the modern environmental movement has endured while many other social movements have declined. Part of the reason for the continued growth of the movement can be found in its ability to mobilize the mass media to focus public attention on environmental issues. Environmentalists recognize that a major part of their strategy to bring about change in society revolves around convincing citizens that it is in their own best interest to change the North American lifestyle. This chapter examines two media strategies used by groups within the environmental movement to bring about this change in consciousness.

Research on the interaction between the environmental movement and the media has been limited; and much of the work that has been done lacks a strong theoretical foundation. James Parlour, in his essay "The Mass Media and Environmental Issues: A Theoretical Analysis," writes about the poorly supported statements made by environmentalists on media-environmental issues:

Although opinions of this kind have a certain rhetorical appeal, their weak empirical and theoretical foundations do little to inspire confidence in their credibility as explanations of the way in which the mass media have portrayed environmental issues. Apart from the research carried out in Canada some six years ago and recently reported by Parlour and Schatzow, the relationships between the mass media, politicians, opinion leaders and the general public have not been systematically explored. (1980:109)

Parlour sought to identify a theoretical framework for the study of the portrayal of environmental issues in the media. After examining a number of theoretical models, he concluded that Antonio Gramsci's concept of hegemony and the dominant ideology thesis developed by Stuart Hall and Raymond Williams provide the best framework for examining how the mass media process information on environmental issues.

Gramsci described the struggle to modify consciousness as part of the "war of position" between conflicting ideologies. He developed the concept of "hegemony" to describe the way dominant classes in society colonize the consciousness of the subaltern classes. Through its control of a nation's social institutions, the ruling class impresses its own values and beliefs on the population as a whole. This ideological dominance is maintained by a constantly changing balance of force and consensus. Hegemony is most effectively maintained when it is supported by the agreement of the majority. Without the support of the subaltern classes, the dominant classes are compelled to resort to force, which exposes the actual power structure and can lead to the collapse of hegemony. One of the major ways the ruling classes maintain consensus is through the ideological domination of the mass media.

Gramsci recognized that "every relationship of 'hegemony' is necessarily a pedagogic relationship" (Gramsci, 1971:350). This process of educational indoctrination takes place throughout society, not just in the schools. The mass media play a central role in educating the public – a function that gives the media their power. This power lies not so much in the media's ability to inform, but in their ability to shape the "perceptions, cognitions and preferences in such a way that" the public accepts its role "in the existing order of things, either because they can see or imagine no alternative to it, or because they see it as natural and unchangeable" (Lukes, 1974:24).

The problem encountered by social movements and their use of media is that they seek to challenge the dominant ideology through an institution that plays a vital role in the dissemination of that same ideology. If ideological hegemony was "airtight," the social movements would probably never be able to challenge the worldview presented by the media. However, there are unresolved contradictions in the capitalist media that make it possible for dissident messages to appear.

First, the media are dependent on the maintenance of the current system, because: "Their very power and prestige deeply presuppose that system. At the same time, they are committed, like members of any other corporate elite, to their own particular economic and political advantage" (Gitlin, 1980:258-259).

This tension between the profit-making aspect of a media corporation and its role as an upholder of the status quo creates a pressure that can sometimes be exploited. TV networks are reluctant to let a "good" story go unreported, especially if there is a possibility that another network will pick up the story. If a group can exploit the qualities that the media use to define a "good" story, it may be able to gain access to the media. For instance, the networks thrive on stories that involve conflict and dramatic visuals. Social movements regularly stage "pseudo-events" (Boorstin, 1961) that give the media a good story and focus attention on an issue.

Even if a group challenges the power structure and manages to make it onto the network news, it does not mean the network is working against the dominant ideology.

Indeed, the hegemonic ideology of bourgeois culture is extremely complex and absorptive; only by absorbing and domesticating conflicting values, definitions of reality, and demands on it, in fact, does it remain hegemonic. (Gitlin, 1980:256; emphasis in original)

A second contradiction is the division between the rhetoric of democratic capitalism and the reality. Hegemony depends on the appearance of consent. It is not unusual for the state to sustain certain ideological myths to preserve legitimacy. Phrases such as "all men are created equal" or "freedom of the press" are frequently used to give the state a moral legitimacy that belies the actual state of social relations. One tactic employed by social movements is to demand that the state live up to its own rhetoric. This can be especially useful if the rhetoric has been incorporated into the legal codes. The problem with this tactic is that it forces the social movement to work within the legal system, which is itself an instrument of hegemony.

During the past twenty years, the environmental movement in North America has used a number of media strategies to exploit the contradictions in the capitalist media. One group, Friends of the Earth (FOE), decided to use the legal system as its instrument for gaining access to the airwaves. Another group, Greenpeace, employed direct-action protest tactics to obtain media coverage. These two case studies can provide important lessons for groups seeking to use the media for progressive change.

Challenging the Rhetoric

In 1971 Friends of the Earth launched a campaign to force the Federal Communications Commission (FCC) to recognize the implicit political messages within many television commercials. Specifically, FOE said that a series of ads run by WNBC in 1969 and 1970 promoting the use of larger automobile engines and the use of high-test leaded gasoline was raising "controversial issues of public importance" and therefore should be subject to the terms of the fairness doctrine.[1] To understand the type of challenge this represented to the U.S. broadcasting system, one must look at the history of the fairness doctrine.

The Fairness Doctrine

The roots of the fairness doctrine can be found in the Communications Act of 1934, which established the Federal Communications Commission as the regulatory agency responsible for the enforcement of the act. From its inception, the FCC considered the airwaves a "scarce natural resource" that could only be used by a limited number of broadcasters. Fearful that one political party might dominate the airwaves, Congress made provisions for the presentation of competing viewpoints in political campaigns in a 1934 Communications Act. In a series of cases culminating in the 1949 *Report on Editorializing by Broadcast Licensees*, the FCC broadened the responsibility of broadcasters to provide coverage of all types of controversial issues, not just those related to political campaigns. In an eloquent statement of its reasoning, the FCC said:

> It is axiomatic that one of the most vital questions of mass communication in a democracy is the development of an informed public opinion through the public dissemination of news and ideas concerning the vital issues of the day.... We have recognized, with respect to such programs, the paramount right of the public in a free society to be informed and to have presented to it for acceptance or rejection the different attitudes and viewpoints concerning these vital and often controversial issues which are held by the various groups which make up the community. It is the right of the public to be informed rather than any right on the part of the government, and broadcast licensee or any individual member of the public to broadcast his own particular views on a matter, which is the foundation stone of the American system of broadcasting.[2]

This is a classic example of the conflict between the rhetoric of the dominant ideology and the reality of the social structure. There is little evidence that broadcasters view the right of the public to be informed as the foundation of the U.S. system of broadcasting. The rhetoric disguises the real foundation of broadcasting, which is the right of broadcasters to make a profit.

Before 1967 the fairness doctrine rarely interfered with the "right" of broadcasters to make money by running product commercials. Commercials were not excluded from the terms of the fairness doctrine,[3] but generally they were not considered to contain political or controversial messages. However, the events of the 1960s raised new questions about which issues were "controversial" and of "public importance." Civil rights, the rising protest over the Vietnam War, consumer advocacy, and the environmental movement all raised questions about what was controversial. The lofty words of the 1949 *Report on Editorializing* were taken seriously by certain members of the public and the FCC was asked to "put up, or shut up."

In a move it almost instantly regretted, the FCC decided to "put up" by agreeing to hear a complaint made by John Banzhaf III.[4]

Banzhaf and Beyond

John Banzhaf complained to the FCC about the refusal of WCBS to carry anti-smoking announcements in response to commercials advocating cigarette smoking. Banzhaf's intervention came at a time when the negative health effects of cigarettes were being hotly debated in the media. In 1964 the Surgeon General had issued a report on the hazards of cigarette smoking, and in 1965 Congress had passed the Federal Cigarette Labelling and Advertising Act. Both of these actions were taken in the belief that there was clear evidence of the dangers of smoking cigarettes. These circumstances led the FCC to rule that cigarette smoking was clearly a "controversial issue of public importance" and that the commercials, though never claiming cigarettes were healthful, clearly raised questions as to the desirability of smoking.

However, the FCC also said that the ruling was "limited to this product – cigarettes" and could not be construed "to imply that any appeal to the Commission by a vocal minority will suffice to classify advertising of a product as controversial and of public importance" (Ginsburg, 1979:578).

Despite the disclaimer, several "vocal minorities" recognized the implications of the Banzhaf decision. Although cigarette smoking was not considered an "environmental" issue in 1967, the basis for the FCC ruling was directly applicable to a number of other environmental issues.

Friends of the Earth was careful in its selection of a test case for expanding the Banzhaf ruling into other areas besides smoking. The issue selected was automobile emissions in New York City. Friends of the Earth maintained that air pollution was a controversial issue of public importance, especially in New York City where the hazards were particularly acute and threatening. In the case that would bear their organization's name, Friends of the Earth argued:

1. The Surgeon General had declared that automobile emissions posed significant dangers to human health and survival.
2. The Environmental Protection Administration of New York City said that air pollution conditions in New York City represented an increasingly serious danger to public health.
3. Serious suggestions for the elimination of private vehicles in New York City were being considered.
4. The commercials in question advocated the use of larger cars and leaded, high-test gasoline.
5. The treatment by the communications media of the relationship of air pollution to automobiles occurs in the context of a public controversy.
6. WNBC-TV had failed to adequately present both sides of the questions raised by the television commercials.
7. The National Environmental Policy Act clearly called for federal agencies to treat environmental quality as a high priority in administering the law.[5]

The FCC refused to hold hearings or oral arguments on the case, saying:

1. While automobile emissions cause serious environmental problems, the same could be said of "a host of other products or services – detergents (particularly with phosphates), gasoline ... electric power, airplanes, disposable containers, etc."
2. While recognizing environmental concerns, the government has not called for the discontinuance of automobiles.
3. The Commission did not have the power to eliminate the air pollution prob-

lems caused by automobiles.

4. The Commission did not have enough information to decide if in fact the commercials being discussed presented only one side of a controversial issue.[6]

The commission went on to say it would not extend the cigarette ruling because such an action would "undermine the present system which is based on product commercials, many of which have some adverse ecological effects."[7]

If the FCC exists to serve the public interest, it would seem logical to assume that it would be interested in limiting advertisements that promote the use of products harmful to public health. Instead, it appears that the FCC's real goal is the preservation of the "present system" of broadcasting. Friends of the Earth was not seeking to limit the advertising of leaded gasoline, it just wanted a chance to present another viewpoint on the use of an environmentally damaging product. By denying that the commercial spots in question "did in fact present one side of a controversial issue" the FCC fulfilled its role as an ideological agent of the capitalist superstructure. As such, it "masked" the class-exploitative nature of the system and preserved the myth that serving the interests of the broadcasting corporations was the same as serving the "public interest." (See Poulantzas, 1965, on the ideological effect of masking.)

The logic of the FCC in the Friends of the Earth case was so contorted that a Court of Appeals remanded the case to the FCC for reconsideration. The Court of Appeals "found this case indistinguishable from Banzhaf in the reach of the fairness doctrine."[8]

Despite the court's ruling, the question of the existence of the Banzhaf case was never settled in *Friends of the Earth* because the parties involved withdrew the petition when WNBC agreed to participate in a campaign to focus attention on the air pollution problem.[9] Several other attempts were made by environmental groups to expand the Banzhaf ruling to other product ads. Two cases that occurred around the same time the FOE case was being heard were the Neckritz case and the so-called Esso case involving the Wilderness Society.[10]

In *Neckritz*, the FCC said that advertisements for a gasoline with an additive called F-310 did not "deal directly with an issue of public importance." The commercials said F-310 was a "major breakthrough to help solve one of today's critical problems ... cleaner air."[11] Using arguments like those in the Friends of the Earth decision, the FCC said the advertisements did not argue a position and that economic and administrative chaos would result if the Banzhaf decision were expanded to include product ads in general.

In his book *The Fairness Doctrine and the Media*, Steven Simmons clearly points out the inconsistencies of the FCC rulings:

> Like previous decisions, the Neckritz decision illustrates the Commission's loose handling of the Banzhaf precedent. In Banzhaf, the FCC, relying on the cigarette health hazard and the unanimous government policy against smoking, held that a fairness obligation was incurred. Yet in Friends of the Earth, when again faced with products involving a health hazard and a government

policy, the Commission ruled that no fairness balance was required. Neckritz ... involved commercials that were more explicit than Banzhaf's in discussing a controversial issue. Here too, however, the Commission avoided fairness treatment. (1978:112)

The other environmental case in 1971 was the *Wilderness Society and Friends of the Earth v. National Broadcasting Company*, sometimes referred to as the Esso case. Esso, a large oil company, ran a series of commercials on NBC television advocating the "fast" development of the Alaskan oil reserves. There was a heated public debate going on at the time concerning the building of the Alaskan pipeline. While the commercials did not specifically mention the pipeline controversy, they did say that Esso could strike a "balance between the need for oil and the needs of nature."[12] The FCC decided the commercials did raise fairness doctrine questions, but the network's subsequent broadcasts adequately covered both sides of the pipeline controversy.

In a partially dissenting opinion, Commissioner Nicholas Johnson pointed out that the network's programming was at least two to one in favour of the pipeline, even when news, interviews, and commercial "spots" were "thrown in the hopper." In a statement that revealed the predisposition of the FCC, Johnson said it was "curious that when a case is difficult or impossible to resolve the Commission usually disposes of it by concluding that the broadcaster wins."[13]

The *Friends of the Earth*, *Neckritz*, and *Wilderness* cases raised serious questions about the nature of television commercials and their latent political content. The cases forced the FCC to initiate an inquiry into the fairness doctrine. Before the inquiry yielded any results, however, several other issues were challenged on fairness grounds.

In *William H. Rodgers Jr.* the FCC ruled that phosphate-based detergent commercials did not raise controversial issues of public importance, despite a large body of government literature advocating a ban on such detergents.[14] In *John S. MacInnis, Consumers Arise Now*, the Commission said that trash compactor commercials were ordinary product ads and not covered by the fairness doctrine, even though compactors prevented recycling as recommended by the National Environmental Policy Act.[15]

The *Sierra Club and the National Council of Jewish Women*, one of the last cases before the FCC issued the results of its inquiry, tried to bring fairness to bear on automobile and gasoline commercials in Los Angeles.[16] The FCC ignored the Court of Appeals ruling in *Friends*, saying that the commercials did not advocate "large" cars or "unleaded" gasoline. Retreating even further from the Banzhaf decision, the FCC said:

We will not extend the fairness doctrine to general product advertisements ... unless the advertisements directly or by necessary inference address a controversial issue of public importance, despite the fact that the use of that product might be related to a controversial issue of public importance.[17]

On July 12, 1974, an era of environmental activism came to an end with the release of the FCC's *Fairness Doctrine Report*.[18] The report laid down the guidelines the FCC would use for deciding future fairness doctrine issues. In dealing with the application of fairness to advertisements, the FCC said there were different rules for different types of ads. Some commercials were actually "direct and substantial commentary on important public issues."[19] The example used by the Commission was a thirty-second announcement urging a constitutional amendment on abortion. The FOE urged broadcasters to treat these advertisements in the same manner as station editorials; that is, the broadcaster should seek out opposing viewpoints.

The FCC made its greatest change in application of the fairness doctrine in the area of product commercials. Referring to the Banzhaf decision, the FCC stated:

> If in the future the Commission is confronted with a case similar to the cigarette controversy, it may be more appropriate to refer the matter to Congress. The Commission does not believe that the usual product commercial can realistically be said to inform the public on any side of a controversial issue.[20]

In one respect the 1974 report was not really a change in FCC policy as much as it was a formalization of the de facto effect of the rulings after Banzhaf. There was not a single case after Banzhaf in which the FCC ruled in favour of the complainant and ordered the broadcaster to present the other side of an issue raised by a product advertisement. It was only when the courts put pressure on the Commission that any action was taken.

Speaking about the "effective use of radio," the FCC said its goal was to foster "uninhibited, robust, wide-open debate on public issues," but it "also stressed that any promotion of this objective must be compatible with the public interest." The FCC noted that "to a major extent, ours is a commercially-based broadcast system" that "renders a vital service to the nation," and it emphasized that "any policies adopted by this Commission, should be consistent with the maintenance and growth of that system and should, among other appropriate standards, be so measured."[21]

One function of hegemony is to define reality in ways that serve the interests of the dominant classes. The actions of the FCC in regard to the fairness doctrine support its role as a hegemonic entity primarily interested in the "growth" of the broadcasting corporations. The FCC consistently defined the limits of the term "robust debate" in a manner that served the broadcasters' interests. By refusing to recognize the ideological content of product commercials, the FCC managed to contain the threat posed by the environmental group's challenges to the dominant ideology. The courts pointed out that the FCC failed to use its own stated guidelines when considering the fairness doctrine. The FCC solved this dilemma by changing the guidelines while continuing to use the rhetoric of the First Amendment.

On August 4, 1987, the Federal Communications Commission abolished the fairness doctrine.[22] The FCC took this action despite strong Congressional support for the doctrine. Congress tried to codify the doctrine,[23] but President Reagan vetoed the bill in June 1987. Most broadcasters rejoiced, while many public-interest groups lamented the demise of the doctrine. Edward Markey (D-Mass.), Chairman of the House Communications Subcommittee, said its elimination revealed the FCC as "ideologically hide-bound. Their blind adherence to a rigid misconstruction of the First Amendment threatens to snuff out debate or discussion of important issues over the public's airwaves."[24]

The 1974 FCC Report eliminated the economic threat posed by the fairness doctrine, but the elimination of the doctrine puts to rest the idea that the public has a right to hear several sides of issues of public importance. The large communication corporations will determine what views are heard on the air in the future. In reality, little has changed, because the FCC rarely supported attempts by citizen groups to challenge ideological viewpoints presented by the broadcast media.

The environmental movement challenged the FCC to live up to its own rhetoric, but its challenge failed to bring about any significant change in the structure. It did succeed, however, in forcing the FCC to consider the possibility of latent political content in commercials. Because it worked within the legal system, the movement had to abide by, and was limited by, the decisions of the FCC and the courts.

If Friends of the Earth had taken its case directly to the public, the ensuing debate might have raised the public's awareness about the environmental issues raised by some product commercials. Of course the question then arises as to the best way to reach the public via mass media, when the media is owned by the very group that may seek to limit public debate on the issue.

Greenpeace and Direct Action

One environmental group that has enjoyed some success in using the media to raise public consciousness of what constitutes an environmental issue is Greenpeace. Instead of working within the legal system, Greenpeace tries to exploit the media's predisposition towards certain types of events, and few groups are as adept at staging events that attract the attention of the international press. Part of the reason Greenpeace has been so successful in its media campaigns is its awareness of how the mass media operate. The roots of this awareness can be traced to the organization's earliest campaign.

Greenpeace was started by several Canadian and U.S. citizens who felt the media were neglecting an important story. On October 1, 1969, seven thousand demonstrators gathered at the U.S.-Canadian border to protest a U.S. plan to detonate a one-megaton nuclear bomb on Amchitka Island, Alaska. The protesters closed the border but failed to attract much attention from the U.S. news media. One of the protestors was Jim Bohlen, a U.S. missile engineer who had fled the United States to prevent his son from being drafted during the Vietnam War. Later Bohlen recalled his disappointment at the coverage the protest received from the mass media: "We thought this was another example of the United States Government keeping information from the people. So we decided to start an organization, informing the public in a way that the media cannot ignore" (Morgan and Whitaker, 1986:113).

The organization was called the Don't Make a Wave Committee, and several of its founding members were experienced journalists who knew just how to keep the media interested in a story.[25] They included, among others: Robert Hunter, a columnist for the Vancouver *Sun*; Ben Metcalf, a former Canadian Broadcasting Corporation freelancer; and Bob Cummings, who wrote for a local underground newspaper. The committee decided to sail a ship, later christened the *Greenpeace*, into the waters near Amchitka Island. The ship never reached the island because it was detained by the U.S. Coast Guard several hundred miles from the test site. The group's immediate goal of getting the U.S. and Canadian press to report on public opposition to the test was a surprising success.

Television and radio crews hounded anyone connected with the *Greenpeace* voyage. Thousands of people throughout Canada demonstrated against the Amchitka test. The *Greenpeace* became the focus of Canadian discontent with the U.S. nuclear testing program in Alaska. The Amchitka blast went forward as planned, but within the next year the U.S. government ceased nuclear testing in the Aleutian Islands. The evidence indicates that the negative publicity generated by the *Greenpeace* voyage played some part in the U.S. government's decision to halt the tests. Today the island of Amchitka is a bird sanctuary.

The first Greenpeace protest demonstrated that a small group of dedicated people with imagination could manipulate the media into covering a story that had previously been ignored. A combination of practical news experience and philosophic insight had guided the *Greenpeace* crew members' interaction with the media. Robert Hunter described the process in his book *Warriors of the Rainbow*:

> For Metcalf, the voyage of the Greenpeace was a campaign like others he had run in the past when he had been paid by politicians to apply his knowledge of the day-to-day mechanics of journalism to get them elected. Image was everything. He knew exactly how to grab headlines, how to drop catchy phrases that would be reprinted, how to play on the reflexes of bored editors. While I had far less practical skill in this department, I had my theory of mind bombs – powerful new images delivered via media – changing mass consciousness. I saw the Greenpeace as an icon, a symbol, as a kind of wobbling control tower from which we might affect the attitudes of millions of people toward Amchitka specifically, and their environment as a whole in general. The screeching static-choked radio on the Phyllis Cormack and the lone radio-phone at Akutan had taught me some of the limits to McLuhan's concept of a "global village," but nothing had yet happened to convince me that the boat was not, after all, a mind bomb sailing across an electronic sea into the minds of the masses. Madison Avenue and Hitler had changed the face of the world through application of the tactic of image projection, and the environmental movement could hardly attempt to do less. (1979:61)

Greenpeace was undermining the consensus that surrounded the issue of nuclear weapons testing. One small ship may not appear to pose much of a threat to the global military establishment, but a measure of Greenpeace's success can be found in the reaction of the French government to Greenpeace protests in Mururoa.

It was Ben Metcalf's idea to place an ad in a New Zealand paper asking for volunteers to sail to the French nuclear testing grounds in Mururoa. David McTaggart, a Canadian expatriate, saw the ad and offered the services of his sailboat, the *Vega*. If there is some doubt about Greenpeace's role in stopping the Amchitka testing, there is little doubt that McTaggart's two voyages to Mururoa and the surrounding publicity forced the French to cease atmospheric testing. McTaggart was beaten, harassed, and ultimately forced to sell his little boat, but before the campaign was over Canadian headlines proclaimed: "French Credit McTaggart for Test End" (McTaggart, 1978:368). Even the government procurer at one of McTaggart's court appeals in France conceded, "It should not be denied that McTaggart may have helped persuade the French government to decide to choose underground tests in place of atmospheric tests" (Morgan and Whitaker, 1986:110).

Despite its apparent success in stopping the nuclear testing under Amchitka and atmospheric testing over Mururoa, it was the whale campaigns that stick in most people's minds when they think of Greenpeace.

The Price of Success

On June 29, 1975, *Greenpeace V* sailed into San Francisco Bay, having just completed a sixty-four-day voyage in which it confronted the Soviet Union's whaling fleet. The ensuing media barrage was unparalleled in the experience of Greenpeace or any other environmental group. Fred Easton, a photographer on the *Greenpeace V*, had managed to capture the firing of a harpoon over the heads of two Greenpeace members in a small inflatable Zodiac dinghy. The harpoon plunged into the back of a sperm whale, exploding on impact, discharging blood and gore as the huge creature died. The personal courage of the men in the boat and the astute awareness of the media allowed Greenpeace to use the image to change the way millions of people thought about whales.

> No network would be able to resist such footage, just as no wire service would be able to ignore the story. As a newsman, I knew we had achieved our immediate goal. Soon, images would be going out into hundreds of millions of minds around the world, a completely new set of basic images about whaling. Instead of small boats and giant whales, giant boats and small whales; instead of courage killing whales, courage saving whales; David had become Goliath, Goliath was now David; if the mythology of Moby Dick and Captain Ahab had dominated human consciousness about Leviathan for over a century, a whole new age was in the making. Nothing less than a historical turning point seemed to have occurred. (Hunter, 1979:229)

A turning point had indeed been reached.

Respectability had been achieved, and it almost destroyed the core organization around which Greenpeace had been built. Suddenly Greenpeace was hot. Newspapers and broadcasters clamoured for a piece of the action. A movie deal was discussed. Before the *Greenpeace V* left San Francisco, its crew was split over how to deal with the media spotlight. One faction wanted to cash in on the notoriety. The Greenpeace organization had always been strapped by lack of funds. Movie deals, book contracts, and distribution rights to Greenpeace-associated paraphernalia seemed an excellent way to raise cash for future campaigns.

Some members of the organization felt such commercialization meant selling out to the very system that was destroying the environment. The "commercial" group won the day. Greenpeace began a period of rapid growth. Local organizations sprang up everywhere, retaining the Greenpeace name but otherwise having little to do with the parent organization. A new emphasis was put on organizational structure, merchandising, and cash flow. Accountants and office managers gained status within the organization.

In some ways, the very success of the whale campaign posed a greater threat to Greenpeace than the angry denunciations of the superpowers. Greenpeace's transformation from a small group of "radical" eco-activists to a large respected environmental organization with a multimillion-dollar budget threatened to change the outlook and goals of the organization. Success has its price and it can be one of the most effective ways of undermining dissident groups.

Greenpeace's success meant that it became part of the environmental movement establishment. Its opinion on environmental issues was sought out. To maintain its credibility with the media, Greenpeace had to conform to the expectations of the media. When ABC signed an exclusive contract with the Greenpeace Foundation of America for footage of another whale protest, it expected more dramatic shots of confrontations between Greenpeace demonstrators and Soviet whalers.

Two ships were launched, the *James Bay* under the control of the Vancouver Greenpeace organization and the *Ohana Kai* belonging to the U.S. group. The whalers ceased their hunt when the *Ohana Kai* sailed into the Soviet fleet. The Greenpeace crew decided to board the main Soviet factory ship but once on board they did little more than talk with the crew. The network was outraged. This was not the type of material it wanted. When the *James Bay* shot some dramatic footage of a whale being killed, ABC threatened to sue unless it got the rights to the killing sequence. Despite the fact that the *James Bay* belonged to the Canadian Greenpeace organization (not the U.S. group that ABC had contracted with) the network got what it wanted. As Bob Hunter put it, "There are certain basic rules. One of them was that you never burned off a major network with whom you had any kind of contract, otherwise your name would never see the light of video in America again" (Hunter, 1979:414). Hunter described the lessons learned from this experience.

If there was any lesson to be learned – or relearned – it was that the mass media, by and large, was not interested in diplomatic exchanges between adversaries; it was not much interested in symbolic meetings at sea.... The only thing besides sex, politics, and sports that grabbed its attention, excited it, made its juices run, was violence. A harpoon being fired in the vicinity of human flesh was news. Dialogue was not news.... Without confrontation – the risk of life and limb – the mass media could not have cared less what we did. (419)

Greenpeace was learning that the mass media could be used to spread the environmental message, but the message would be framed to fit the media's worldview. It is a worldview dominated by Nielsen, not Muir. Information about Greenpeace's activities would be distributed only if it was exciting enough to entertain news audiences – or at least news producers and advertisers.

One of the secrets to Greenpeace's success has been its ability to use emotionally charged images to counter the effects of negative framing by the mass media. No matter what words accompany the image, it is difficult to undermine the impact of a clip showing Greenpeace members risking their lives to protect whales or seals. In later campaigns Greenpeace members bathed in the effluent discharges from chemical plants to show the effect on unprotected skin. The media might portray such activities as crazy, or it might have an official spokesperson claim that the discharge was not harmful, but the rash and boils on the skin of the Greenpeacers make for a powerful image not easily subverted.

Has Greenpeace found a way to overcome the influence of the media's framing devices? The answer would appear to be a qualified yes, but more research needs to be done on the subject. On wildlife issues Greenpeace has been very successful. The International Whaling Commission has declared a moratorium on all commercial whaling. The problems of pirate whalers and whaling done under the guise of "scientific research" remain, but the killing has been greatly reduced. Although there have been no "scientific" measurements or surveys, there does appear to have been a significant change in attitudes towards whales in the past twenty years. Greenpeace is undoubtedly responsible for some of this change in consciousness.

Despite its successes, though, Greenpeace is not necessarily an adequate model for using the media to change consciousness. Greenpeace is most successful in areas that are peripheral to the primary interests of the dominant classes in North American society. As Todd Gitlin puts it, "The closer an issue is to the core interests of national political elites, the more likely is a blackout of news that effectively challenges that interest" (1980:5). Greenpeace's anti-nuclear weapons campaigns have received far less coverage than the whale campaigns. Part of the problem can be traced to the lack of dramatic visuals. How is it possible to show the immorality of an underground nuclear test? However, the coverage surrounding the sinking of the *Rainbow Warrior* suggests that something other than the lack of a good story directs the way the media reports nuclear weapons testing.

The Rainbow Warrior

Shortly before midnight on July 10, 1985, two explosions ripped through the hull of the *Rainbow Warrior*, a ship used by Greenpeace to protest French nuclear testing. One crew member, Fernando Pereira, was killed, but before the smoke settled on the incident the casualties would include the French Minister of Defence and the Chief of the French Intelligence Service. The world media had a heyday. The combination of scandal, espionage, and violence made it a hot story. In the next two months, prestigious papers like *The New York Times* gave the incident extensive coverage. The *Times* ran more stories on the *Rainbow Warrior* sinking than it had on all other Greenpeace-related stories in the previous five years. There were articles on the details of the investigation by New Zealand police, the reaction of the French people, and the impact on the French political scene. But the general impression given was that the bombing was an isolated, though dramatic, action on the part of the French. No historical background was given on France's violent actions against Greenpeace in the early 1970s. Even after France admitted to planting the bomb, the term "state-sponsored-terrorism" was rarely used. One can't help but wonder how the bombing would have been described if it had been done by Libya or Iran.

No serious questions about the French nuclear testing were raised, nor was any attempt made to review the effects of the U.S. nuclear tests in the Pacific. These omissions are significant, because the *Rainbow Warrior's* last mission was to evacuate Rongelap, a Pacific island covered with nuclear fallout from one of the hydrogen bomb tests on Bikini. The evacuation received little attention in the U.S. press. This is not to say the mass media *consciously* omit information that might reflect negatively on the U.S. nuclear weapons testing program. The media are part of the hegemonic structure and consciously or unconsciously reflect the ideology of the dominant classes in society. As Stuart Hall puts it:

> Ideology is a function of the discourse and of the logic of social processes, rather than an intention of the agent. The broadcaster's consciousness of what he is doing ... is indeed, an interesting and important question. But it does not substantially affect the theoretical issue. The ideology has 'worked' in such a case because the discourse has spoken itself through him/her. Unwittingly, unconsciously, the broadcaster has served as a support for the reproduction of a dominant ideological discursive field. (Hall, 1982:88)

This brings us back to the question of how an agent of hegemony can be used to bring about a positive change in social consciousness.

Conclusion

My research suggests that it is possible to exploit the contradictions within the capitalist media to present alternatives to the dominant worldview. Both Friends of the Earth and Greenpeace attempted to gain access to the media. The direct-action tactics of Greenpeace were more successful than the legal manoeuvres of

FOE. Working within the legal system means dealing with another hegemonic institution. If the threat to the status quo is too great, the laws can be rewritten to prevent any meaningful challenge to the dominant ideology. However, the actions of Friends of the Earth did help expose the emptiness of the first-amendment rhetoric used by the FCC.

Greenpeace has had a great deal of success in exploiting the contradiction between the media's role as upholder of the status quo and their hunger for dramatic, though critical, stories with powerful visuals. However, the evidence suggests that the media still fulfil their role as a hegemonic institution. They do this by ignoring or negatively framing those stories most threatening to the core interests of the ruling classes. The elimination of whaling does not threaten dominant economic or political interests; therefore, Greenpeace could generate substantial and relatively "unshaped" news coverage of its protests. However, even when Greenpeace manages to focus attention on nuclear weapons testing, it only succeeds in questioning whether tests should be conducted in Amchitka or in the atmosphere; not whether such tests should be conducted at all. It does raise the issue and that in itself is an important step. Hegemony is most effective when the public is too unaware of its own self-interest to even ask questions about issues like nuclear weapons testing.

Greenpeace challenges the "common sense" notion that nuclear weapons testing increases the security of the North American people. By removing the hegemonic "blinders" that such a notion sets on public debate, Greenpeace is helping to create a new level of consciousness. The struggle that remains is not an easy one, but as Gramsci put it: "The first step in emancipating oneself from political and social slavery is that of freeing the mind" (Quoted in Davidson, 1977:77).

Notes

1. *Friends of the Earth v. F.C.C.*, 449 F. 2d (D.C.Cir. 1971), p.1164.
2. Federal Communications Commission (FCC), *Report on Editorializing by Broadcast Licensees*, Washington, D.C., 1949, pp.1246,1249.
3. See *Sam Morris*, 11 F.C.C. 198 (1946) and *Controversial Issue Programming*, F.C.C. 57, 572 (1963) for early FCC pronouncements on the application of the fairness doctrine to product advertisements.
4. WCBS, 8 F.C.C. 2d 381 (1967), *Banzhaf v. F.C.C.*, 405 F.2d 1082 (D.C. Cir. 1968).
5. *Friends of the Earth v. F.C.C.*, 449 F. 2d (D.C.Cir. 1971), p.1164.
6. Ibid., p.1167.
7. Ibid., p.1168.
8. *Friends of the Earth v. F.C.C.*, 449 F.2d (D.C. Cir. 1971), p.1171.
9. *Friends of the Earth*, 39 F.C.C. 2d (1973), p.564.
10. *Alan F. Neckritz*, 29 F.C.C. 2d 807 (1971 aff'd, 502 F 2d (D.C. Cir. 1974), p.411; *Wilderness Society*, 31 F.C.C. 2d (1971).
11. *Alan F. Neckritz*, p.812, quoting *Friends of the Earth*, 24 F.C.C. 2d (1970), pp.743, 807.
12. *Wilderness Society*, 22 R.R. 2d (1971), p.1027.
13. Ibid., pp.1035,1037.

14. *William H. Rodgers Jr.*, 30 F.C.C., 2d (1971), p.640.
15. *John S. MacInnis, Consumers Arise Now,* 32 F.C.C. 2d (1971), p.837.
16. *Sierra Club,* 45 F.C.C. 2d (1979), p.833.
17. *Sierra Club,* 51 F.C.C. 2d 569 (1975).
18. *The Handling of Public Issues Under the Fairness Doctrine and the Public Interest Standards of the Communications Act,* 48 F.C.C. 2d 1 (1974) 30 R.R. 2d.
19. Ibid., p.1264.
20. Ibid., p.1265.
21. Ibid., pp.1266, 1267.
22. United States, Federal Communications Commission, "Memorandum Opinion and Order," Washington, D.C.: GPO, 1987.
23. United States, Senate, S. 742, 100th Cong., 1st Session, Washington, D.C.: GPO, 1987.
24. "Fairness Held Unfair," *Broadcasting,* 10 (August 1987), p.63.
25. Some of the information on the relationship between Greenpeace and the media was developed as part of an ongoing study. See also Cassidy, 1987:18-23.

References

Boorstin, Daniel J. (1961). *The Image: A Guide to Pseudo-Events in America.* New York: Atheneum.
Cassidy, Sean D. (1987). "Greenpeace: When Journalists Become Advocates." *The Steward Quarterly,* 1,1:19-23.
Davidson, Alastair (1977). *Antonio Gramsci: Towards an Intellectual Biography.* New Jersey: Humanities Press.
Devall, Bill and George Sessions (1985). *Deep Ecology.* Salt Lake City: Peregrine Smith Books.
Ginsburg, Douglas H. (1979). *Regulation of Broadcasting.* St. Paul: West Publishing Co.
Gitlin, Todd (1980). *The Whole World Is Watching: Mass Media in the Making and Unmaking of the New Left.* Berkeley: University of California Press.
Gramsci, Antonio (1971). *Selections from the Prison Notebooks of Antonio Gramsci,* ed. and trans. Quintin Hoare and Geoffrey N. Smith. New York: International Publishers.
Hall, Stuart (1982). "The Rediscovery of Ideology." In Michael Gurevitch, Tony Bennett, James Curran, and Janet Woollcott, eds. *Culture, Society, and the Media.* New York: Methuen & Co.
Hunter, Robert (1979). *Warriors of the Rainbow.* New York: Holt, Rinehart and Winston.
Kazis, Richard and Richard L. Grossman (1982). *Fear at Work: Job Blackmail, Labor and the Environment.* New York: Pilgrim Press.
Lukes, Steven (1974). *Power: A Radical View.* London: Macmillan Press.
McTaggart, David with Robert Hunter (1978). *Greenpeace III: Journey into the Bomb.* London: William Collins Sons & Co.
Morgan, Robin and Brian Whitaker (1986). *Rainbow Warrior: The French Attempt to Sink Greenpeace.* London: Arrow Books.
Parlour, James W. (1980). "The Mass Media and Environmental Issues: A Theoretical Analysis," *International Journal of Environmental Studies,* 15:109-121.
Poulantzas, N. (1965). *Political Power and the Social Classes.* London: New Left Books and Sheed & Ward.
Simmons, Steven (1978). *The Fairness Doctrine and the Media.* Berkeley: University of California Press.

Communication, Politics, and Society: The Case of Popular Media in Quebec

Marc Raboy

To UNDERSTAND QUEBEC, sociologists and political scientists have traditionally referred to notions such as development, dependency, cultural division of labour, class relations, and national consciousness (see, for example, McRoberts and Posgate, 1980). I would add to these the notion of communication. As much as by anything else, Quebec is distinguished by the particular relationship of communication to social and political life. In one sense, *all* Quebec media have a certain emancipatory component, to the extent that they aid and abet Quebec's cultural resistance to the centrifugal forces of the great North American melting pot. At the same time, this very quality makes Quebec media an agent of fragmentation within the national entity known as Canada.

Even presuming the maintenance of a distinctive society in Quebec, there is still a continuous struggle to define what that society is and will be, and media have been decidedly a part of that struggle as well.

Media were first introduced to Quebec by American revolutionaries seeking to extend their influence by striking at the weak spot of British North America in the years following the Declaration of Independence. French Canada's first newspaper publisher, Fleury Mesplet, was set up in business by none other than Benjamin Franklin – although British government contracts kept him there. The relationship between media and the state in Quebec as well as the U.S. connection (see Lamonde, 1984) is thus older than the political structure of Canadian confederation, which dates only from 1867.

Quebec's mainstream media have historically exhibited a certain ambivalence with respect to their place in North America, not unlike that of Quebec society on the whole. Quebec's mass-circulation daily newspapers, for example, have generally been among the most grey, most conservative, and least independent on the continent. On the other hand there has always been a European-style daily press of opinion, which continues unto this day.

Radio and television have contributed to breaking down the barriers of isolation, at the same time as they have helped maintain the indigenous culture. In the 1950s, when television was new and there was only one station available to francophone Québécois, the weekly soap opera *The Plouffe Family* was watched regularly in up to 85 per cent of households. At another level, jurisdiction over broadcasting has been a constitutional and political issue in Canada as long as there has been broadcasting. The federal government has exclusive jurisdiction over broadcasting in Canada, but every Quebec government since 1929 has claimed a stake in broadcasting and argued for a larger provincial role (see Raboy, 1986a).

In his classic study of Canadian society, *The Vertical Mosaic*, sociologist John Porter (1965) noted the preponderance of "intellectual journalists" in articulating the values of change in Quebec society. The same is true of Quebec political life. In 1980, when Quebec voted in a historic referendum on the future of its place in Canada, the political leaders of both sides, René Lévesque and Claude Ryan, were former prominent journalists who had given up influential careers to enter active politics.

The focus of this chapter is not on the general place of media in Quebec, however, but on a particular set of experiences with popular uses of media. Distinctive in North America because of its main language, religion, class structure, and social history, Quebec in the past thirty years has been the setting for some unique examples of social and political uses of media. Taken together, these uses of media provide important insights into the limits and possibilities of democratic media, including:

- the criticism of mainstream media from a perspective of popular movements;
- the challenge to ideological hegemony and the logic of the marketplace from within mainstream media, in the form of struggles involving journalists and other media workers;
- the attempts to create autonomous alternatives to mainstream media;
- direct action aimed at appropriating space in the media;
- strategies to gain access to media by achieving newsworthiness;
- popular intervention to influence the mandate of state media apparatuses and state policies with regard to media.

All of these elements have been present in Quebec at one time or another since 1960, and they have cumulatively resulted in creating a distinctive media culture and a situation in which media are considered as part of the normal terrain of social struggle.[1]

Media and Quebec's Quiet Revolution

Quebec society in the 1940s and 1950s was dominated by a clerical conservative ideology embodied in the ruling political party, the Union Nationale, which had first been elected in 1936. The election of a reform government in June 1960 signalled the opening of a new era that has come to be known as the "Quiet Revolution."

The hallmark of the Quiet Revolution was a series of structural reforms and social innovations rooted in the modernization of the Quebec state and appended institutions, such as the education and social services system. For the most part, Quebec's mainstream media, especially the daily press, actively supported the reform movement, and the media themselves underwent considerable upheaval during the early part of the decade. In fact, major labour conflicts at Montreal's largest newspaper, *La Presse* (1958), and at Radio-Canada (1958-59) actually preceded the 1960 elections, heralding the broader social changes to come. In the early 1960s, media were thus seen as responsible social institutions playing an important role in the prevailing consensus in favour of social change, and the media generally agreed to play such a role (Benjamin, 1979).

As early as 1963, disillusionment began to set in about the degree and extent of the reforms. New and radical forms of social and political opposition began to emerge in the way of violent attacks on symbols of anglo-colonial domination, the organization of citizens committees around radical reformist demands in inner cities, and an increase in labour militancy, especially in the newly organized public sector.

The cracks in the consensus were most clearly evident in events surrounding *La Presse.* The newspaper was closely tied to the ruling Liberal Party and had been a staunch supporter of the reform phase of the Quiet Revolution, investing staff and resources in popularizing the government reforms for its mass readership. In 1961 it had hired a former labour movement journalist and outspoken critic of the previous regime, Gérard Pelletier, as its editor-in-chief, and Pelletier had stocked his newsroom with young, free-spirited college graduates, many of them with close ties to the emerging opposition movements.

As social agitation heightened, so did tensions between the *La Presse* journalists and the paper's board of directors. Pelletier sat on the fence, torn between a genuine liberal commitment to a socially responsible press and the inevitability of the rights of ownership. When *La Presse* typesetters affiliated with the International Typographers' Union went on strike in September 1964, the newspaper immediately locked out the reporters. The paper remained closed down for seven months.

The *La Presse* conflict of 1964-65 has often been cited as the signal of the end of the Quiet Revolution. It was certainly a watershed as far as public perception of the mainstream media was concerned. Before the newspaper returned to publishing, Gérard Pelletier was fired as editor (he went on to enter federal politics at the side of Pierre Trudeau, for whom he served as minister of communications and later ambassador to Paris and the United Nations). Many of the dynamic elements of the reporting staff left mainstream journalism, and a new tabloid competitor was launched on the Montreal market (*Le Journal de Montréal*, now the highest circulation daily in Quebec). The struggle around *La Presse* was a symbol of the new social conflict in Quebec, and when it was over the mainstream media by extension were considered in the camp of the political status quo (Godin, 1972).

Throughout the 1960s and 1970s, labour conflicts in the media paralleled social conflicts in the surrounding society, and media workers' unions would generally identify with opposition social groups. Media owners and managers were camped on the other side, the side of power, and the lines were clearly drawn.

This critical perception of the place of the media was further heightened by changes in the political economy of Quebec media. Public opinion in Quebec was alerted to the problem of concentration of media ownership in 1967 when *La Presse* was sold to a conglomerate that already owned three smaller dailies. In 1969 and again in 1972, public pressure prompted the Quebec National Assembly to convene a special parliamentary commission on freedom of the press. Throughout the 1970s and 1980s, journalists and public-interest groups regularly spoke out against ever-increasing concentration in the press and broadcast media. But while journalists' unions and their professional associations pressed for legal controls on the concentration of ownership, union and popular movement leaders also called for the creation of autonomous media outside the control of capital or the state.[2]

Alternative Media

Small but influential radical journals had played an important part in the genesis of the Quiet Revolution. The most famous of these prior to 1960 was *Cité libre*, which had numbered among its editors the future prime minister of Canada, Pierre Trudeau, the journalist Gérard Pelletier, and, briefly, the revolutionary nationalist Pierre Vallières (author of the anti-colonialist classic *White Niggers of America*).

In 1963 a new political journal called *Parti pris* appeared, moving the level of intellectual social criticism in Quebec sharply to the left. Describing itself as "pro-independence, socialist, and anti-clerical," it was the first intellectual rallying point of left-wing nationalism in Quebec. In its pages the concerns of the international youth movement of the 1960s were linked with the specific Québécois demands of socialism and national independence.

Parti pris represented a rupture with the *Cité libre* generation of anti-nationalist, Catholic progressives. It soon spawned other journals of the left, ranging from the militant and action-oriented *Mobilisation* to the more scholarly and academic *Socialisme*. Both types left their mark on Quebec's political culture, the first in the form of agitation and propaganda vehicles for various action groups, the second in a particular Québécois brand of Marxist sociography.

Parti pris itself published until 1968, when it collapsed under the weight of a political split characteristic of sixties politics in Quebec: the question of whether or not to support the new Parti Québécois formed by a coalition of defectors from the Quiet Revolution's Liberal Party and electorally inclined supporters of Quebec independence. Some *Parti pris* veterans eventually served as "organic intellectuals" of the PQ after it took power in 1976, while others went into the labour movement, the extraparliamentary nationalist movement, and organizations of the extreme left.

The political situation was further polarized in 1966, with the electoral defeat of the Liberals and the return to power of the Union Nationale. Not beholden to the progressive coalition that had elected the Liberals, the government moved strongly against the labour movement, charged nationalist spokesmen with seditious conspiracy, and generally sought to demonstrate to Quebec's traditional elites that all change can be reversed. The resulting increase in radical militancy had a further impact on communications.

From 1967 on, dozens of "community newspapers" appeared in working-class neighbourhoods of Quebec cities, as well as in rural areas. In 1968 the president of the Confédération des syndicats nationaux (CSN), Marcel Pepin, in a historic document called *Le Deuxième front* (The Second Front), denounced Quebec's commercial media for placing profit above the public interest and called on the union movement and its supporters to create independent vehicles for "people's" or "popular" information. By 1969 a co-operative formed by a coalition of labour and community groups had begun publishing a left-wing weekly newspaper, *Québec-Presse*, and several smaller-scale initiatives had sprung up as well. In the late 1960s and early 1970s, the ideologies of radical nationalism, socialism, and community action were interlaced in dozens of media experiences, usually linked loosely or organically to oppositional social and political groups but free of ties to either capitalist or state interests.

Québec-Presse combined a philosophy of alternative information with a democratic structure and provided an unprecedented degree of autonomy for its editorial staff, which was recruited on the basis of both politics and professionalism. Billed as "popular response to cultural domination," the paper was the first attempt by opposition groups to penetrate the mass market. While it published for five years, constituting an important pole of solidarity for a generation of social activists, *Québec-Presse* was never free of financial crisis. One of the legacies of the experience was the understanding of the limits of establishing self-sufficient autonomous media in a small market. With a weekly circulation of about thirty-five thousand, *Québec-Presse* could not survive after the union federations pulled the plug on it in 1974. But while it published, the paper played an indispensable role in the evolution of Quebec's social movements. These were years of crisis, and *Québec-Presse* was a journal of record, vehicle of mobilization, and cultural unifier.

A second large-scale autonomous media operation of the period was the Agence presse libre du Québec (APLQ). Like many of the media projects of the period, its creators included former students and disaffected young professionals. As a news agency, the APLQ had minimal production costs and was therefore less fraught with financial problems than a journal like *Québec-Presse*. In 1971 it began providing a weekly information package to subscribing activist groups. It addressed "collectivities" rather than individuals, and sought to establish a two-way communication network by soliciting news from its subscribers. In a context where mainstream media were highly centralized in a few cities and generally inaccessible to movement groups, the agency successfully linked several hundred disparate groups around Quebec and provided them with a means of communication. This project self-destructed in 1976 in a period of ultra-left radicalization marked by the "liquidation" of dozens of projects deemed to be politically unsound (see *Mobilisation*, 1976).

The late 1960s and early 1970s thus provided a rich range of alternative press experiences, each with its own legacy. In general, these projects showed the difficulty both of sustaining financially ambitious projects in a limited market and of placing a communications undertaking in the direct service of a political project, rather than allowing it to serve the general interests of a movement while retaining editorial and organizational autonomy.

Direct Action

Aside from a critical approach to mainstream media manifesting itself in the militant actions of media workers, and along with the attempts to create autonomous media, the early 1970s also provided examples of direct attempts by activists to take media into their own hands. The occasions were the two major social upheavals of the period, the so-called "October crisis" of 1970 and the general strike in the public sector in 1972.

The October crisis refers to the suspension of civil liberties and occupation of Quebec by the Canadian army following the kidnapping by radical nationalists of the British trade commissioner and a provincial cabinet minister in October 1970. The crisis has been described by some analysts (for example, Latouche, 1975) as a struggle over the means of communications, because in the early stages the kidnappers of the Front de libération du Québec (FLQ) and the authorities both used mainstream media to muster public support. As one contemporary commentator put it, official information was caught in its own trap, as the FLQ successfully manipulated institutional news values to keep the upper hand ("B.R., Journalist," 1971). Unquestionably, the high point of the adventure from the FLQ's point of view was the broadcasting of its manifesto on national television by the Canadian Broadcasting Corporation – the only one of its demands to be fully granted. The manifesto hit a responsive public chord, as for the first time a radical critique of Quebec society was made directly to its intended audience.

The 1972 events were a different version of the same phenomenon: the direct appropriation of the means of mass communication by social activists in time of crisis. This time, however, the protagonists were union members at the base of the labour movement, and their target was local broadcasting outlets. During a province-wide general strike called to protest unsatisfactory contract negotiations in the public sector, dozens of unionists in some twenty cities and towns around Quebec occupied local radio and television stations for periods ranging from a few minutes to several days, broadcasting their own version of events and trying their hands at cultural programming as well.

In general the events of 1970 and 1972 contributed to popular consciousness about media in Quebec and gave activists a taste for direct involvement.

Challenges from Within

If labour conflicts in the Quebec media had been a common feature of the political context since the late 1950s, increasingly in the 1960s and 1970s the conflicts were marked by the links that media workers made between their working conditions, control of production, and the nature of their product.

Quebec journalists considered themselves actively involved in the reform movement of the early 1960s. As public attitudes towards the reforms turned critical, militancy among journalists increased. By the late 1960s, most French-language print and electronic journalists in Quebec were unionized with the CSN – the independent, combative union federation that had issued the "second front" call in 1968. As social agitation in Quebec grew, so did the journalists' determination not to be used as mere transmission agents for the elites who controlled both private and public media institutions. In 1969 this concern crystallized in the creation of the FPJQ (Fédération professionelle des journalistes du Québec), a professional organization that would become the main agitator for "the public's right to information" in the 1970s.

Quebec journalists were among the direct targets of police and legal repression in the October crisis of 1970, being subjected to various forms of police and employer harassment. More than a dozen journalists were arrested and detained for varying lengths of time, and several were fired or removed from sensitive positions for criticizing their employers' coverage of the crisis (see Féderation professionelle des journalistes du Québec, 1971).

Journalists carried on a sort of newsroom guerrilla warfare campaign in the mainstream press through the 1970s. Again, *La Presse* was a major site of confrontation. In October 1971 the newspaper shut down, sparking massive demonstrations of support for the journalists and their critique of the paper's news policy. The union, meanwhile, published a self-managed daily newspaper called *Le Quotidien Populaire* (People's Daily).

In 1972, unions of journalists and other communication workers formed the FNC (Fédération nationale des communications), affiliated with the CSN. In subsequent years, both the FNC and FPJQ published widely and organized around social issues related to media and information, despite important rivalries between professionally oriented and primarily syndicalist factions among them.

Interestingly, journalists were one of the rare professional groups to continue militant union activity in the relative social calm that accompanied the election of the Parti Québécois in 1976. In 1977-78, an unprecedented wave of strikes in the media paralysed *La Presse* yet again, as well as Quebec City's *Le Soleil*, the private radio network Radiomutuel, the provincial public-educational television network Radio-Québec, the dailies *Montréal-Matin* and *The Montreal Star* (which did not survive the conflicts). At *La Presse* and *Le Soleil*, professional clauses relating to journalists' control over the integrity of their stories were at the root of the conflict. In 1980-81, long strikes shut down the newsroom of Radio-Canada and the daily *Le Devoir* (whose journalists had won creation of a joint worker-management news policy committee following a previous conflict in 1975).

Thus, the mainstream media have been at the heart of social conflict and conflict surrounding media in Quebec.

Propaganda, Politics, and Communication

In addition to the role of mainstream media, alternative media, struggles involving media workers, and direct action on media, we must consider the media strategies of radical and reformist political groups. These were basically of three sorts.

To a greater extent than the rest of North America, Quebec was marked by a proliferation of extreme left parties and groups in the early 1970s. Generally, these movements took a Leninist view of communication as political propaganda, and they created their own media (usually newspapers or magazines). Under their influence, many of the autonomous projects of the earlier period, such as the APLQ, were either transformed into propaganda vehicles, or, more often, were "liquidated." This current was characterized by the conscious subordination of ideological and cultural activity to a political line.

The second type of political communication involved a specific experience of the Parti Québécois. In provincial elections in 1973 the PQ received about 30 per cent of the popular vote but only 6 out of 110 seats in the Quebec National Assembly. The PQ leadership decided to compensate for its lack of a parliamentary platform by launching a daily newspaper, *Le Jour*, openly committed to Quebec independence and a general program of social democracy. The newspaper began publishing in February 1974 and attracted many professional journalists and a readership equal to that of the critical (but federalist) intellectual daily, *Le Devoir*. *Le Jour* published for two years, in spite of serious advertiser boycotts, but experienced a spiralling series of conflicts between its staff and party leaders over editorial and management policy. The newspaper was shut down less than three months before the November 1976 election that brought the PQ to power.

Meanwhile, between these currents of neo-Bolshevism and social democracy, new movements began to emerge around social issues such as feminism, ecology, sexuality, and urban life (see Raboy, 1986b). In some cases these movements spun off interesting alternative publications, but the most important political challenges to established authority have relied on traditional communication strategies involving public relations and the use of mainstream media to get messages across. The most striking example of this was the case of the Montreal Citizens' Movement, a municipal party formed in 1974, whose electoral fortunes rose and fell in waves of media approval and disapproval until it took power at city hall in 1986. In the late 1970s and early 1980s, several important periodicals with loose ties to popular movements came and went (*Le Temps fou*, 1978-82; *Presse libre*, 1981-82). The most durable were those that could rely on support rooted in political conviction (such as the feminist *La Vie en Rose*, 1981-87 and the union-based *Mouvements*, 1983-87). At the same time, a number of serious attempts to launch new non-sectarian media of the left have floundered due to a lack of institutional support: The union federations, for example, have been reluctant to participate in any project involving a coalition of popular groups, preferring to rely on internal means of communication to reach their members and on massive advertising campaigns in the mainstream media to communicate with the public.

State Intervention and Popular Participation

While opposition movements in Quebec focused their attention on the locations of power, one of those locations, the Quebec state, was engaged in a power struggle of its own.

In 1968 Canada adopted a new Broadcasting Act, stating, among many other things, that "facilities should be provided within the Canadian broadcasting system for educational broadcasting" (Canada, 1968: s.2[i]). The federal government proposed to create a new agency that would provide facilities to each province, and each province would in turn control production and programming within its own territory.

Every Quebec government since 1929 had asserted the province's claim on broadcasting. The conservative nationalist premier, Maurice Duplessis, went so far as to enact legislation in 1945 enabling the province to set up a radio network but, under threat from Ottawa, Quebec did not execute the law.

A Canadian Supreme Court judgment of 1931 had given exclusive jurisdiction over broadcasting to the federal government, but Quebec saw a loophole: constitutionally, the provinces had clear control of education – so which level of government could then claim authority over "educational broadcasting"?

Reaction to the federal proposal in Quebec ranged from scepticism to outrage. Forty years earlier, a federal royal commission (Canada, 1929) had proposed a similar formula for all of public broadcasting, only to have the plan rejected in favour of a central organization, which became the CBC.

In 1967, Quebec began experimenting with an educational television project known as TEVEC, through which broadcasts were prepared by the Department of Education and broadcast in time purchased from CBC or private stations. Ontario had announced similar intentions, and its Department of Education would soon be broadcasting over a UHF frequency licenced to the CBC. But Ottawa's proposal to furnish an infrastructure for educational broadcasting was about to be rejected out of hand by Quebec.

During intensive constitutional negotiations between Ottawa and the provinces in February 1968, the Quebec government claimed authority over educational broadcasting by virtue of its exclusive powers in education. Quebec then announced its intention to create an educational broadcasting organization to be known as Radio-Québec.

Both Ottawa and Quebec introduced educational broadcasting legislation in March 1969 (around the same time as both governments were in the process of creating cabinet-level departments of communications). But it was Ottawa that backed down from a constitutional (and political) showdown over broadcasting, and its proposed bill creating a Canadian Educational Broadcasting Authority was withdrawn in November 1969, just as the Radio-Québec legislation was taking effect.

Radio-Québec had been actually operating for about a year by this time and was well into production. The law enabled it to own broadcasting facilities as well as produce programs. For the first time within the framework of Canadian federal-provincial relations in communications, a province would have its own broadcasting service.

In the Quebec National Assembly, the Liberal opposition supported Quebec's constitutional right to jurisdiction over educational broadcasting and acknowledged the historic importance of the legislation, but the Liberals also made a vigorous and lengthy critique of the proposed composition and operation of Radio-Québec. Liberal communications critic Yves Michaud (later editor of *Le Jour*), an outspoken advocate of the freedom and responsibility of the press, attacked the close relationship between the government and Radio-Québec that the legislation provided. Michaud called instead for an independent agency.

So while the government's constitutional position on broadcasting could be the basis of a political consensus, there was a wide divergence of opinion concerning the form of the Radio-Québec project, particularly with respect to the Quebec state. In 1969, Quebec's Union Nationale government was perceived in liberal and progressive circles as repressive, if not reactionary, with respect to civil liberties and traditional North American notions of freedom.

Indeed, the debate over Radio-Québec highlighted many of the evident contradictions inherent in asserting "national sovereignty" in communications. Having built a consensus and affirmed its right to national autonomy over the means of cultural production (as, for example, Canada had long done vis-à-vis the United States), the Quebec government viewed those means as an effective extension of itself. Critics outside the government saw the issue in terms of the ideal potential of broadcasting and the proper relationship between media, the state, and the public, while the representatives of the Quebec state reduced the question to one of national interest.

But even after Ottawa withdrew from educational broadcasting, provincial agencies were still barred from holding broadcasting licences until 1972. Quebec therefore began by transmitting programs over closed-circuit cable systems. When Radio-Québec received approval to operate broadcasting transmitters in Montreal and Quebec City in 1974, Quebec communications minister Jean-Paul L'Allier announced that Radio-Québec would not be an ivory tower in which programs were conceived at the top and merely transmitted to a receiving public. Quebec educational television would be more than a mere means of intellectual exchange. Mechanisms to ensure public participation would be worked out.

But even at this early stage a gap was appearing between the promise of Radio-Québec and its actual performance. A crippling four-month labour conflict in 1973-74 revealed Radio-Québec to be a bureaucratic organization, characterized by hierarchical functioning and self-censorship on the part of creative personnel. By the time Radio-Québec began broadcasting on its own UHF frequency in January 1975, it was already under public fire for failing to meet expectations for truly different television programming. Later that year, public hearings on Radio-Québec's programming and development demonstrated a strong public demand for a democratic, decentralized educational network, with a strong regional thrust (see Institut canadien d'éducation des adultes, 1974,1975).

Under the Parti Québécois government (1976-85), Radio-Québec expanded and came to occupy an important place in the francophone-Quebec television spectrum. Following a further study of its own, the PQ decided to restructure Radio-Québec along the lines recommended by the public hearings, and in 1979 a new law created a series of nine regional committees composed of community representatives to make programming and policy decisions. At the same time, Radio-Québec's central board of directors was expanded from seven to twenty-one members to include regional representation.

From 1980-85 Radio-Québec's regional production tripled (while overall production increased by only 30 per cent). A government study in 1985 reported that people in areas served by Radio-Québec regional production offices considered the provincial broadcaster "their" television (Canada/Quebec, 1985). Yet regional programming never received more than about 15 per cent of the Radio-Québec budget.

The PQ government never made full use of the cultural apparatus at its disposal to advance the cause of Quebec independence. In 1980 it organized a referendum seeking a mandate to negotiate a new political arrangement with Ottawa (enigmatically known as "sovereignty-association"). When that failed, it made a fundamental shift from politics towards economics as the lever for Quebec's self-determination, and by 1982-83 – along with most governments in the Western world – it was treating communications as a sector of economic and industrial rather than sociocultural development (Quebec, 1982, 1983). Soon, Radio-Québec was being redefined as a more traditional television network (see Société de radio-télévision du Québec, 1985). Advertising was introduced, and there was talk of privatization.

When the Liberals were re-elected in December 1985, they immediately cut $8 million of the network's $60 million budget by dismantling the regional decision-making structures and closing down most of the regional production facilities. In March 1987 a Quebec ministry of communications report recommended that Radio-Québec could still serve a useful purpose; as a springboard for launching Quebec cultural industries into the international francophone market; and as a foothold from which Quebec could demand a role in establishing Canadian communications policy (Quebec, 1987).

Thus a media that began as a vehicle of cultural sovereignty and became an instrument of social development took on an increasingly economic function in the late 1980s. Educational broadcasting, repatriated to Quebec, was a major terrain of struggle over democratization during the 1970s. While the Quebec state proved in the end to be no more receptive to the democratic impulse, the fact that it was closer to the people made it an easier object of social action.[3]

Community Broadcasting
Finally, the combination of state and popular interests spawned a further distinctive media practice in Quebec: community broadcasting.

The introduction of community broadcasting in Quebec has to be seen in the context of the general approach to state intervention that characterized the Quiet Revolution – an approach distinguished by the widespread use of community organizers (known as "social animators") to involve local communities in planning their own economic and social development. Following a pilot project in a depressed area of eastern Quebec, the Quebec government (or rather, its technocrats) adopted community "participation" in health care, social services, and education as an ideological value (see Godbout, 1987).

In 1967 the ministry of education launched a program known as TEVEC (*té-vé-communautaire*, or community television) in the Lake St. John region north of Quebec City, in which social animation techniques were employed to get the community to participate in producing adult education material aired during time purchased from local television stations. Quebec went on to experiment with other methods of "de-schooling" education in the 1970s, but an important germ had been unleashed, in Lake St. John at least, as people got a taste of direct, local involvement in producing television content. In 1970, the first community to become involved in cable-supported "community television" was in the small town of Normandin, in Lake St. John.

A federal program know as Challenge for Change (or Société nouvelle) was also instrumental in the origins of Quebec community media. Set up in 1967 (1969 on the French side), Challenge for Change was designed to use communications to promote new ideas and provoke social change in the "fight against poverty." The Normandin project was directly aided by Challenge for Change.

When they were not already integral parts of government programs (as in the case of TEVEC and Challenge for Change), community media were often financed by short-term grants from two federal government programs set up in the early 1970s: Opportunities for Youth and Local Initiatives Projects. In 1973 the Quebec government, through its Ministry of Communications, began providing regular funding of community radio, television, and newspapers through a special program of aid to community media (PAMEC). Quebec has tended to see support for community media (and educational broadcasting) as a way to recapture some of the broadcasting space constitutionally occupied by Ottawa. It has been the only Canadian province to directly support community media over an extended period (see Canada, 1986, ch.19).[4]

Community broadcasting's link with the state has been the subject of vigorous polemical discussion in Quebec (see, for example, Council for the Development of Community Media, 1977). The early community media of the 1960s were criticized for failing to live up to their initial promise of interactivity and for becoming limited, small-scale versions of mass media. Interestingly, the first attempts to create alternative electronic media in the late 1960s and early 1970s did not designate themselves as community broadcasters. Montreal's Radio Centreville, for example, initially called itself a "neighbourhood radio" (*radio de quartier*) and a "people's radio" (*radio populaire*), only adopting the community label later to qualify for state support.

Some community media grew out of and maintained ties with activist groups in the "popular movement." With the general demobilization and retreat from left-wing militancy of the late 1970s and early 1980s, certain community broadcasting operations emerged as focal points for popular intervention, as well as providing information alternatives in a context of increasing concentration and uniformity in the mainstream media.

In many cases, despite the constraints imposed by government purse-strings, community media were working models of democratic communication. In the original Normandin experiment, 150 villagers took part in choosing themes, researching, interviewing, editing, and otherwise manipulating technical equipment during three hours of nightly television distributed by cable through five towns in the region (see Girard, 1985). The experience led to the creation of Quebec's first community broadcasting council, in which individual members and representatives of some fifty community associations participated regularly. Later, as community television took hold and spread, similar councils were formed in other regions of Quebec (see Canadian Radio-Television Commission, 1974).

Quebec community television thus developed as an associative form of communication, made possible by provincial state subsidies and federal regulatory provisions.

The Canadian Radio-Television Commission (CRTC) in its earliest policy statements on cable (CRTC, 1969) urged cable operators to provide a community channel, and a Canadian Senate committee investigating ownership and control of Canadian mass media reiterated this expectation (Canada, 1970). But while the CRTC encouraged cable companies to provide for community programming, it did not make it obligatory. Of 387 cable companies licenced in 1972, only 139 provided some form of community programming, and "very, very few of these gave open access" (Rosen and Herman, 1977:87).

In 1975 the CRTC announced new regulations making the provision of a community channel a requirement for every cable undertaking in Canada (Canadian Radio-Television Commission, 1975a). At first the CRTC said that licensees would be further required to devote at least 10 per cent of gross annual subscription revenue to operating the community channel, but following an outcry from the industry it retreated from this position and decided to regulate the extent of cable company contributions. Instead, the CRTC said it would "expect licensees to allocate a reasonable percentage of their gross subscriber revenue for the ongoing operation of the community channel" (Canadian Radio-Television Commission, 1975b:14).

The CRTC still held out high hopes for the role that could be played by community programming, most significantly "its ability to turn the passive viewer of television into an active participant" (Canadian Radio-Television Commission, 1975b:5). But it was not prepared to oblige the cable entrepreneurs to support community programming with their profits.

More importantly, community television was not seen as a new sector, to be

fully developed to meet the needs that could not be filled by either national public broadcasting or commercial private broadcasting. The possibility of commu-
nity-controlled cable *systems*, as opposed to community-access channels within
privately owned systems, was never seriously explored. The CRTC's policy of
moral suasion depended entirely on the benevolence of the cable companies,
while resting on the paternalistic premise that local programming, unlike national
programming, required no public resources. Under the Canadian regulations, a
means of distributing community programming was provided, without the means
to produce the programming. The only exception, to a very limited degree, was
in Quebec.

But even in Quebec, community television has suffered from a lack of autonomy. The CRTC model interjected the cable undertaking between community
broadcasters and the regulatory authority, providing a politically convenient inter-
mediary to be the first line of defence against "questionable" programming. Local cable companies, rather than a federal authority, would watch over the content
of community programming.

In radio the situation was somewhat different. Community radio became possible as the result of a 1973 CRTC policy proposal for FM radio. Within a year, community radio stations took root in Vancouver (B.C.), Kitchener (Ont.), Chicoutimi
(Que.), and Montreal. But here too, only the Quebec government was willing to
systematically fund community radio, albeit again in a limited way, and aside from
college campuses and northern Native communities (which constitute a case that
would have to be studied separately), community radio has been largely restricted
to Quebec. Community radio stations provide the only local programming services available in some sparsely populated regions where commercial broadcasters
are not interested to tread. But in Montreal, where two community radio stations
attract significant audiences, the CRTC has refused to allow those stations to increase their transmission power, thus helping to protect a heavily saturated market for commercial broadcasters (see Bréniel, 1987; *Le Devoir*, 1987).

By 1986 there were twenty-one community radio stations operating in Quebec, and another six were being organized. In community television, meanwhile,
there were thirty-three active associations, and four in formation. Together, radio
and television involved about 450 full and part-time workers, 4,000 volunteers,
and 42,000 supporting members. The main source of revenue came in the form of
Quebec government grants, although radio was increasingly able to finance itself
partially through advertising, and about 10 per cent of the television stations'
budgets came in the form of contributions from cable companies –cable companies servicing organized community television associations contributed an average $6,000 apiece in 1986 (Canada, 1986).

The total sum of money involved was paltry, however: $3.8 million for radio
and less than $2 million for television, about a third of the total coming in grants
from Quebec. In the same year, Radio-Québec's budget was close to $60 million;
the Canadian Broadcasting Corporation received about $900 million from the fed-

eral government; and commercial advertising revenue for radio and television in Canada surpassed $1.5 billion (Canada, 1986).

In 1986 the federal Task Force on Broadcasting Policy recommended that community broadcasting be officially recognized as a distinct sector in the Canadian broadcasting system, "on an equal footing with the public and private sectors which it complements" (Canada, 1986:153). The task force commended the Quebec government for its support of community broadcasting and suggested that the federal government collaborate with the provinces in finding further support. Shortly thereafter, however, the Quebec government announced drastic cuts to the PAMEC program and said the community broadcasters would have to become self-sufficient.

By the end of the decade the future of Quebec community broadcasting was uncertain, but the vision of the community broadcasters was clear. To them, community broadcasting was "seen to be an instrument of service to the collective development of the community," a form of communications that considers the public "first of all as citizen, and not as consumer" (Regroupement des organismes communautaires de communication du Québec, 1987).

Conclusion

This overview of the Quebec experience since 1960 has demonstrated the extent to which popular struggles surrounding media have reflected the array of social forces active at any given moment. In this, two general phenomena are notable: on the one hand, the way social movements use media to deal with their need for social communication; on the other hand, the way communication through media can become in itself a form of sociopolitical action.

The fabric of this action is what we might call "culture." The action itself we might qualify as "cultural communication," a useful conceptual category for appreciating the range of activity observed in Quebec with respect to media. For example, the failure of propaganda strategies, of the left or right, can be seen as the shortcoming of a strictly political approach that ignores the cultural dimension. But, as indicated earlier, there is also in Quebec a certain inevitable complicity between the most conservative media and the most radical; the complicity lies in the shared quality of cultural resistance that both provide vis-à-vis the outside.

This is not to suggest culture as a leveller of social barriers or as a mediator of social conflict. Indeed, there are within Quebec society at least two clearly defined and opposing political cultures: a culture of conservative nationalism, and a communitarian culture. The particularly troublesome nature of the Quebec state arises from the fact that both political cultures see the Quebec state as an agent of social development. The ambiguities inherent in the media experiences of the 1970s and 1980s in which the Quebec state was directly involved stem from this duality.

In the earlier period, media initiatives were somewhat simpler to characterize: The typical alternative social or political movement of the 1960s emerged with no consciously articulated strategy for communication. Gradually, as its critical perspective on society expanded, a critical awareness of media set in, leading to the integration of some sort of action with respect to media and the movement's general action plan.

At least three types of media practice emerged from this context: the creation of alternative media, direct action aimed at media, and attempts to influence media from within. At the extremities of the spectrum of media-directed action were attempts to use media as propaganda and attempts to market movements to the mainstream media.

The experiences of educational and community broadcasting were singular examples that have the added feature of central involvement on the part of the Quebec state – a state, it is essential to recall, with relatively little sovereignty over matters related to communication. Within the general Canadian context, educational and community broadcasting are part of the enlarged public sector that came into being in the 1970s, holding out a promise of decentralization and democratization (see Lorimer and McNulty, 1985). In Quebec, these sectors took on a particularly political overtone.

By the late 1980s the thwarting of popular aspirations with respect to Radio-Québec pointed to the fact that the Quebec state is, after all, a state, and should not be viewed as necessarily more benevolent or more democratic than its Canadian parent. The crisis in community broadcasting pointed to the dangers inherent in a financial dependency relationship between movement and state.

There is an important distinction to be made between the media projects of the 1960s and 1970s, which attempted to function with maximum autonomy and in political opposition to the domination of state and capital, and those of the 1970s and 1980s, which were politically less clearly situated. Under the sign of "community," for example, many popular media practices were, in the 1980s, subjected to the normative influence of state subsidy programs and regulatory procedures (see Sénécal, 1981).

On the other hand, community media were still an important breach in the social firmament. For Quebec was not exempt from the worldwide current of conservatism, and in fact it is not unusual for manifestations of the geopolitical climate to become more pronounced in Quebec. (Scholars often wonder whether Quebec is the least advanced of the advanced industrial countries, or the most developed of the underdeveloped countries; in either case, its status places it on the periphery of world affairs, subjecting it to the shock waves of development.)

Private-sector mainstream media in Quebec today are increasingly concentrated in the hands of fewer and fewer powerful owners, and it is virtually impossible for small entrepreneurial or independent non-profit media to break into the market. In the public sector, the tensions between Quebec and Ottawa are marked by a retreat of both governments from their traditional responsibilities. In the small space that remains between capitalist and state-based initiatives, the generation of activists that came of age in the 1960s is wiser but reluctant to embark on new adventures, while for the most part the younger generation of Quebec is less inclined to view media in a sociopolitical sense.

In this context, a strategy based on the demand for basic democratic human rights with respect to communication appeared appropriate, and in the early 1990s popular initiatives focused on the centre of the system: policy intervention with respect to such questions as the defence of public broadcasting, demands for access and fair representation, media literacy education, democratization of media. At the same time, people involved in autonomous media initiatives were aware of the need to deal with such questions as marketability and quality as well as social purpose.

The legacy of the previous thirty years was the knowledge that success or failure of these initiatives would depend on two things: establishment of a "rapport de force" with the dominant social and political forces, and discovery of a cultural link with a popular constituency.

Notes

1. A number of excellent texts are available in English for readers wishing more detailed background on Quebec. For a general history, see Linteau, Durocher and Robert (1983). In addition to McRoberts and Posgate (1980), for an overview of the social history and contemporary political context see Milner and Milner (1972), and Fraser (1985). On the context of Quebec media in Canada, see McCormack (1981, 1983). For more detailed studies of some of the material covered in this article, and related matters, see Raboy (1984, 1990). For an official view of the Quebec government's position on culture and communications, see French (1987).

2. Regarding concentration of ownership in the Canadian media, see Canada (1970, 1981, 1986). For a polemical and descriptive account of the phenomenon in Quebec, see Keable (1985). Since 1987 alone the following developments have occurred: the Canadian Radio-Television and Telecommunications Commission approved the sale of Quebec's largest private television station, Télé-Métropole, to Quebec's largest cable distributor, Vidéotron; the Quebec government sold its holdings in newsprint production to a consortium formed by the Quebecor publishing chain (*Le Journal de Montréal*) and British press magnate Robert Maxwell; the UniMédia newspaper chain was sold to a holding company owned by Toronto financier Conrad Black, publisher of the *Daily Telegraph* (London).

3. Canada's Broadcasting Act was completely revised in 1991 and now recognizes both educational and community broadcasting as integral parts of the Canadian broadcasting system. Meanwhile, jurisdictional questions surrounding communications and culture were once again in the foreground in the debate over Canada's constitutional future. Several official reports commissioned by the Quebec government urged the province to demand repatriation of all powers in these sectors, while Ottawa's proposals tabled in September 1991 offered provincial governments the possibility of owning and operating full-fledged public broadcasting undertakings, subject to federal regulation.

4. The irony of all this was not lost on a group of French researchers who studied Quebec community media in the mid-1970s and noted the dependency of oppositional electronic media in Quebec on state support. In Europe, where state intervention in the cultural sphere has a long tradition, autonomous "médias libres" were flourishing, while in free enterprise North America, granting agencies were in full bloom. See Barbier-Bouvet, Beaud and Flichy (1979).

References

"B.R., Journaliste" (1971). "Une information totalitaire, prise à son propre piège." In Jean-Marc Piotte, ed., *Québec-occupé.* Montreal: Parti pris.

Barbier-Bouvet, Jean-François, Paul Beaud and Patrice Flichy (1979). *Communication et pouvoir: mass médias et médias communautaires au Québec.* Paris: Anthropos.

Benjamin, Jacques (1979). "Pouvoir politique et médias au Québec," *Communication et Information,* 3,1:67-77.

Bréniel, Pascale (1987). "Les radios communautaires, coincés entre la communauté et la rentabilité?" *Le 30,* 11,2:16-18.

Canada (1929). *Report of the Royal Commission on Radio Broadcasting.* Ottawa: King's Printer.

Canada (1968). *Broadcasting Act.* Statutes of Canada 1967-68, c.25.

Canada (1970). *Report of the Special Senate Committee on Mass Media.* Ottawa: Information Canada.

Canada (1981). *Report of the Royal Commission on Newspapers.* Ottawa: Minister of Supply and Services Canada.

Canada (1986). *Report of the Task Force on Broadcasting Policy.* Ottawa: Minister of Supply and Services Canada.

Canada/Quebec (1985). *The Future of French-Language Television.* Ottawa/Quebec City: Department of Communications/Ministère des communications du Québec.

Canadian Radio-Television Commission (1969). "Community Antenna Television." Public announcement, May 13.

Canadian Radio-Television Commission (1974). *A Resource for the Active Community.* Ottawa: Information Canada.

Canadian Radio-Television Commission (1975a). "Policy Announcement on Cable Television." Public announcement, February 17.

Canadian Radio-Television Commission (1975b). "Policies Respecting Broadcasting Receiving Undertakings (Cable Television)." Public announcement, December 16.

Council for the Development of Community Media (1977). "Community Media and the Ideology of Participation." In Armand Mattelart and Seth Siegelaub, eds., *Communication and Class Struggle.* Vol 2. New York: International General, 1983.

Confédération des syndicats nationaux (1968). *Le Deuxième Front.* Montreal: CSN.

Fédération professionnelle des journalistes du Québec (1971). *Le Dossier "Z."* Montreal: FPJQ.

Fraser, Graham (1985). *PQ: René Lévesque and the Parti Québécois in Power.* Toronto: Macmillan of Canada.

French, Richard D. (1987). "The Francophone Summit," *Canadian Journal of Communication,* special issue, December 1987:47-53.

Girard, Anne (1985). *Les télévisions communautaires au Québec, d'hier au demain.* Quebec City: Ministère des communications du Québec.

Godbout, Jacques T. (1987). *La démocratie des usagers.* Montreal: Boréal.

Godin, Pierre (1972). *L'information-opium: Une historie politique du journal "La Presse."* Montreal: Parti pris.

Institut canadien d'éducation des adultes (1974). *Radio-Québec pour qui?* Montreal: ICEA.

Institut canadien d'éducation des adultes (1975). *Le défi de Radio-Québec: Démocratiser la télévision.* Brief to the public hearings on the orientation of Radio-Québec, October. Montreal: ICEA.

Keable, Jacques (1985). *L'information sous influence.* Montreal: VLB Editeur.

Lamonde, Yvan (1984). "American Cultural Influence in Quebec: A One-Way Mirror." In Alfred O. Hero Jr. and Marcel Daneau, eds., *Problems and Opportunities in U.S.-Quebec Relations.* Boulder, Col.: Westview Press.

Latouche, Daniel (1975). "Mass Media and Communication in a Canadian Political Crisis." In Benjamin D. Singer, ed., *Communications in Canadian Society.* Toronto: Copp Clark.

Le Devoir (1987). "La radio communautaire CIBL-FM devra bientôt décider de son avenir," April 8.

Linteau, Paul-André, René Durocher and Jean-Claude Robert (1983). *A History of Quebec.* Translated by Robert Chodos. Toronto: Lorimer.

Lorimer, Rowland and Jean McNulty (1985). "The Case for and Structuring of Regional, Local and Educational Community Broadcasting." In Colin Hoskins and Stuart McFadyen, eds., *Canadian Broadcasting: The Challenge of Change.* Edmonton: University of Alberta.

McCormack, Thelma (1981). "Revolution, Communication and the Sense of History." In Elihu Katz and Tamos Szecsko, eds., *Mass Media and Social Change.* London: Sage.

McCormack, Thelma (1983). "The Political Culture and the Press of Canada," *Canadian Journal of Political Science,* 16,3:451-472.

McRoberts, Kenneth and Dale Posgate (1980). *Quebec: Social Change and Political Crisis.* Toronto: McClelland and Stewart.

Milner, Sheilagh Hodgins and Henry Milner (1972). *The Decolonization of Quebec: An Analysis of Left-Wing Nationalism.* Toronto: McClelland and Stewart.

Mobilisation (1976). *Liquidons le spontanéisme, l'opportunisme et l'économisme.* Pamphlet.

Porter, John (1965). *The Vertical Mosaic.* Toronto: University of Toronto Press.

Quebec (1982). *Bâtir l'avenir.* Quebec City: Ministère des communications du Québec.

Quebec (1983). *Le Québec et les communications: Un futur simple?* Quebec City: Ministère des communications du Quebec.

Quebec (1987). "Bilan et perspectives de la Société de radio-télévision du Québec (Radio-Québec)." Quebec City: Ministère des communications du Québec.

Raboy, Marc (1984). *Movements and Messages: Media and Radical Politics in Quebec.* Toronto: Between the Lines.

Raboy, Marc (1986a). "Public Television, the National Question, and the Preservation of the Canadian State." In Phillip Drummond and Richard Paterson, eds., *Television in Transition.* London: BFI Publishing.

Raboy, Marc, ed. (1986b). *Old Passions New Visions: Social Movements and Political Activism in Quebec.* Toronto: Between the Lines.

Raboy, Marc (1990). *Missed Opportunities: The Story of Canada's Broadcasting Policy.* Montreal and Kingston: McGill-Queen's University Press.

Regroupement des organismes communautaires de le communication du Québec (1987). "Observations relatives aux recommandations du groupe de travail sur la politique de la radiodiffusion" (Brief to the House of Commons Standing Committee on Communications and Culture), March 18.

Rosen, Earl and Reg Herman (1977). "The Community Use of Media for Life-Long Learning in Canada." In Frances Berrigan, ed., *Access: Some Western Models of Community Media.* Paris: UNESCO.

Sénécal, Michel (1981). "Médias communautaires: état de marginalité ou marginalité d'Etat," *Revue internationale d'action communautaire,* 6,46:29-42.

Société de radio-télédiffusion du Québec (1985). *Radio-Québec Maintenant.* Montreal: SRTQ.

Vallières, Pierre (1971). *White Niggers of America.* New York: Monthly Review.

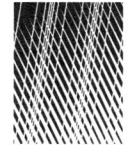

Part V

Social Movements, Media, and the Third World

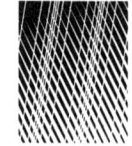

From Manila to Manhattan: An Analysis of the New York Times Coverage of Aquino's People Power Movement

David A. Frank

WHEN JAMES FENTON, the British journalist, travelled with members of the National People's Army (NPA) into the mountain forests of the Philippines during the early months of 1986, he was surprised to learn that many of the insurgents had seen *Rambo* on the army's Betamax (Fenton, 1986). Borrowing from Tony Orlando and Dawn's 1973 hit, "Tie a Yellow Ribbon Round the Old Oak Tree," leaders and members of "People Power" adopted yellow as the movement's colour (Friend, 1986). In response to Republican Senator Paul Laxalt's suggestion (Laxalt, 1986), on November 3, 1985 Ferdinand Marcos announced a snap election on *This Week with David Brinkley*. That American culture is pervasive in the Philippines and that the U.S. media have influenced the course of Philippine history is the consensus of most informed observers.

The U.S. mass media was at the centre of the snap election; often shaping as well as reporting the actions of those involved. In a book written for The Asian Society, Hernandez (1986) concludes that the mass media played a "crucial role" in the final hours of the Marcos regime. Johnson (1987) and Bonner (1987), in their thorough accounts of the snap election and its aftermath, document in detail how Marcos and Corazon Aquino both courted the U.S. media and often saw *The New York Times* and CBS as more important than the indigenous media.[1] Increasingly, it has become apparent that leaders and members of social movements (particularly leaders and members of social movements in the Third World) recognize that they must address the global as well as the local audience.

Social Movements in the Global Village

The Philippine controversy provides the rhetorical scholar with an example of a social movement in a non-Western setting attempting to appeal to a global audience. I am hopeful that this study might help to illuminate how movements make use of the media to achieve non-violent social change. As such, this investigation may help to expand our understanding of the rhetorical strategy of social movements. First, Steward, Smith, and Denton (1984:81) have urged critics to study how movements employ the mass media. They write, "We need to study how social movements employ the media and how the media report social movements." For those who do not have direct access to the movement, *the mediated image is the movement.* The make-up of the mediated message is, in turn, shaped and framed by the hegemonic assumptions and routines used by the media to report the actions of the movement (Gitlin, 1980). Movement members and leaders who are aware of these assumptions and routines may be able to adapt their messages to these assumptions and routines. There is strong evidence that the leaders of both the People Power movement and the Marcos regime were quite aware of the inner workings of the U.S. mass media. The Philippine economy is intertwined with U.S. interests, and changes in Philippine political and military power have been dependent, in large part, on U.S. colonial interest. While a discussion of the history and politics of Philippine culture is beyond the scope of this paper (for excellent histories of U.S. colonization efforts in the Philippines, see May and Nemenzo, 1986; Bresnan, 1986), the fifty-year colonization of the Philippines by U.S. military and commercial interests has made the U.S.-Philippine relationship particularly important to Philippine domestic politics. Hence, the U.S. audience was critically important in the Marcos-Aquino drama. The People Power movement was well received by that audience, in part because the movement leaders were able to make use of and adjust to the routines of the U.S. media.

As Todd Gitlin and others have noted, the media will attend to movements that are flamboyant and confrontational; violent confrontations will almost guarantee media coverage. The media will also report movements headed by media-certified celebrity leaders (Gitlin, 1980). In addition, the U.S. media routine of "impartiality" guarantees that "both sides" of a controversy will be heard; particularly when an attack has been made upon the credibility of a belligerent. If the movement does not confront and does not have a celebrity leader, it is likely that the movement will not be covered by the media. Hence, Cathcart (1976) may be right (but for reasons different than those he presents) that a movement must confront to exist – that is, the social movement that does not confront may not be reported. If it is not reported, it does not exist for those who are dependent on mass media coverage for their information on a movement's existence and actions.

Coverage of Philippine affairs by the U.S. media confirms this theoretical perspective. In the four-week election period, the three major networks devoted 180 minutes to Philippine news (Bain, 1986). Between 1972 and 1981 these same networks presented three stories a year on Philippine issues. A review of the coverage patterns of *The New York Times* provides additional support. *The New York Times* presented thirty-two articles on Philippine affairs in January and February of 1985. During the first two months of 1986, the *Times* reported on Philippine matters in some 264 articles. The number of reports receded to sixty-one during the initial months of 1987. Obviously, the U.S. media focused on the Philippines because of the drama of the elections and the success of People Power. Aquino received media attention because she was able to confront Marcos in a manner consistent with the expectations of the U.S. mass media. The depiction of the movement by the *Times* reveals how the movement adjusted to the media and how the media adjusted to the movement; and how the *Times* reported on a non-violent movement as well as a movement headed by a woman in a non-Western setting. An additional factor is the mix of symbols, rituals, and actions of movement adherents in Asia cultures – cultural signs that are quite different from those observed in Western settings. The confrontation between the forces of Aquino and Marcos elicited a melange of these cultural signs.

The New York Times in the Philippines: January 1, 1986-March 1, 1986

The New York Times, with its key role in both national and international affairs, is read by the power elite and helps to set social, political, and international agendas (Sigal, 1973; Kadushin, 1974). Television networks often turn to the *Times* for stories deserving of attention. In addition, Gitlin (1980:301) found, to his surprise, "that the *Times*'s and CBS's frames for covering the [new left] movement were not so different after all, that roughly the same analytic model could be brought to bear on both television and newspapers."

Rosenblum (1981:124-125) has noted the particularly powerful influence of the *Times* on other newspapers and journalists in the reporting of international affairs: "The *New York Times* by itself plays an enormous role [in international journalism]. Even at the AP and the UPI, night editors anxiously await early editions of the *Times* to see what foreign stories the paper saw fit to print."

The New York Times, its editor A.M. Rosenthal, and the *Times*'s Philippine correspondent Seth Mydans were important factors in the Philippine drama. On December 16, 1985, Corazon Aquino was interviewed by Rosenthal, Mydans, and foreign affairs editor Warren Hoge. The interview turned out to be a major setback for Aquino's campaign, because Rosenthal, an avowed anti-communist, concluded that Aquino was weak and ill prepared and that she would allow communism to gain ground in the Philippines. For Rosenthal, Aquino's remarks on the National People's Army (NPA), the "Marxist" insurgents, implied that she would not be "tough" on communism. Aquino had suggested that the majority of the NPA militants were not really devoted to communism and that if elected she would encourage dialogue and a cease-fire with the NPA. Rosenthal believed that "his correspondents had been too soft in their reporting on the Sandinistas before and after they came to power, wanted to be sure that his correspondent in Manila, Seth Mydans, didn't make the same errors when reporting about the NPA" (Bonner, 1987:393).

The December 1986 issue of *Commentary* contained an article suggesting that the NPA was the new Khmer Rouge. Rosenthal had read this article and, reportedly, it influenced his conclusion that communism had to be stopped in the Philippines and that Aquino was not an appropriate choice as president. Rosenthal not only urged Mydans to report the Philippine controversy from the Rosenthal point of view, but also influenced people in the State Department and the White House along the same lines. "His opinion was very influential for a long, long time around the White House," Secretary of State Shultz said later. In the weeks that followed both Reagan and those of his advisers who wanted to stick with Marcos often said in their attacks on Aquino: "This is what the editor of *The New York Times* thinks of her" (Bonner, 1987:395).

The Aquino campaign learned from the interview fiasco and reacted by hiring the New York public-relations firm of D.H. Sawyer. Marcos had hired the U.S. public-relations firm of Black, Manafort, Stone and Kelly. As Bonner (1987:397) notes, "It was symbolic of the Philippine election that both candidates had retained American public relations firms and that those firms concentrated on American, not Philippine, audiences." The Sawyer firm created a public-relations campaign designed to meet the formats and assumptions of the U.S. mass media. This campaign was relatively successful for it altered, in part, the rather dismal depiction and portrayal of Aquino and the movement provided by *The New York Times* in its December 1985 interview.

While the U.S. audience was of critical importance to the ultimate success of the movement, Aquino was unable to gain access to her home audience. Marcos controlled the Philippine media and had placed a blackout on press coverage of her activities. If Aquino was to achieve success in the February snap election, she needed to gain media attention at home and favourable media depictions in the United States. The strategy created by the Sawyer firm, with the somewhat reluctant acceptance of Aquino, was moderately successful in helping the movement achieve both goals. The strategy was, in part, based on three themes.

First, the *Times* interview revealed the need to train Aquino in the art and science of media management. Cory Aquino is a deeply private, religious woman. She appeared to be uneasy in public, and to Rosenthal and other Westerners she appeared to be weak, naive, and more like a housewife than a national leader. Mark Brown, a Sawyer employee, helped Aquino prepare for news conferences and other media events and went to work on her "image." He aimed at creating an appearance of toughness, competence, and integrity (Brown, 1986). Brown created mock press conferences in which Aquino prepared and enacted responses to meet the questions of nasty and suspicious reporters (Bonner, 1987:398).

Second, the issue of communism had to be presented in a manner palatable to the U.S. audience. While many voters in the Philippines did not see communism or the NPA as an important issue on the nation's agenda, policy-makers in Washington and in the editorial rooms of *The New York Times* viewed the conflict in the Philippines through East-West, Communist-Free World templates (Bonner,

1987). The U.S. military bases (Subic naval base and the Clark Air Force field) were seen as barriers to communist encroachment and critical to U.S. interests.

The American elite, it seems, did not have a clear view of the NPA. The NPA has no ties with and receives no support from foreign communist regimes (Rodriguez, 1985); is not dogmatically committed to Marxism-Leninism-Maoism (Lande, 1986); is not monolithic (Nemenzo, 1985); has built roads, schools, and provided basic services not provided by the Marcos regime (Bonner, 1987); and had grown in strength because of the corrupt practices of Marcos. Yet, even though the politics of the NPA (the so-called Philippine communists) were not high on the Philippine agenda, the U.S. policy-makers perceived communism to be the important issue.

Aquino had announced that she would appoint communists to her cabinet if they renounced violence. In addition, she had expressed opposition to the presence of U.S. bases on Philippine soil. In response to advice from her public-relations firm, she reversed these positions. In early January she announced that no communists would serve in an Aquino cabinet. She also announced that she would honour an agreement allowing the U.S. bases to remain until 1991.

Third, for the benefit of both the U.S. and Filipino audiences, Aquino's campaign had to be personalized. That is, Marcos had to become the centre of attack and controversy. Aquino was a reluctant campaigner, and personal attacks did not come easily for her. However, her staff successfully persuaded her to alter her campaign tactics, and rhetorical assaults on Marcos became part of her style. Such attacks, centring on the graft and fraud that was the mark of the Marcos regime and on Marcos's war record, led to the much-needed media attention. According to Bonner, the attack strategy "was based on the principle in American journalism that a person about whom something negative is said is to be given an opportunity to respond."

> This meant that Marcos would be called upon to answer the charges about his real estate holdings and his war record.... Since anything Marcos said was news, the Philippine television stations naturally ran excerpts of Marcos's television appearances. In order to make sense of his denials, Philippine journalists had to provide some background on the charges. Thus did the scandals reach the Philippine people. (Bonner, 1987:402-403)

Mark Brown worked with the Aquino movement and writes:

> The attacks succeeded in overcoming the Philippine press censorship of her campaign: They forced Marcos to respond, however indirectly, before his own media. For although the attacks were initially only reported in the foreign press, once Marcos responded to them the government controlled media could report Marcos's replies.... As the election approached, Aquino became adept at bouncing stories into the domestic press by way of the international press and Marcos's outraged response. (Brown, 1986:163)

The media-based strategy was responsive to the assumptions and routines of the U.S. media. As the analysis of the *New York Times* coverage of the Aquino-Marcos drama especially illustrates, the strategy did help to reverse the negative portrayal that was the result of the December 1985 interview.

Patterns of Coverage

A. Aquino, the Communist

The communist theme dominated coverage of the Philippines during the initial weeks of 1986 (Jan. 1-14). The *Times* reported on a Marcos rally in Taytay and underscored his claim that "armed communists rebels" were campaigning for Aquino (1-6-86). Predictably, there are articles reporting the response by Aquino, who stated that she would allow communists into her cabinet if they renounced violence; later she would announce that she would not appoint communists to her cabinet (1-7-86; 1-10-86).

Two remarkably imprescient opinion editorials helped readers frame the events. Raymond Bonner argued that the Philippines was "hurtling" towards an inevitable full-scale civil war and that the snap elections would not prevent violence and bloodshed (1-12-86). Max Singer suggested that Marcos had the potential to win a fair election and might institute progressive reforms (1-12-86).

B. Marcos, the Sick Crook

From January 14 to 22, the *Times* included a report of Representative Solarez's findings that Marcos may have acquired millions of dollars of property in the United States (1-16-86). A report also suggested that he was ill (1-17-86). The *Times* recorded Marcos's denials of these reports (1-20-86).

C. Marcos, the Phoney Hero

Between January 23 and 25, several important articles were published on Marcos. A front-page article reported on declassified U.S. Army records that demonstrated that Marcos had not been a heroic guerrilla leader and that his claim to be a wartime hero was untrue (1-13-86). Marcos had claimed to be a war hero for some twenty years and had used this as a theme for his campaign against Aquino. The *Times* also reported on attacks made by Aquino on Marcos. She called him a "dying dictator" and argued that the phoney war record was proof of Marcos's deception (1-24-86). Marcos defended himself, declaring that the attacks on his war record were absurd.

D. A Non-Communist Future

The *Times* recorded a dramatic shift of allegiance between January 26 and February 2. On January 26, the paper indicated that the Reagan administration had concluded that the departure of Marcos was important to a non-communist future in the Philippines (1-26-86). An article the same day summarized the "setbacks" that Marcos had endured (1-26-86). On the 27th, an editorial attacked Marcos for fabricating his World War II record and suggested this evidence was important for Filipinos to consider in evaluating Marcos as a candidate (1-27-86). Seven articles during this time period detailed Marcos's responses to the various allegations. Marcos employed direct attacks on those who had attacked him: He suggested that the international observers who were scheduled to observe the election were "meddlers and interventionists"; he asserted that Benigno Aquino, Jr., who had been murdered, was his secret supporter and that if elected, Cory Aquino would declare martial law; he declared that Western journalists often behaved like communists; he stated that the United States was meddling in the election and favoured Aquino; he denied that his rule had been corrupt and that all attacks on his war record and finances had been "orchestrated" through the foreign press under the direction of Aquino aides. On this last point, he was close to the truth (1-26-86; 1-27-86; 1-28-86).

The January 28 report on an Aquino rally in Manila marks a public shift in the Seth Mydans coverage. In this article, Mydans writes that Aquino is sincere, honest, and willing to sacrifice herself for the good of the country (1-28-86). Two articles during this time period make note of the "huge crowds" that had gathered to support Aquino during campaign rallies (1-28-86; 2-1-86).

E. The Election: A Potential Threat to U.S. Interests

The *Times* provided heavy coverage of the Philippines from February 2 to February 9. Mydans's article of February 2 detailed the support gained by the Aquino movement and mentioned that the movement had gained widespread support from middle-income and high-income Filipinos (2-2-86). Mydans wrote that further U.S. support for Marcos, in light of the popularity of Aquino, could threaten U.S. interests. Several articles were devoted to the election process. One article focused on the power of the Marcos presidency and on the various advantages that Marcos and his supporters maintained over Aquino (2-3-86; 2-4-86). The *Times* reported on a "detailed" speech by Aquino in which she attempted to present herself as a strong, substantive politician who was ready and able to deal with the communists. Aquino also attacked Marcos, calling him a "Philippine Pharaoh" (2-4-86).

One article during this time period reported on "American related issues." The military bases and communist insurgency were said to be the primary U.S. concerns in the upcoming elections (2-6-86). A February 7 report indicated that Filipinos were "determined" to vote despite intimidation and fraud at the polling booths (2-7-86).

F. A Fraudulent Election

From February 7 to 14, many reports and articles in the *Times* highlighted the widespread corruption of Marcos's supporters; international and national elections oversight teams had reported gratuitous fraud. Senator Richard Lugar, no friend of communism, accused the Marcos government of attempting to warp the elections (2-8-86). As was his pattern, Marcos accused the oversight teams of manipulating the voter figures against him (2-9-86). The Reagan administration, according to a mid-week report, was "disturbed" by the reports of widespread fraud (2-9-86). Later in the week Mydans reported that international election observers had witnessed significant fraud on the part of the Marcos campaign (2-10-86).

On February 11, the *Times* reported President Reagan's infamous remark that there had been fraud committed by both sides (2-11-86). On the same day, the *Times* editorialized that there should be a strong response to "Marcos's theft of the election." Reagan then announced that he would send Philip Habib to assess the situation (2-12-86).

The *Times* criticized Reagan for suggesting that both sides had been guilty of fraud (2-13-86). A Flora Lewis column argued that Reagan should urge Marcos to step down (2-13-86). In addition, a bipartisan consensus had emerged in Congress. Republican Robert Dole and Democrat Sam Nunn agreed that the United States should not support a regime that had been improperly elected (2-14-87).

G. Non-Violent Action

The *Times* focused on Aquino and the "People Power" movement from February 14 to 20, with the question of strategy and tactics appearing as a central concern. Aquino was reported to be considering a form of direct action and acts of civil disobedience (2-14-86). Two reports of violence (2-14-86; 2-15-86) appeared during the week. These reports provided an appropriate prelude to a letter, printed in full by the *Times*, from the Roman Catholic Bishops of the Philippines (2-15-87). The letter indicted the fraud of the election and urged Filipinos to make use of non-violence as the strategy of opposition. While the goals of the opposition were deemed just by the bishops, the means used to achieve these goals were considered to be as important. The bishops concluded the letter by suggesting, "Our acting must always be according to the Gospel of Christ, that is, in a peaceful, nonviolent way."

Reagan reversed his position on the fraud issue (2-16-86) and blamed Marcos for the fraud and violence. Marcos responded to the bishops by demanding that they prove their charges and suggested that he might have some of the clergy arrested (2-16-87). Representative Solarez, in an opinion editorial, urged the United States to disassociate itself from the Marcos government (2-16-87).

Aquino declared the birth of a non-violent campaign designed to bring down the Marcos regime (2-17-86). She called for a one-day nationwide strike, cancellation of classes, boycotts of Marcos-controlled banks, and delayed payments of utility bills, and she suggested that these actions were "experiment[s] with nonviolent forms of protest." Pope John Paul II, on the same day, expressed support for the bishops. To a nation in which some 80 per cent of the population adhere to the Catholic faith, the Pope stated: "I pray ardently that the Lord may help that dear nation find the peaceful and just way, without violence on any side, as is required for the true good of the entire Philippine community" (2-17-86).

Senator Lugar, the head of the U.S. delegation of observers, concluded that

Marcos should step down (2-18-86). The Senate voted 85 to 9 in favour of a resolution condemning the electoral corruption, and Secretary of State Shultz denounced the "fraud and widespread fraud and violence" perpetuated by the Marcos regime (2-20-86). Marcos responded by damning "foreign intervention" and guaranteed that he would charge those who engaged in civil disobedience with sedition and rebellion (2-20-86).

H. On the Soviet Union, Communism, and the Fall of the Marcos Regime
Good news for the Marcos campaign came from an unexpected quarter: The Soviet Union congratulated Marcos on his victory (2-20-86). Flora Lewis, in an opinion editorial, found it curious that the Reagan administration could support Nicaraguan and Angolan "freedom fighters" but not oppose Marcos (2-20-86). Anthony Lewis also suggested that a new consensus on human rights had emerged in the United States as a result of the tactics used by Marcos. The *Times* editorialized that the United States needed to use economic sanctions to push Marcos out of office (2-21-86). Marcos defended himself and suggested that his enemies came from abroad (2-22-86). Another article suggested that Marcos owned $300 million in New York City real estate (2-22-86).

The Philippine defence minister, Jaun Enrile, and the deputy chief of staff, Fidel Ramos, quit the government and took over the defence headquarters (2-23-86). These men represented many in the Philippine military who had grown to hate Marcos. The Soviet Union "stepped up" its support of Marcos (2-23-86). Aquino called for Filipinos to support Enrile, Ramos, and the other officers who had abandoned Marcos (2-23-86). Another article recounted the loss of support experienced by Marcos among the Philippine population (2-23-86).

Articles by James Reston, Stanley Karnow, Owen Harries, and Mortimer Zuckerman commented on what should be done in the Philippines (2-23-86). Reston called for Marcos to resign. Quoting an *Economist* article, he feared that further support for Marcos might lead to the storming of the presidential palace, the closing of the two bases, and a communist takeover of the Philippines. Karnow wrote that "the biggest challenge on the horizon is the rise of the communist-led new people's army" and suggested that the United States could do little to affect the future. Harries urged policy-makers to keep Marcos until a superior alternative appeared: "The case for removing Mr. Marcos forthwith turns essentially on whether Mrs. Aquino would do a better job of pulling the country together, and in particular, of combating the Communist New People's Army." Finally, Zuckerman argued that Marcos needed to step down and that the United States should pursue such an option to "enhance the prospect of democracy and retard the Communist insurgency."

President Reagan urged Marcos to avoid the use of force and threatened the termination of military aid if force were used (2-24-86). When a non-violent rally was held in Manila, the *Times* compared it to a 1960s anti-war rally: "Throughout, the scene evoked anti-war demonstrations in the United States of the 1960's.

Young men and women handed flowers and candy to soldiers. They planted daisies inside the barrels of their rifles. Priests and nuns knelt before the marines in the field's tall weeds and prayed (2-24-86). Again, the *Times* presented an article on the "Communist Movement" in the Philippines, but the piece suggested that the New People's Army was unlikely to play a major role in an Aquino government (2-24-86).

The White House, backed by an emerging Congressional consensus, called for Marcos to give up the presidency and offered him a refuge in the United States (2-25-86). The People Power movement with the assistance of the military seized the government-controlled radio and television stations. Aquino was sworn in as president of a provisional government. The Soviet newspaper *Pravda* asserted that the United States had assisted in a plan to overthrow Marcos and a *New York Times* editorial urged Marcos to step down (2-25-86). Tom Wicker lauded the power of the Philippine people and their choice to carry out a non-violent movement (2-25-86).

I. Marcos to Guam and Aquino to the Presidency

Marcos left the Philippines for Guam and the Reagan administration recognized Aquino as president (2-26-86). Filipinos celebrated the departure of Marcos without looting or engaging in unruly behaviour (2-26-86). Aquino moved quickly to exercise presidential power and informed some of the country's most powerful men of the role they would play in her government (2-26-86). President Reagan congratulated Aquino on the democratic outcome of the election.

Aquino formed her cabinet with military men in positions of great power. The *Times* reported that the New People's Army would continue insurgency actions (2-27-86). Anthony Lewis, in an opinion editorial, suggested that U.S. influence in the Philippines demonstrated that U.S. policy could be used to achieve peaceful change (2-27-86). One of the first acts initiated by the new president was to release thirty-four political prisoners.

Once again, the *Times* devoted a front-page article to the "Rapid growth of Communist insurgency in the Philippines" (2-26-86). This would be "a serious threat" to Aquino's efforts to promote democracy and economy. On the same day, two articles were published on the enormous wealth of the Marcos. Other articles reported that many Filipinos expressed great joy in reaction to the ascension of Aquino and were almost "giddily hopeful" that she would raise the standard of living. Many reportedly felt that twenty years with Marcos could not possibly be worse than a future with Aquino.

Implications

How did the People Power movement make use of the media and how did the media make use of the movement? The Aquino campaign staff, with its public-relations firm in part calling the shots, appeared to have reversed the dismal impression Aquino left with the *New York Times* editor after the December 1985 interview. That the editors came to hold a favourable view of Aquino is supported by a January 28, 1987, editorial: "Her achievements cry out for applause. The Philippine Republic is now the liveliest democracy in Asia, and more remarkably, the armed forces are committed to upholding that freedom" (1-28-87). This reversal may be due, in small part, to the media strategy adopted by Aquino and her public-relations firm. She carefully altered her position on the communist issue, making it acceptable to the U.S. audience. She went on the attack and kept the media's attention on the faults and weaknesses of Marcos. The U.S. mass media is regulated by the practice of giving those who are attacked an opportunity to respond. Aquino's attacks elicited responses from Marcos, which were reported by the *Times*. As such, this strategy also allowed the Aquino movement to break the media blackout that had been imposed by Marcos on the indigenous Philippine media; for when Marcos defended himself in public, the Philippine government media reported his message.

I do not wish to overestimate the influence of the media on U.S. elite perception. The shift in Aquino's favour may have been due to a number of other factors as well. Regardless, there is evidence that the favourable coverage of the mass media had a substantial impact (Bain, 1986).

In addition, Aquino continued to confront Marcos in an active but non-violent manner. She was a colourful, media-certified leader. Dressed in yellow and holding high the laban sign, she was visually attractive to reporters. The *Times* did not report on the non-violent dimension of the campaign until the final confrontation, and when the approach was reported it was covered in a positive fashion. Indeed, one reason why the movement gained popularity in the United States may be that the movement purposefully elected to make use of non-violent action. This strategy, linked with the conclusion that the movement had garnered the support of many middle-class and upper-class Filipinos, may have led the readers of *The New York Times* to a favourable view of Aquino and her movement – demonstrating that a movement committed to non-violence can make use of colourful media-oriented strategies and achieve a modest success.

Significantly, *The New York Times* missed some important dimensions of the confrontation in the Philippines and overdramatized other factors, and since *The New York Times* serves as a major source of information on social movements in the non-Western arena, the defects in its coverage should be of some concern. One example is the communist theme that echoed throughout the paper's coverage of the Philippines. U.S. writers and policy-makers were inordinately concerned with the NPA, and this concern possibly served to filter out a clear view of the 60 per cent of Filipinos who are desperately poor. To view the Philippines through the East-West template is to miss the local factors that make up the Filipino culture. Rhetorical critics who possess at least a partial understanding of a given culture can help in the identification of such oversights.

The *Times* also did not devote much attention to the actions and rhetoric of the Catholic church during this time period. The Filipinos are a deeply religious people, and many (among them Cory Aquino) are practising Catholics. The Catholic station Radio Veritas was a major source of information for the People Power movement and Cardinal Sin provided indispensable leadership. The readers of the *Times* learned little about the role of the Catholic church in the movement or about Cardinal Sin.

The interface between the study of social movements and media becomes increasingly important as leaders and members of social movements in non-Western settings become cognizant of the need to make use of the mass media to influence popular perceptions. In the past, social movements have used premodern means of communication and have not included the mass media in strategy planning. The Aquino movement stands as an example of how a social movement can respond, in a modestly effective way, to the demands of the modern mass media. Leaders and members of social movements devoted to non-violent change have much to learn from the Philippine example.

Notes

***The author expresses his thanks to Professor Robert Cathcart, Queens College, for the suggestion that social movements might be studied in the context of the global village.

1. I will be using Johnson (1987) and Bonner (1987) to assess the coverage of the Philippines by *The New York Times*. Both works earned strong reviews in *The New York Times Book Review*. Bain (1987:9) suggests that Johnson's book "may well be the best book on the Ferdinand Marcos-Corazon Aquino election campaign and on the People Power that toppled a tyrant." I rely heavily on Bonner because his work documents how *The New York Times* functioned with respect to the Philippines. There are few other published documents on this particular subject.

References

Aquino, C. (1986). "Speech at Harvard University, 20 Sept 1986." *Boston Sunday Globe*, November 21.

Bain, D. (1986). "Letter From Manila," *Columbia Journalism Review*, May/June.

Bain, D. (1987). "Charade at Malacanang Palace," *The New York Times Book Review*, June 14.

Bartu, F. (1986). "The Philippines: Farewell to Illusions," *Swiss Review of World Affairs*.

Bonner, R. (1987). *Waltzing with a Dictator*. New York: Times.

Bresnan, J., ed. (1986). *Crisis in the Philippines*. Princeton: Princeton University Press.

Brock-Utne, B. (1986). *Education for Peace*. New York: Athene.

Brown, M. (1986). "Aquino, Marcos and the White House," in "The Snap Election," *Granta*, Vol.18 (Spring).

Cathcart, R. (1976). "Movements: Confrontations as Rhetorical Form," *Southern Speech Communication Journal*, 43.

Clad, J. (1986). "Which Way is Up?" *Far Eastern Economic Review*, November 6.

Editorial (1987). "Democracy in the Philippines," *The New York Times*, January 17.

Fenton, J. (1986). In "The Snap Election," *Granta*, Vol.18 (Spring).

Frank, D. (1982). *In Search of Peace: The Rhetoric of Nonviolent Action*. Dissertation, University of Oregon.

Frank, D. (1981). "Shalom Aschev: Rituals of the Israeli Peace Movement," *Communication Monographs*, 48.

Friend, T. (1986). "Philippine-American Tensions in History." In Bresnan (1986).

Gitlin, T. (1980). *The Whole World is Watching: Mass Media in the Making and Unmaking of the New Left*. Berkeley: University of California Press.

Hernandez, C. (1986). "Reconstituting the Political Order." In Bresnan (1986).

Ileko, R. (1985). "The Past in the Present Crisis." In R. May and B. Johnson, eds., *The Four Days of Courage*. New York: Free Press, 1987.

Kadushin, C. (1974). *The American Intellectual Elite*. Boston: Little, Brown.

Lande, C. (1986). "The Political Crisis." In Bresnan (1986).

Laxalt, P. (1986). "My Conversations with Ferdinand Marcos: A Lesson in Personal Diplomacy," *Policy Review*, Summer.

May, R. and F. Nemenzo, eds. (1986). *The Philippines After Marcos*. New York: St. Martin's Press.

Nemenzo, F. (1985). "The Left and the Traditional Opposition." In May and Nemenzo (1986).

Resource Center for Philippine Concerns (1986). "From the Publishers," *Solidaridad II*, 10.

Rodriguez, F. (1985). *The Marcos Regime*. New York: Vantage Press.

Rosenberg, D. "The Philippines: Aquino's First Year," *Current History*, 86.

Rosenblum, M. (1981). *Coups and Earthquakes*. New York: Harper.

Sharp, G. (1973). *The Politics of Nonviolent Action*. Boston: Porter Sargent.

Sharp, G. (1986). "Foreword: A Brave Example to the World." In M. Mercado, *People Power*. Manila: Reuter.

Sigal, L. (1973) *Reporters and Officials*. Lexington: D.C. Heath.

Steward, C., Smith, C., and Denton, R. (1984). *Persuasion and Social Movements*. Prospect Heights: Waveland.

Aliran and the Struggle for Freedom of Expression in Malaysia

Stephen A. Douglas and Sara U. Douglas

IN THE LATE 1980s events in Malaysia provoked a crescendo of controversy about the condition of that country's political system. The worst fears were expressed in a December 1986 headline in *The Bulletin* (Australia): "Shades of Marcos as Malaysia Slides Toward Totalitarianism" (Pinwill, 1986). It is a startling comparison, for until recently virtually all observers would have ranked Malaysia as the most democratic among the varied political systems of Southeast Asia. And the governing elite's rhetoric continues to stress and claim continuity with a liberal, moderate, and tolerant political tradition. Ironically, these claims gain some credibility from the very existence within Malaysia of escalating cries of alarm about vanishing freedoms and "democracy in fetters."

While there is no lack of attention to these claims and counterclaims in journalistic quarters, more scholarly considerations of Malaysian politics have dealt with freedom of expression only peripherally. Recent studies have emphasized instead the regime's utilization of such approaches to conflict management as co-optation and neopatrimonial bargaining. Especially where the challenge from a newly mobilized Islam is concerned, these techniques have been explicated in the works of Crouch (1982), Gale (1981), Barraclough (1985), Funston (1980), Mauzy (1983), and others. Although many aspects of intra-elite alignments and actions have been illuminated nicely in these studies, they do not adequately address the problem of maintaining democratic politics in a relatively prosperous multicultural society experiencing rapid social mobilization. Among the omissions is the valiant role played by scattered idealists, individuals, and organizations whose willingness to hold government to its proclaimed principles stands between the regime and its total domination of political discourse.

In the long run the authoritarian trend may prevail, and all channels for expression of opposition or discontent may simply be shut down. For the time being, such conspicuous and conclusive repression is not the government's style. A small opening remains for expression of dissent, an opening so hazardous that it is breached only because of the presence in Malaysia of a handful of courageous and resourceful people who insist on speaking out in opposition to the regime. Their dedication to freedom is matched by their persistent and creative use of media. Their activism not only serves to inspire and reassure other Malaysians who are potential resistors; it also has begun to receive enough attention in such regional media as *Far Eastern Economic Review* and *Asiaweek* and in various non-governmental organization circles that it may serve to inspire democratic, oppositional groups in neighbouring countries. Not all individuals who champion free and critical political speech operate within the same organizational framework. But one "social reform" society, Aliran, is clearly the most vigorous and prominent of the progressive organizations.

More frequently than once a week the newspaper-reading public encounters statements by Aliran on a wide range of societal issues. Detailed and generally more sharply oppositional discussions are published in the journal, *Aliran Monthly*. Aliran also produces books and audio-cassettes and has plans to produce video-cassettes. The organization also has made plans for outreach, mainly through study circles, to unskilled workers and related disadvantaged sectors. Although Aliran's membership is small, probably less than 250, it is large enough to have a surprising impact in a country where a substantial proportion of the 16.5 million population has little experience with democratic principles and practices.

Aliran (Aliran Kesedaran Negara or, loosely, "national consciousness trend") is a social movement, multi-ethnic in its philosophy, policies, programs, and membership, and it is the first, though no longer the only, organization of its kind in Malaysia. Formed in 1977 for the purpose of raising social consciousness and encouraging social action and social justice, it seeks to maintain a comprehensive concept of change that is bound to no particular time frame and no specific issue.

While Aliran's public philosophy, which has been formulated into thirty-three basic principles, promotes social and economic justice and political freedom in fairly abstract terms, the organization's day-to-day struggle is shaped by the severity of ethnic conflict in Malaysia. It is a country in which substantial Chinese and Indian minorities are systematically disadvantaged by legislative, administrative, and even constitutional provisions. Whereas most political actors representing both the minorities and the Malay majority accept a form of communal corporatism as the political framework, Aliran, along with such like-minded associations as the Malaysian Bar Association, The Consumers' Association of Penang, and the Institute for Social Analysis, does not.

A fifteen-member executive committee, elected at the Annual General Meeting, comprises Aliran's official policy-making body. A former professor of political science at Universiti Sains Malaysia in Penang, Dr. Chandra Muzaffar, has been the organization's only president. A forceful and articulate speaker and an energetic and skilled writer, Muzaffar has a vigour and devotion that are obviously crucial to the organization's effectiveness and even survival. In fact, this extensive reliance upon and identification with an individual leader is recognized as a serious liability. Yet in its brief twelve years' existence Aliran has emerged as the most active organization of its type in Malaysia. And as it jousts with the Malaysian political establishment, Aliran badly needs the legitimacy that it derives from its growing international reputation.

Since its inception Aliran has been in the thick of most significant national controversies. In the 1980s, however, a confluence of critical events generated some exceptionally intense and visible exchanges on freedom of expression. On the one hand, a series of financial scandals involving public figures provoked Aliran and kindred organizations to campaign for public disclosure and prosecution of corrupt officials. On the other hand, the 1986 economic decline stemming from low commodity prices and, more recently, a schism within the dominant United Malay National Organization (UMNO) put the government on edge and probably enhanced greatly the temptation to suppress criticism from vocal but politically weak groups. Under these conditions the crucial but precarious role of Aliran can best be analyzed through consideration of three related dimensions of the struggle for freedom of expression in Malaysia. The three are, first, the debate over the Official Secrets (Amendments) Act, 1986; second, the recurring conflicts over regulation of societies; and, third, the limitations of the mass media.

The Official Secrets (Amendments) Act, 1986

The government's bill to amend the Official Secrets Act (OSA) was the immediate cause of the December 1986 *Bulletin* headline and the focal point in 1986 of the debate on liberalism in Malaysia. Finally adopted on December 5, 1986, by a parliamentary vote of 131 to 21, the amendments created new categories of secrecy, empowered many public officials to classify documents according to those categories, and stipulated mandatory imprisonment of at least one year for any person convicted of possessing or receiving (unless "contrary to his desire") information so classified. Finer points of legalistic interpretation inevitably came into play in the debate; however, the larger issues were broadly political. On the government's side the justification for making national security a priority was based on three imperatives related to stability, as succinctly expressed by the attorney-general: "The amendments to the Official Secrets Act would ... ensure (1) economic growth and (2) racial harmony and that there would be (3) no provocation to overthrow the Government" (*The Star*, Nov. 8, 1986:2).

Speaking for Aliran, Chandra Muzaffar made a strong and direct response: "It is a pity that the Attorney-General has merely mouthed a series of hackneyed clichés about 'national security,' 'economic growth,' and 'racial harmony' in trying to justify the OSA amendments" (Muzaffar, 1986:23). Aliran was not alone in arguing that the justifications for the OSA amendments were feeble and wrong. With obvious approbation a group of journalists cited *The Economist* statement linking press restrictions to negative economic growth: "It is likely to ... frighten off foreign investment and stifle the ideas needed for further growth" (*The Star*, Nov. 8,

1986:15). Similarly, the claim that inter-ethnic conflicts and sensitivities require special efforts to suppress potentially provocative information was met by the argument that, to minimize suspicion and misunderstanding, it is especially important for channels of communication to remain open and free in multiracial Malaysia. Moreover, limitations on freedom of expression would only aggravate the already excessive Malaysian rumor mill.

In the context of a series of revelations about self-serving practices among public officials, the OSA issue also became a vehicle for renewed and intensified charges of corruption. Most issues of *Aliran Monthly* featured denunciations of financial scandals and other ethical misadventures of public officials and UMNO party leaders. The main thrust of the attack was summarized in a *Star* editorial:

> Indeed, the new amendment seems designed to enable corrupt officers who sell secrets to make even more money. After all, they can now claim that they are taking bigger risks. Further, another new section, enabling anyone in the administration to classify anything secret, could encourage corruption. Officers can now stamp ordinary bits of information secret to enhance their value in the information black market." (*The Star*, Nov. 23, 1986:8)

This argument was only slightly more cynical than other frequently expressed questions, such as: How can government agencies and officials be held accountable when an OSA prevents the public from being informed of their activities? How can an uninformed public participate meaningfully in any civic affairs? How, in the face of OSA restrictions, can scholars conduct research on such topics as national economic trends? Recognizing that these questions implied the need for positive action to ensure freedom of information, Aliran played a leading role in organizing a Freedom of Information Campaign Committee. The Committee's immediate purpose was to combat the OSA, but with passage of the amendments certain the more distant objective of promoting a freedom of information act took precedence.

In early December 1986, the government, proclaiming a commitment to responsiveness and flexibility, announced revisions in the OSA amendments bill. The new version specified a narrower range of documents subject to classification and provided that only public officers appointed by a minister or chief minister of a state could classify documents as secret. Generally critics of the amendments were not mollified. For wavering members of parliament belonging to the Barisan Nasional coalition, however, the changes helped to provide a rationale for going along with the coalition's parliamentary whip. None of the members broke ranks, and debate on the OSA ended abruptly with the decisive affirmative vote. Any notion that this stronger legislation would immediately curb political disharmony, however, was strikingly contradicted by subsequent events. As the unprecedented contest for the presidency of UMNO developed in early 1987, for example, the incumbent's penchant for secrecy and advocacy of the OSA amendments became an issue for the challengers (*Asiaweek*, 1986). The OSA controversy, sparked by Aliran, had thus contributed to a fundamentally significant conflict within the governing party.

In addition, the controversy stimulated a number of organizations to new levels of activism. The Freedom of Information Campaign Committee attracted some independent, individual supporters. But for almost all of its resources, including its mass membership, the committee depended upon a number of constituent organizations. These included the National Union of Journalists, the Malaysian Bar Council, the Malaysian Trades Union Congress, the Environmental Protection Society of Malaysia, the Selangor Graduates Society, the Federation of Malaysian Consumer Organizations, the Malaysian Association of Engineers, and, especially, Aliran. Two political parties, the Democratic Action Party (DAP) and the Malaysian People's Socialist Party (PSRM), were active in the oppositional campaign; the DAP worked closely with other organizations while the PSRM staged more demonstrative events, including a rally in Johore Baru at which a copy of the amendments bill was burned. Many local groups also expressed strong opposition to the bill, among them the Justice and Peace Commission of Penang, the Selangor and Federal Territory Consumers Association, the Johore Civil Rights Committee, the Christian Family and Social Movement (Ipoh), the Kuching Reporters Fellowship, the Sabah Christian Fellowship, and the Kuala Lumpur and Selangor Chambers of Commerce and Industry. At least one international body, the Confederation of ASEAN Journalists, lent its voice to the cause.

Societies, Registration, and Group Politics
Except for the Confederation of ASEAN Journalists, all of these organizations come under the purview of the Societies Act of 1966 and are subject to its enforcement by the Registrar of Societies, an agent of the Home Ministry. A relic of colonialism, the Societies Act requires that any club, company, partnership, or association of seven persons or more be registered and report annually any changes in bylaws, officers, financial condition, and so forth (Douglas and Pedersen, 1974). Whereas critics regard this legislation as onerous, the prime minister, Dr. Mahathir Mohamad, had said, in effect, "Don't worry, we don't use societies' registration as a means of suppressing opposition." A similar contention in the OSA debate was somewhat more credible: Mahathir claimed that only three people had been prosecuted under the original Official Secrets Act between 1957 and 1986. The opposition's retort that the correct number is more like five did not detract greatly from his point – that the OSA had not been abused through excessive application. Deregistration is a different matter, however; during the last three months of 1980 alone, eighty-six associations were deregistered "for various violations" (Aliran Kesedaran Negara, 1981: 357). And this was a period when Aliran itself was feeling the pressure of the registrar's scrutiny.

In October 1980 Aliran issued a statement questioning the inequitable consequences of salary increases and subsidized loans for some public employees. Appearing as a letter to the editor in the *Star* newspaper and signed by Chandra

Muzaffar as president of Aliran, the statement was relatively brief and moderate in tone. Yet it was specifically mentioned by the Registrar of Societies as the basis for his subsequent order giving Aliran until November 10, 1980, to provide reasons why its registration should not be cancelled. During the ensuing weeks Aliran officers sought to resolve the crisis first through private discussions with officials in the Ministry of Home Affairs and then through extensive public pleading of their case. At one point, Deputy Home Affairs Minister Sanusi Junid told parliament that Aliran was guilty of taking the matter to the public. This publicity campaign, to which Aliran readily admitted, involved not only press releases and letters to public officials but also letters to selected private individuals and potentially sympathetic organizations. It propelled Aliran to an elevated level of visibility and it contributed, apparently, to the association's survival.

This last point would be difficult to prove beyond any doubt. A more timid Aliran might have survived as well. The fact is, however, that Aliran's quick, well-publicized criticisms generate so much visibility that the organization cannot simply and inconspicuously be silenced. In addition to setting forth alternative views, Aliran's statements thus provide a form of defence against the state that the organization denounces. In a sense, Aliran cannot afford subtlety and indirection. Its executive committee's widely disseminated reaction to the government's March 1988 proposal to revise the Societies Act accordingly included such comments as: "When one is so blatant about the perpetuation of one's self-interest, doubts begin to arise ... about ... justice and fairness. It has now reached a point when the leadership does not even attempt to camouflage its obsession with its own position and powers" (Committee Against Repression, 1988:95).

From the regime's point of view, if control or acquiescence cannot be achieved, perhaps the next best thing is some degree of balance between the left and right poles of opposition. Conservative Islam pulls so hard in one direction that at times the generally countervailing pressure of progressive politics manufactured by Aliran and related groups may actually be welcomed by authorities who wish to appear moderate, balanced, and, of course, "liberal." This formulation oversimplifies a dynamic political environment in which interests determined by emergent commercial and financial relationships are superimposed uneasily onto traditional communal and regional rivalries, and in which religion and ideology may take unexpected if temporary turns. But in the face of such complexity, political leaders may be all the more likely to seek and employ simplifying perspectives.

In any event official and legalistic attempts to discourage dissent throughout the 1980s instead provoked it. In 1981, when the government introduced amendments to strengthen the Societies Act, extensive protests materialized. The Malaysian Bar Council staged an illegal demonstration outside of parliament, and a newly created Secretariat of the Conference of Societies assumed the task of coordinating and sustaining opposition to regulation of voluntary associations. The Freedom of Information Campaign Committee, which was formed in 1986, thus may be seen as a sequel, albeit with a different issue at stake, to the Secretariat.

Other issues stimulated mobilization and coalescence of progressive organizations. Among these are the plan to bury nuclear waste near the village of Papan in Perak state, the proposed commercial development of the Bukit Cina burial site in Malacca, and the imposition of unfavourable wage and working conditions on civil servants and other public employees. All of these issues have been cited in surveys as illustrative of the growing capability of Malaysian citizens to mount determined and effective responses to unpopular government policies (Das, 1986; Muzaffar, 1986a).

As a key participant in the Secretariat of the Conference of Societies, Aliran is foremost among a handful of public-interest organizations that have established themselves as particularly voluble, "thorns in the flesh of the country" according to one government official (Aznam, 1987). In the late stages of the OSA debate, ominous statements about "certain groups" suggested that patience in official circles was wearing thin. The following excerpt from a position paper signed by Gurmit Singh, President of the Selangor Graduates Society, (SGS), exemplifies the "thorniness" of such groups:

> Most of us have been very concerned about mass media (especially press) freedom in Malaysia. On numerous occasions SGS has called for some democratization in the ownership, management and operations of all forms of media in the country. But, alas, the response has been negative and the recent coverage of the General Elections by the media has dramatized the absence of any meaningful democracy in this sector!
>
> We have grown up saddled with the Official Secrets Act (OSA), one of the many repressive laws bequeathed to us by our colonial masters on Merdeka Day. The years of Independence, instead of lessening the restrictions, have instead seen three tightenings of this particular piece of legislation, the latest proposal ... being the unkindest cut of all. This example of overkill has even moved our controlled and docile press (including the Organization of Newspapers Editors) to protest!
>
> In a way, this move should not be a surprise. It seems to be part of a pattern that started unfolding in January 1985 when the Prime Minister began hitting out against critics of his policies. The innuendoes have intensified in 1986 and the Government has been hypersensitive to criticisms over the BMF and Memali affairs. This move may be the masterstroke to gag all critics (not just journalists) by depriving them of any means of finding out how the country is run. SGS views this move as tantamount to imprisoning public accountability. (Singh, 1986:11)

Needless to say, the Selangor Graduates Society joined Aliran on the roster of seven organizations and parties accused of "trying to destroy the country's political and social fabric" (*The Star*, Dec. 15, 1986:1). The other five included the Consumers' Association of Penang, Environmental Protection Society of Malaysia, the Bar Council, Democratic Action Party (DAP), and Parti se-Islam Malaysia (PAS). The disclosure of this list of seven occurred just after the passage of the OSA amendments and followed a buildup of ominous references to "certain groups" that were trying to destabilize and destroy the government. The implicit threat of official and coercive action against the groups was magnified by occasional speculation, even by the prime minister, about certain associations' receipt of financial support from Zionist sources.

Without knowing the extent to which such comments from official sources are purposeful and orchestrated, it is nonetheless reasonable to conclude that they are intimidating. In private, Aliran activists readily admit as much. Yet publicly, the targeted groups react with characteristic speed and firmness. The president of the Bar Council responded to publication of the "list of seven" by stating that the allegations of the government spokesman were "untrue, mischievous, and misconceived." The Consumers' Association of Penang issued a release labelling the government's position "outrageous." At a more ideological level, denigration (if not harassment) of groups is consistent with the regime's negative view of Western-style pressure-group politics. The prime minister, for example, has explicitly labelled interest groups as the worst aspect of democratic politics because their activity "ensure[s] that a minority will have a greater say in the affairs of a country than their numbers justify" (Selvaratnam, 1982:261).

Not-So-Critical Journalism

In the related area of mass media regulation, the Malaysian government has adopted a more directly repressive approach. Aliran, accordingly, has moved freedom of the press to centre stage in its struggle to check the regime's authoritarian machinations. The May/June 1986 number of *Aliran Monthly* reported on an instance of suppression of a newspaper, the *National Echo*, in some detail. Staffed by a group of idealistic journalists determined to resist all incentives to self-censorship, the *Echo* encountered close scrutiny from another agency of the Ministry of Home Affairs, the Special Branch of the police. Admonitions from the Special Branch to reporters and editors alike were rejected, with the editors doubting that the government would do anything so blatantly repressive as directly ban the newspaper. Apparently they were correct. Instead, various government agencies and representatives expressed their unhappiness with the newspaper to the *Echo*'s owner and reminded him that his many business interests depended upon government contracts and co-operation. When the newspaper staff rejected the owner's directive for more moderate presentation of views, the owner brought production of the paper to a halt (Fong, 1986).

Virtually no one claims that the press in Malaysia is free to publish all bad news, including criticism, along with the good. No one, that is, other than those occupying the highest positions in the government. Foremost among these is the prime minister, who asserted during the mid-1986 general election campaign: "There are now freer reports and comments in our newspapers and magazines, more than at any other time in the history of Malaysia. Often these are without foundation and only seek to sow confusion and doubt. This is the price of democracy. The government's only weapon is truth and positive action" (*New Straits Times*, July 26, 1986:12). The summary view of more critical observers, however, is diametrically opposed. Commenting on the same election campaign, the *Aliran Monthly* said: "The Barisan leadership's cynical manipulation of television in particular in the General Election was a clear indication that it had hardly any regard for values such as fairplay and evenhandedness. Television was not the only medium of mass communication it abused with total contempt. Almost all the dailies in nearly every language were transformed into instruments of party propaganda" (Muzaffar, 1986b:24).

Aliran's view of the problem relies partly on the allegation that the domestic press is severely self-censored in response to the government's preferential treatment of co-operative journalists and ominous advice to those inclined to be more critical. An example of government advice was a speech in which Deputy Prime Minister Ghafar Baba asserted, "Writers are free to contribute ideas including criticisms of the Government but they must criticize constructively and objectively." He went on to advise journalists against "making assumptions" and added, in language that might have been borrowed from communications with the ownership of the *Echo*, that publishers, in "guiding" their writers, should do so "taking into account the social environment and the administrative system" (*New Straits Times*, April 12, 1987:7). While the meaning of such remarks is anything but clear, it is not unreasonable to suppose that people responsible for selecting and formulating news stories would have felt that any reportage that might be construed as non-constructive or non-objective could put their careers in jeopardy. And the same reaction seems equally appropriate to the prime minister's previous pronouncement in his National Day speech, as blithely reported by the *New Straits Times*: "Dr. Mahathir advised the people not to use the freedom of the Press [sic], which was claimed to exist in other countries, as a yardstick for judging the local mass media" (*New Straits Times*, Aug. 31, 1986:1).

It is one thing for a government to make pronouncements that could inhibit press coverage and content. It is another for a government to mobilize the press in support of policies or positions or, simply, of incumbents. This is the transgression to which Aliran has objected most strenuously. One of two recent and outstanding cases in point was the so-called constitutional crisis in 1984 during which a virtual news blackout – the issue was deemed sensitive – was followed by a strong governmental publicity campaign. As one observer described this development: "The press was 'turned on.' It was time to bring the people into the issue: mass rallies in all the state capitals; full coverage. Articles and editorials appeared, recalling the nationalist struggle against the colonial power and the people's aspirations for democracy" (Tan, 1984). A second case involved the general election campaign of mid-1986. The major complaints emphasized the press's tendency to carry Barisan Nasional releases in full text while opposition statements were trimmed, buried in inconspicuous locations, or neglected altogether. Most news-papers carried a series of sharply exaggerated – if not scurrilous – pro-Barisan car-toons without any indication that these were paid advertisements. The *Straits Times* group regularly praised Barisan candidates and policies in its ostensibly ob-jective coverage of the campaign and election.

Parties and organizations – like Aliran – critical of the government and put off by the media seek to publish their own weekly, monthly, or less regular journals and pamphlets. These, of course, are especially vulnerable to the legal apparatus of press regulation. One highly visible message that excessive criticism would not be tolerated was the 1983 withdrawal from the Institute for Social Analysis of its permit to publish its hard-hitting magazine, *Nadi Insan*. The message was strongly reinforced by passage of a Publication and Print Act (1984) and subsequent amendments (1987), which require annual renewal of each publishing permit, deny any appeal to the judiciary by publishers whose permits are revoked, and give the home minister "absolute discretion" in restricting publication (Commit-tee Against Repression, 1988:18-20). This legislation simply added to the avail-able bases for government action against wayward printing presses; previous pros-ecutions under the Sedition Act, the Internal Security Act, and Essential Security Cases (Amendments) Regulations (ESCAR), though infrequent, already had put journalists on notice.

In the case of *Aliran Monthly*, a partial and somewhat whimsical ban has been in effect since 1983, when Aliran first requested permission to publish the *Monthly* in Bahasa Malaysia as well as English. Even though most issues of the monthly have included one or more articles in Bahasa Malaysia and, furthermore, there is doubt whether the law requires a separate permit for each language of publica-tion, the Home Ministry flatly denied the request.

By 1985 direct restriction of even the foreign press was becoming more com-mon, and in a sense Aliran was thus in the company of the *Far Eastern Economic Review* and the *Asian Wall Street Journal*, whose Kuala Lumpur correspondents were expelled from the country in 1985 and 1986 respectively. (In the case of James Clad of the *Far Eastern Economic Review*, prosecution under the OSA had resulted in conviction and a $4,000 fine (DAS, 1986:60-62). Ultimately, in the *Asian Wall Street Journal* episode, the prime minister charged that foreign press cover-age of Malaysian economics and finance was biased in favour of Zionist efforts to subvert Malaysian economic development.

These experiences of foreign journalists undoubtedly have a chilling effect on domestic journalists as well. Consistent with allegations of self-censorship, some Malaysian journalists have begun to defend an "Asian model of journalism in which the press works with the government to build a national consensus" (Lau, 1987). The thorough and persuasive analysis of this problem in *Aliran Monthly* (May/June 1985) was not only critical of the press establishment but also linked the problem to Malaysia's social and political structure and relied upon, among other sources, Ellul's study of propaganda (Muzaffar, 1985).

The scarcity of this type of analysis points to another sector in which politically relevant expression is problematic, namely the intellectual community. The recent history and political prospects of academics and scholars reveal a strikingly familiar pattern. A stiffly prohibitive law or two, though infrequently invoked, combines with cautionary (and in this case sometimes insulting) admonitions to give pause to would-be critics within university circles. The key legislation affecting campus life is the University and University Colleges Act. Although it delimits student activity particularly severely, it also "allows government officials to dominate university councils" (Muzaffar, 1986a:143) and generally contributes to an atmosphere best described as lethargic and suppressed. Chandra Muzaffar's resignation from the faculty at Universiti Sains Malaysia was at least partly an expression of frustration with the conditions foisted upon and accepted by most intellectuals.

A small assortment of recent paperback books represents another mode of expression for critics of the government. But most of the authors, like Chandra Muzaffar, have no formal association with any university. The most visible of these volumes, all of which appeared in the second half of the 1980s, are Muzaffar's *Freedom in Fetters*, Lim Kit Siang's *Malaysia: Crisis of Identity*, Kua Kia Soong's *Of Myths and Mystification*, K. Das's *The Musa Dilemma*, and the multi-authored *Tangled Web: Dissent, Deterrence, and the 27 October 1987 Crackdown in Malaysia*. Each seeks in an aggressively outspoken fashion to expose a wide range of shortcomings in the country's governance. Typically, however, inference that this avenue of protest is secure must be qualified by an ominous exception, in this case the prosecution and conviction under the Internal Security Act of the printer and publisher of a 1983 book entitled *Oppressors and Apologists*. The sentence, handed down in July 1987, was limited to a fine of $800. But the case revealed again the availability to the regime of means of repression and a disposition, however unpredictable and sporadic, to use them.

Conclusions

There is, then, a strained incompatibility between the governmental preference for compliance and positive feedback on the one hand and a persistent set of critics who organize and publish and protest on the other. In the current Malaysian political milieu, in fact, the state's pursuit of acquiescence frequently provokes noisy dissent. A further irony is that Barisan leaders themselves can then cite their failure to silence all opposition as evidence that the regime is open and tolerant. A *New Straits Times* article thus appeared under the headline: "Criticisms a Sign PM's Liberal, says [Minister of Education] Anwar" (*New Straits Times*, April 14, 1987:4). But an attempt to comprehend trends and undercurrents must go beyond the observation that there is political cacophony in Malaysia. While that observation fairly contradicts any description of this system as totalitarian, it neglects a number of reverberating factors that are revealed by Aliran's struggle and help explain the infirmities of democracy in Malaysia.

Aliran's emphasis on clarity and openness is noteworthy because one aspect of Malaysian politics that seems to moderate discussion, soften the edges of conflict, and sustain, among other things, confusion about the real significance of repressive legislation is a style of ambiguity. Perhaps related to the circumlocutory style of Malay speech and underlying cultural complexities, politics in Malaysia has been described as consisting of especially imprecise bargains, threats, and promises. Just what is the significance, for example, of the constitutional provision that Islam is Malaysia's official religion? "Politics of ambiguity" apparently was first applied to Malaysia by Cynthia Enloe (1970). Other scholars have found the term apt, and more than one contributor to *Negara*, the publication of the government's Department of National Unity, has borrowed the concept and presented it as a positive feature of Malaysian politics.

Whether it is a virtue or a fault, and it seems likely that a case could be made both ways, the ambiguity in the application of restrictions on speech and association is clear enough. Perhaps the most fundamentally ambiguous issue is the notion that "sensitive issues" may not be discussed. Most general surveys of Malaysian politics dutifully report that in 1971 the Sedition Act was amended to disallow public discussion of the powers and privileges of the king and sultans, the laws on citizenship, the status of Malay as sole national and official language, and the special rights and privileges of the Bumiputra peoples. Yet most people who spend even a little time in Malaysia know that such topics are discussed frequently. And if the meaning and limits of the "sensitive issues" proscription are vague, it should be less surprising that other restrictions on freedom of expression, such as the OSA and societies registration and press controls, are uncertain in intent and application.

Of course Aliran's explicit and confrontational approach is out of step with the politics of ambiguity and thus, to some extent, at odds with the dominant cultural biases in Malaysia.

If Aliran's survival therefore seems unlikely, some hope may be drawn from the particular configuration of interests and parties that has obtained in Malaysian politics for the last several years. According to the triangular model already touched upon, a government confronted by oppositions that are ideological enemies may find ways to benefit from their enmity. Parti se-Islam Malaysia (PAS) and related Islamic groups generally press for more extensive Islamicization. Aliran, the Democratic Action Party, and other parties and groups criticize the government from a very different, roughly leftist, point of view. Occasionally these different sets of opponents join forces for momentary expressions of shared grievances. In general, however, the progressive opposition is so fundamentally different from PAS and other Islamic elements that pressure from one of these directions tends to counteract pressure from the other. It is in the regime's interest, as long as either of these sets of opponents is at all active, to allow the other to be similarly vocal and visible.

Part of this balancing act consists of co-optation and other forms of rewards and inducements calculated to keep both sets of challenges in the game, each largely dependent upon governmental favours in its quest for some advantage over the other. Additionally, the same function may be attributed to legislation which is, in principle, ominously restrictive. In practice these regulations, such as the OSA, Societies Act, and various press controls, are applied with restraint and discretion and thus become another mechanism for fine-tuning the balance between the left and right opposition. Related official pronouncements, sometimes incorporating the ultimate ambiguous reference to "certain groups," operate similarly. The strain towards harmony as well as the resultant dissonance thus may be seen as part of the same elaborate process of encouraging opponents to recognize their rivalry. Thorough and even-handed enforcement would minimize these uses of control and would even tend to drive the Islamic opposition and the liberal-reformist opposition together.

An adequate analysis of this hypothesis would require a separate study of considerable depth. One of the most suggestive illustrations of a decision reflecting the regime's purposeful manipulation of controls is the recent reiteration of the Home Ministry's rejection of Aliran's request for permission to publish its magazine in Bahasa Malaysia (*The Star*, May 10, 1987:5). One can at least infer from this policy that Aliran's mobilization of progressive (and largely non-Malay) discontent is acceptable, fitting within the sort of fluid equilibrium that the triangular model presupposes. A more direct appeal from Aliran to Malays, however, could be disruptive of the balance – it would be threatening not so directly to the regime perhaps as to the right-wing opposition.

Finally, the model of authoritarian practice provided by Singapore should not be overlooked in any attempt to understand the state of dissent and repression in Malaysia. In fact, their identification with the Southeast Asian region in general means that Malaysian government officials refer to peers who are themselves more committed to stability and, accordingly, to restrictions on political activity and speech, than to civil liberties. In their pursuit of investment and assistance of all kinds from the United States, Japan, and other Western sources, the six ASEAN countries – Malaysia, Singapore, Thailand, Indonesia, the Philippines, and Brunei – have found these priorities most welcome. But, more particularly, from the beginning of the Mahathir administration it has been Singapore that has served as the unacknowledged source of many ideas about governance. In one way or another most of the regime's slogans and public campaigns can be seen as emulating Singaporean programs of a year or two earlier. And justifications of suppression that are pegged to economic growth, political stability, and racial harmony also may be borrowed from Singapore's playbook. This demonstration effect is especially apparent in the area of press controls. In the late 1980s Singapore's well-deserved reputation for vigorous guidance of domestic newspapers was augmented by some highly publicized actions against the foreign press. In the late 1980s a new law allowing severe limitations on circulation within Singapore and a series of harsh pronouncements about the foreign media (defending, for example, the government's exclusion of foreign correspondents from virtually all official press conferences) undoubtedly made it easier for Malaysian authorities to withstand criticism of their own ban on the *Asian Wall Street Journal* and regular censorship of foreign newspapers and magazines. More recently, Singapore's Prime Minister Lee Kuan Yew introduced a libel suit against the Kuala Lumpur newspaper, *The Star* – a manoeuvre against the press that was all the more visible in Malaysia.

On May 21, 1987, the government of Singapore detained sixteen church workers and community organizers under that country's Internal Security Act. In reacting strongly against that repression, Chandra Muzaffar must have had in mind his own organization's vulnerability to similar action (Muzaffar, 1987).

Indeed, five months after the arrests in Singapore a similar action was carried out in Malaysia. By the end of November 1987 this sweep, called "Operation lallang," had resulted in detention and interrogation of at least 106 Malaysians (Aznam, 1989). In most cases, including that of Chandra Muzaffar, the "preventive detention" rationale (also borrowed from Singapore) was a euphemism for intimidation; and it failed spectacularly. After nearly two months of harsh confinement, Chandra Muzaffar was released whereupon he immediately resumed his high profile as champion of human rights and forceful critic of the regime and its policies. The arrest had magnified his international stature, and in 1989 he was awarded the prestigious Benda Prize by the Association for Asian Studies. His courageous idealism is clearly an inspiration to other progressive individuals and groups in Malaysia – and a powerful testimony to the importance of carrying on the struggle for freedom of expression.

References

Aliran Kesedaran Negara (1981). *Aliran Speaks*. Penang.

Aliran Monthly (1981). February/March.

Asiaweek (1986). "A Liking for Contest," December 7:28.

Aznam, Suhaini (1987). "The Unofficial Thorns," *Far Eastern Economic Review*, January 1:16-18.

Aznam, Suhaini (1989). "Tales of Torture," *Far Eastern Economic Review*, January 12:20-21.

Barraclough, Simon (1985). "Cooptation and Elite Accommodation in Malaysian Politics," *Journal of Contemporary Southeast Asia*, March:308-318.

Barraclough, Simon (1984). "Political Participation and Its Regulation in Malaysia," *Pacific Affairs*, Fall:450-461.

Committee Against Repression in the Pacific and Asia (1988). *Tangled Web: Dissent, Deterrence and the 27 October 1987 Crackdown in Malaysia*. Haymarket, NSW, Australia: CARPA.

Crouch, Harold (1982). *Malaysia's 1982 General Election*. Singapore: Institute for Southeast Asian Studies.

Das, K. (1986). *The Musa Dilemma*. Kuala Lumpur: K. Das.

Douglas, Stephen A. and Paul Pedersen (1984). *Blood, Believer, and Brother: The Development of Voluntary Associations in Malaysia*. Athens: Ohio University.

Enloe, Cynthia (1970). *Multi-Ethnic Politics: The Case of Malaysia*. Berkeley: Centre for South and Southeast Asian Studies, University of California.

Fong, Michael (1986). "Why the Echo Was 'Killed'," *Aliran Monthly*, May/June:14-15.

Funston, John (1980). *Malay Politics in Malaysia*. Singapore: Heinemann Educational Books.

Gale, Bruce (1981). *Politics and Public Enterprise in Malaysia*. Singapore: Eastern University Press.

Jomo, K.S. (1985). *The Sun Also Sets: Lessons in Looking East*. Kuala Lumpur: INSAN.

Karim, Gulrose, ed. (1987). *Information Malaysia*. Kuala Lumpur: Berita Publishing.

Lau, Emily (1987). "Two Views of Freedom," *Far Eastern Economic Review*, March 12:29-30.

Mauzy, Diane (1983). *Barisan Nasional: Coalition Government in Malaysia*. Kuala Lumpur: Marican and Sons.

Muzaffar, Chandra (1987). "ISA Arrests in Singapore," *Aliran Monthly*, May/June:2-4.

Muzaffar, Chandra (1986-1987). "A-G Should Not Be Excused for His Excesses," *Aliran Monthly*, December/January:23.

Muzaffar, Chandra (1986a). *Freedom in Fetters*. Penang: Aliran.

Muzaffar, Chandra (1986b). "The 1986 General Election: Means and Ends," *Aliran Monthly*, September/October:24-27.

Muzaffar, Chandra (1985). "The Press," *Aliran Monthly*, May/June:1-6.

Pinwill, William (1986). "Shades of Marcos as Malaysia Slides Towards Totalitarianism," *The Bulletin*, December 16:80.

Segal, Jeffrey (1983). "The Third Time Around," *Far Eastern Economic Review*, March 31:14.

Selvaratnam, V. (1982). "Malaysia in 1981: A Year of Political Transition." In *Southeast Asian Affairs 1982*. Singapore: Institute for Southeast Asian Studies.

Singh, Gurmit (1986). "Democraticize the Malaysian Media," *Aliran Monthly*, November/December:11.

Szende, Andrew (1986). *From Torrent to Trickle: Managing the Flow of News in Southeast Asia*. Singapore: Institute of Southeast Asian Studies.

Tan Boom Kean (1984). "Orwell's Year in the Malaysian Press," *Far Eastern Economic Review*, September 20:40-41.

Teoh Jin-Inn (1975). "Community Relations in Malaysia," *Negara*, June:7.

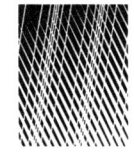

The Transmission and Reception of International Labour Information in Peru

Peter Waterman

Internationalism exists as an ideal because it is the new reality, the nascent reality. It is not an arbitrary ideal, it is not the absurd ideal of a few dreamers or utopians.... The development of heavy industry, the emergence of big factories, destroys small industry and ruins the small artisan; but it at the same time creates the material possibility for the realization of socialism and creates, above all, the will to bring this to realization.... Socialism, trade unionism, did not thus spring from some work of genius. They sprang from the new social reality, the new economic reality. And the same is true of internationalism.... Capitalism, under the reign of the bourgeoisie, does not produce for the national market; it produces for the international market.... Its product, its merchandise, recognizes no frontiers; it struggles to surpass and subjugate political restrictions.... In consequence of this international web the big European and United States banks become completely international entities.... The circulation of capital, through the banks, is an international circulation.... The owner of a textile mill in Britain is interested in paying his workers less wages than the proprietor of a textile mill in the United States, so that his merchandise can be sold more cheaply, more advantageously and abundantly. And this causes the North American textile worker to interest himself in the non-reduction of wages of a British textile worker. A fall of wages in the British textile industry is a threat to the worker of Vitarte, to the worker of Santa Catalina. In virtue of these facts, the workers have declared their solidarity and their fraternity over frontiers and despite nationalities. The workers have seen that when they fight a battle it is not only against the capitalist class of their own country but against the international capitalist class.... In this century everything tends to link, everything tends to connect, peoples and individuals. In other times the setting for a civilization was limited, small; in our epoch it is almost the whole world. The British colonizer who settles in a primitive corner of Africa brings to this corner the telephone, the wireless telegraph, the automobile.... The progress of communica-

tions has to an incredible extent mutually bound the activity and history of nations....
Communications are the nervous system of this internationalism and human solidarity.
One of the characteristics of our epoch is the rapidity, the velocity, with which ideas spread,
with which currents of thought and culture are transmitted. A new idea that blossoms in
Britain is not a British idea except for the time that it takes for it to be printed. Once
launched into space by the press, this idea, if it expresses some universal truth, can also be
instantaneously transformed into an internationalist idea.
                           –Jose Carlos Mariategui, "Internationalism and Nationalism," 1923

THIS IS AN EXPLORATION into the national-level transmission of information and ideas about workers and labour movements of other countries. To the best of my knowledge there exists no such research anywhere in the contemporary world, and I know of no such historical research either. However modest the present exercise, it is concerned with one of the great issues of the labour movement historically. The *Communist Manifesto* of 1848 distinguishes communists from others by the fact that "In the national struggles of the proletarians of different countries, they point out and bring to the front the common interests of the entire proletariat independent of all nationality" (Marx, 1935:219). It ends with the more famous appeal: "The proletarians have nothing to lose but their chains. They have a world to win. Workingmen of the world, unite!" (241).

The concern of this chapter is with how self-declared socialists today propagate such internationalism. The survey was first carried out in Peru because I happened to visit that country while trying to set up a project on the democratization of international labour communication (Waterman, 1986). Situated between the naked Andes and the empty Pacific, Peru may be one of the Latin American countries most isolated from the rest of the industrialized capitalist or communist worlds. It may be virtually uninvolved in the changing international division of labour that is tying the countries of Southeast Asia so closely to the latest technical and commercial developments of industrial capitalism (Wad, Norlund and Brun, 1986; Southall, 1987). But it is also a country in which the working class and popular sectors have been repeatedly rebellious, and in the mid-1980s its United Left electoral alliance was capable of gaining 20 to 30 per cent of the vote in municipal and national elections. It is, furthermore, the country of Jose Carlos Mariategui (1894-1930), one of the great creative spirits of early 20th-century Marxism.

Mariategui was a journalist, popular educator, labour organizer, and founder of both the first General Confederation of Peruvian Labour (CGTP), and the Peruvian affiliate to Lenin's Third International (Kapsoli, 1980; Quijano, 1981; Vanden, 1986; Angotti, 1986). In the book *Historia de la Crisis Mundial* there are items on the world crisis, the collapse of the Second International, European labour and socialist revolutions, revolutionary and socialist movements in China and India, and the Mexican Revolution. In Mariategui's essay on nationalism and internationalism, his argument deals with the reality of the world market, the idea of internationalism, its implications for labour, the internationalist consciousness and behaviour of workers, and, finally, the role of communication in the creation and spread of internationalism.

I carried out my 1986 enquiry in the city that honours Mariategui with numerous street names, in unions that use his image as their symbol, and amongst the party left that was united around his name. My subject begins where the quotation from Mariategui ends: with communication as the nervous system of internationalism and solidarity.

Methodology

I began this study with no theoretical framework in mind and no theoretical ambitions either. My title uses common-language terminology: "transmission," "information." While communications specialists might consider this terminology simplistic or feel that it mystifies the actual relationship examined, I consider it adequate for beginning an equally simple task. I do not wish, moreover, to let theoretical discussion stand in the way of access to material by the labour activists I am writing about and for. In the course of the survey I develop certain categories as I reflect on and try to make sense of the material. In the conclusion I go a little further, considering the theoretical and strategic implications of the findings already conceptualized. Even there, however, I hope to remain accessible to interested labour activists internationally.

As for my research strategy, the whole exploration was carried out in a week or two, spread over four to five weeks, which was the time available between other tasks. I carried out interviews with the following labour leaders and media specialists as "transmitters": 1) leaders of the major trade union confederation, the communist-led CGTP (General Confederation of Peruvian Workers); 2) leaders of the FNTMMSP or Federacion Minera (National Federation of Mine, Metal and Steel Workers of Peru, the Mineworkers Federation); 3) those responsible for the well-established bimonthly labour magazine, *Cuadernos Laborales*, and for the new labour radio program, "La Jornada."

I held open-ended interviews of about thirty minutes in English or Spanish as appropriate, structured loosely around a number of issues: international labour coverage in the dominant media, in the labour and socialist media, in the interviewee's own particular media; identification of any new tendencies; future possibilities or necessities; local worker knowledge of or interest in labour abroad; national and international sources for international labour news. I examined the following media, all of which were providing exclusive or extensive coverage of labour nationally: 1) *Amauta*, a new weekly paper associated with the PUM (United Mariateguian Party); 2) *Cambio*, a new weekly magazine associated with the Izquierda Unida (United Left); 3) *Unidad*, weekly of the PCP, the pro-Soviet Communist Party of Peru; 4) *Prensa Obrera*, a Peruvian paper of the Trotskyist tradition; 5) "La Jornada," the labour radio program; 6) occasional labour and socialist pamphlets and teaching materials; 7) *Labor*, the labour newspaper set up by Mariategui in the late 1920s.

The examination methods were simple and their application restricted. I attempted, where possible, to obtain a run of serials covering several months, and using these I measured foreign labour coverage (in some cases, any foreign coverage) as a percentage of total space. I made notes on matters of interest. It was not possible in practice to obtain serials covering the same period. One-off (single) items were examined without any common methodology being applied. No attempt could be made to evaluate either the circulation or impact of these items.

Background

Peruvian political parties of the left – a collection of over forty groups – bloomed and flourished with the return of parliamentary rule in 1980. A spurt of neo-liberalism in 1980-85, under President Fernando Belaunde, ended in economic and national depression amidst increasing social violence. Voters did not, however, opt for the far left but rather for the middle-of-the-road Apra Party, which appeals particularly to the middle classes. The Peruvian political scene, in theatrical terms, consisted in 1986 of a tussle between the Apra and the self-styled Marxists of the Izquierda Unida (IU), who got 20 to 30 per cent of the votes in national and municipal elections and ruled Lima and several other cities. Lurking in the wings to the left was Sendero Luminoso (the Shining Path terrorist movement). Offstage to the right, and surrounding the whole theatre, were the tanks of Peru's bloated armed services. In June 1986, during the Lima conference of the Socialist International, there was a prison mutiny of virtually unarmed Sendero detainees, who were then massacred by the military.

Of the 2.2 million "adequately employed" workforce, 1.6 million can technically be organized in trade unions. The rest are not legally allowed to form labour organizations because they are members of the armed forces or work in factories employing less than five workers. In practice, about half the potentially organized (860,000) were members of some 4,781 trade unions in 1982. Most of these unions were worker (*obrero*) organizations, although there were also over 600 white-collar (*empleado*) unions and some 900 mixed (blue-collar and white-collar) unions. Over half of all the trade unions in Peru were formed and recognized under the radical military regime of Velasco (1968-75).

Most Peruvian unions are formed in a single-establishment place of work and then join up in sector-based federations, which in turn belong to national confederations. There are two main confederations. The General Confederation of Peruvian Workers (CGTP) was founded by Mariategui in 1929 and is affiliated to the World Federation of Trade Unions (WFTU) in Prague. The Confederation of Peruvian Workers (CTP), an Apra Party stronghold, was founded in 1944 and is affiliated to the Brussels-based International Confederation of Free Trade Unions (ICFTU).

The CGTP has had a chequered history. After three years of existence, it was banned by dictator Sanchez Cerro. In 1944 a new confederation (the CTP) was formed by both the Communist Party (PCP) and the Apra and quickly took over the leadership. Disputes between the two groups led to the Communists leaving the CTP and eventually reorganizing the old CGTP in 1968. At first the Moscow-oriented leadership supported the reformist military government of Velasco, which caused several groups, including miners, teachers, and metalworkers, to leave or criticize the Confederation and adopt a more radical class-conscious (*clasista*) stance. This meant that many of Peru's more independent unions were born and tested in struggles that were not only for their own "economic" benefit but also directed against the military dictatorship. This earned them broad popular support, expressed in a series of general strikes against the military regimes. But it also meant that some labour groups were disorientated when a civilian government came to power in 1980 and their demands suddenly appeared more self-interested. The radical left did not succeed in forming its own confederation. In the 1980s, parallel to the formation of the Izquierda Unida coalition of Marxist parties, many of the more radical unions decided to join or rejoin the CGTP, by far the most influential labour organization in Peru. Although the Communists have lost control of various national federations over the years, they still firmly control the CGTP apparatus itself. Today all key sectors of the economy have trade unions and most of them belong to the CGTP.

Over two-thirds of unionized labour is probably in unions affiliated to the CGTP. The Apra confederation, CTP, lost influence from the 1960s as the party desperately sought power through a series of compromises with its former oppressors. Its appeal faded, in Peruvian eyes, as the military government made an effort to set up its own confederation, the Confederation of Workers of the Peruvian Revolution (CTRP), and the Christian Democrats, a minor force in Peruvian politics, set up the National Confederation of Workers (CNT). Neither centre prospered and in 1986 they probably accounted between them for less than 5 per cent of the organized workforce.

In President Alan Garcia's speeches, organized workers were located at the upper end of the social pyramid that he liked to sketch. His emphasis, partly due to Apra's dwindling influence among organized workers, was on the millions of peasant farmers and the underemployed at the base of his pyramid. Nevertheless, Apra activists were trying at this time, with some success, to win over unions in mining and other sectors. Even left-wing trade union leaders admitted that the struggle had so far been "clean," contrary to general expectations before Apra took office in July 1985.

The shifts and crises of the past two decades in Peruvian politics and labour history have thrown up a generation of labour leaders absorbed by national struggles. On the positive side, this could be seen as a desire by the left to avoid dependence on foreign models and draw from the long local history of struggle. But it also means that few labour leaders currently turn for lessons to the experience of workers and unions in other countries (NACLA, 1980, 1986; Reid, 1985; Arellano, 1986a,b).

The Transmitters

Interviews

1. The CGTP: The CGTP leaders were not only articulate but also had knowledge of – and a quite distinctive set of attitudes towards – the media. The main note they struck on the topic of the dominant media was that of its power. The terminology used was that of "domination by a few press agencies," the "monopoly control" and "censorship and self-censorship" of the local press, the "one-sided and fragmented" nature of the information given. Although my question was about coverage of labour internationally, the replies did not relate to this specifically. The same was the case with a question concerning international labour coverage in the local socialist and labour media. Here the dominant note struck was that of weakness. The terminology used was that of the "impossibility of defending," of "being unable to use radio or television," or the "weakness of the left press," the "lack of sufficient resources," of "splits within publications."

I asked why Mariategui's newspaper *Labor* had been able to give so much space to labour internationally so many years ago while the contemporary left seemed to be unable to do so:

> In the time of Mariategui the organization was smaller, and trade union politics were less contaminated. Today it is much more difficult, there is ideological contraband, the confusion of the working class is much more intense, earlier there was no TV. The work [of communication?] today is more extensive, it requires improved technology, a better-organized press. It is impossible today to reach workers only with speeches, bulletins and magazines. These don't meet the need.

I asked about any felt need for increasing international labour information. "Of course, this is an obvious necessity if we want better communication, mutual information. We would be gradually moving in the direction of a New International Press Order to confront the information multinationals." What use, if any, was made of new technical means of communication? Apparently little, if any. One affiliate was said to have a video monitor and camera. The telex was expensive but was used for important declarations to the outside world or for seeking and expressing solidarity. Concerning knowledge of national or international sources for international labour information, the interviewees also had little to say, although earlier one of them had mentioned Cuba's state agency, Prensa Latina, as "the only left-wing press [agency] that distributes news of the left."

It was interesting to note not only the somewhat pessimistic tone of the CGTP's responses but also the "statist" orientation in the alternatives visualized. The pessimism is not simply due to being communist, or pro-communist, since Soviet communism has traditionally tended more to triumphalism than to defeatism. Nor is it a matter of ignorance, since the leaders were well aware of the importance of the media and also of the international demand for a New World Information and Communication Order (an inter-state project). The CGTP's worries about the media were matched by a certain inability to answer questions in a specific manner. The leaders were also evidently unaware of such non-state Latin American sources of labour information as ALAI (Agencia Latino-Americana de Informacion, or Latin American Information Agency, in Quito and Montreal), and Informativo Tercer Mundo, a tape-cassette information service based in Santiago, Chile (Salinas and Gomez, 1987). And although, finally, they were sensitive to the need for new and appropriate means of communication to reach Peruvian workers today, the leaders were evidently neither informed of nor engaged in attempts to create such a system.

2. **The Mineworkers Federation:** The Federation was a major force in the development of "independent class" unionism in Peru in the 1970s, when the CGTP was compromised with the military regime. It was in 1986 again a leading force within the CGTP. I met a group consisting of the Assistant Secretary and the officers responsible for press and international relations.

On international labour coverage in the dominant media, they complained of its control by foreign agencies and its distorted nature. What of the main existing labour or socialist media? They spoke of the limitations of the left media, its restricted coverage. They felt that the weekly papers *Amauta* and *Cambio* gave little coverage to labour nationally – a view that those with knowledge of left media in other countries might not immediately endorse. They felt that these weeklies gave sufficient information on, for example, Libya and Nicaragua. In the face of the dominant media reports on Poland, they said: "There arises another kind of information, manipulated by other types of political tendencies, mainly the Peruvian Communist Party, in which it is suggested that the Polish workers were infiltrated by – at the service of – the CIA. From other sources we have managed to understand that this was a movement against a clique which had usurped power, which had taken the name of socialism but distorted its objectives." They also pointed out that the Mineworkers Federation had approved a motion of support for the Solidarity movement at its congress.

The group was much more positive on future communication necessities and possibilities. The members interviewed thought it would be possible to use the Mineworkers International Federation (MIF) to obtain information or explore new possibilities. They were interested in possibly training some of their own people to work on international communication. The leaders thought that workers were interested in international information. They were beginning to build up correspondents nationally for the radio programs, to tape songs and poems and to organize themselves around available media.

The Federation leadership seemed, in sum, to share the position of the CGTP leaders both on the shortcomings of the dominant media and on that of the left in general – as well as on its own media in particular. There was, however, a difference in attitude from the CGTP. This difference was not limited to Federation criticism of media manipulation by communists. It was a matter, firstly, perhaps, of the contrast between the state-dependence of the CGTP and the media activity of the Federation. It came out secondly, and possibly consequently, in the contrast between the quasi-fatalistic attitude of the CGTP and the sober yet positive attitude of the Federation towards new communication possibilities. The Federation's orientation is based on a certain international knowledge and experience built up through recent years, even if this may not have been effectively communicated to the mass of the members.

3. **Cuadernos Laborales and "La Jornada":** Although the first was published by the ADEC (Association for Legal Defence and Training) and the second is based on the ATC (Association for Work and Culture), we can consider these jointly. ADEC and ATC share the same building and at the time of the survey were moving towards a merger. *Cuadernos Laborales* was a well-established bimonthly magazine of labour news and analysis, printing some two thousand copies mostly bought by labour activists, either from their organizations or from bookstores and bookstalls. "La Jornada" – along with its associated audio-tape service – was a new daily radio program, broadcasting news and interviews in an attempt to surpass the shortcomings of the *prensa chica* (little press) of the unions (Sulmont, 1981) that fail to reach beyond a local and trade-union constituency in Peru. The editor of the magazine, Amalia Mendoza, and the producer of the radio program, Hans Landolt, were young and both spoke English.

With respect to international labour coverage in either the dominant or left media, the opinions of this pair coincided more or less with each other and with what earlier interviewees had to say. As far as their own products were concerned, Mendoza said that it was not worth looking for international labour coverage in *Cuadernos*, even though it had made a certain contribution in this sphere. Landolt guessed, correctly, that international labour coverage in "La Jornada" would be around 5 per cent. Sources for the material he broadcast were primarily the Santiago-based tape-cassette service, Informativo Tercer Mundo. He also made use of a Bolivian bulletin on miners and Brazilian material from the Workers' Pastorate. He had, finally, done interviews with visiting public-sector unionists from Colombia.

Was it possible to see any new tendencies in international labour communication in Peru? Landolt thought not. But he also thought that the development of *clasista* unionism in Peru provided a basis for future internationalism. The class unionism of the 1970s, he said, distinguished itself both from Western-type "free trade unionism," represented locally by the pro-government unions, and the Eastern-bloc-aligned unionism of the communists. He said the new tendency represented a revival of the 1920s project of united and democratic (member-controlled) unions. The international policy of this tendency was one of non-affiliation, while recognizing the necessity for relations with unions abroad. On existing national and international sources for international labour information, Mendoza placed particular stress on the International Labour Organization (ILO); ATC turned to the ILO whenever it needed information on labour relations abroad or input on new legislation due to be introduced in Peru. And what kind of information did they think would be necessary in the future? Amalia Mendoza said:

> I remember going to a conference organized by the Friedrich Ebert Foundation [development organization of the West German Social Democrats – PW] on the social contract in Spain ... in which you have the participation of the state, the workers, and the employers. And they invited union leaders from the main unions in Spain. And they spoke of the need of the workers to even give way on some of the typical worker demands in exchange for participation, and the right to present alternatives to the government to fight the crisis in Spain.... [This implies] not only solidarity amongst the workers but from the workers towards the ... unemployed sectors of the population. Union leaders in the audience were asking questions more directed towards, well, what about the workers' demands? And is it possible for workers to give up benefits for other sectors of the population? And I think mainly the intellectuals, here, the people who work in the [resource] centres, are ... taking up this idea and talking with the unions.

It was interesting in these two interviews to note, firstly, that these two communications projects, associated with the development of autonomous, democratic, and class unionism in Peru, had been even less engaged in the production of international information than some of the more traditional socialist media; and secondly, that both interviewees were very open to the use of such material (after the interviews both said that the questions asked had stimulated their awareness of the necessity for international labour information); and thirdly, that both – separately – highlighted the importance for Peru today of the Spanish social contract process. It was only in response to direct questions that they also declared interest in alternative worker plans (a phenomenon apparently unknown to them) and in general strategy questions. When Amalia Mendoza said that there was pressure on labour to come up with alternatives in the current situation, and when she talked of the interest of intellectuals in the Spanish experience, the question arises of whether the pro-labour intellectuals are possibly interested in a different kind of international labour information from the unions. We should not make too much of this, because we do not have enough evidence to be able to do so, but it should be borne in mind. Elsewhere there was coincidence between what they and earlier interviewees had said. But *Cuadernos Laborales* and "La Jornada" are – as became clear from further interviews – media *for* unions and workers rather than controlled by them. We do need to be aware of the different information/communication needs amongst all the relevant parties or levels – including the national unions themselves and the workers at the base.

4. **Tentative conclusion:** These three interviews provide a limited base for any kind of generalization, yet it remains important to draw tentative conclusions. Perhaps we should first make explicit what has so far been only implicit, that we are dealing with self-avowedly socialist groups only, that they belong to different socialist traditions, and that they represent different labour movement levels or

practices. The CGTP is the recognized national left union confederation but it is also a traditional communist one. The Mineworkers Federation exists at a lower institutional level but it is also a major force in "independent and class" unionism, critical not only of the right but also of the CGTP and communism. *Cuadernos Laborales* and "La Jornada" are pro-labour media, produced outside a union or party structure by socialist intellectuals who see such support activities as more fruitful than the traditional practice of providing an intellectual vanguard or revolutionary leadership for the workers. This particular activity is, moreover, one closely linked with independent class unionism in general and the Mineworkers Federation in particular.

The contrast we have already identified between the CGTP and the Federation is, however, clearly one of orientation, not level. The crucial difference is, perhaps, the contrast between the apparent inertia of the CGTP on international and communication issues, and the innovatory and experimental attitude of the Mineworkers Federation. In any case, it is not difficult to see an interrelationship between the different elements in the CGTP position: the notion of powerfully manipulating capitalist media, the organization's own media inactivity, its dependence on the state or inter-state activity for a solution, and a consequently reasonable pessimism about the possibility of the CGTP itself changing the situation. One additional element in its inactivity, of course, may be the assumption that the international communication function is carried out by the PCP and its paper, *Unidad*, thus making the CGTP's own activity here unnecessary. When comparing the attitude of *Cuadernos Laborales* and "La Jornada" to that of the others, one must note the possibly differing information interests of international labour transmitters. It is a commonplace of left political debate in Peru that there is a dangerous gap between the left parties (largely associated with the Izquierda Unida) and the social movements in the workplace, squatter settlements, or rural communities (Ames, 1986). Those working in the *centros* (resource centres) are always aware of a tension between themselves and those whom they claim to be serving (in relationship to women's centres in Peru, see Carillo, 1986). There might also exist different information interests between levels within labour organizations as such. The leadership of the Mineworkers Federation, for example, might have an interest in international union relations or in international labour information quite distinct from that of its member unions – or their worker members.

Analyses

1. **Amauta:** This was a new tabloid weekly, associated closely with the United Mariateguian Party (PUM), itself part of the IU. The PUM was a Leninist vanguard party but the tabloid did not give this impression: it appeared more to be a non-party organ of the left. It was professionally produced and attractively laid out. It had adopted the name of Mariategui's own cultural and political periodical, and its extensive coverage of labour and other popular struggles within Peru suggested that it was attempting to follow in his tracks. Its international coverage,

however, was limited. The eleven issues examined (not a complete run) contained some 214 pages, of which only 18-19 were of an international character, this amounting to only some 8.4 per cent of total space. Little of this international coverage was on labour, trade unions, or the labour movement. There were three items on the Socialist International – due, of course, to the June 1986 meeting in Lima. The May Day issue (April 30, 1986) noted the hundredth anniversary of the event. But the issue made no mention of the international labour movement except for passing editorial reference to the Russian, Cuban, and Nicaraguan revolutions. Most of the foreign coverage was of what we might call a "National-Democratic" character (that is, anti-imperialist, anti-authoritarian) rather than being specifically "Labour" or "Socialist."

2. **Cambio:** This was another new tabloid weekly magazine, this time associated with the IU. It began publication on April 17, 1986, in a glossy format but had to adopt cheaper paper after a couple of months. It was, like *Amauta*, a professional and attractive publication, devoting much space to labour and other popular struggles in Peru. It also gave the impression of having more extensive international coverage. This turned out on examination to be due to its greater number of pages and a large number of short items. I examined eleven of its fourteen issues, amounting to some 302 pages, exclusive of commercial advertisements. Of this total, only 26-27 pages contained items of an international character, amounting to 7.6 per cent of the total. Its May Day issue also managed to avoid explicit mention of labour outside Peru, even in union or party advertisements mentioning Chile, El Salvador, and the socialist states. Once again, the coverage seemed to be of a National-Democratic rather than a specifically Labour nature.

3. **Unidad:** This is the attractive tabloid weekly of the pro-Soviet Peruvian Communist Party. In July 1986, amongst the congratulations of much of the Peruvian left, it published its one-thousandth issue. I had access to an incomplete run of twelve issues published between February 6 and June 21, 1983. At that time *Unidad* had six pages, with the back page usually carrying an international solidarity story or picture and others reserved for foreign news. Of the total of 192 pages in the issues examined, 40 contained international coverage, amounting to some 21 per cent. Labour coverage – except for items celebrating the life enjoyed by working people under communist regimes – was nil. During this period, for some Peruvian reason, there was a regular column for extracts from Lenin, mostly about the nationalization of banks. The tabloid also celebrated a Marx anniversary at some length. (I refer to this type of material as "Marxist.") Much space was given to coverage of communist countries and to speeches by the leaders of these countries, to book reviews by writers from these countries and to articles on the world communist movement. Items under this heading amounted to some nineteen pages, around half of total international coverage and almost 10 per cent of total space in the paper. We could characterize this type of material as "Socialist State." Most of the other foreign material in these issues of *Unidad* falls under the National-Democratic category.

4. Prensa Obrera: In 1986 this was a biweekly tabloid, but in 1984 (before a major crisis of Peruvian Trotskyism) it was a weekly. It appeared at the time with six to eight pages. I was able to examine a complete run, from August 8, 1984, to February 22, 1985, including twenty-one issues totalling 130 pages. Of these there were thirty-four pages of international coverage, amounting to 26 per cent of the total available space: the highest amount so far found. International labour news (workers, unions, strikes, movements) came to around twelve pages, some 9 per cent of the space – again the highest found. It may be that this proportion is accounted for by the British miners' strike and the anniversary of Trotsky's death, both of which fell in the period. It is also evident, however, that the Trotskyists give major importance to labour protest internationally, since they also covered strikes in Brazil and Bolivia. I call this "Foreign Labour" coverage. There were in *Prensa Obrera*, moreover, and again for the first time, items on labour internationalism: the solidarity of the Peruvians with the British miners' union, and the international policy of a British Trotskyist party. Before we characterize this material as simply "Socialist Internationalist," however, we should note certain special feature of these items. The defence of the British mine union's approach to the Libyan unions identified with the Libyan regime and its state-approved unions in much the same way as the PCP did with the Soviet type. The international policy document of the British Trotskyists itself made as good as no mention of working-class internationalism. Perhaps such material should be called "International Party" coverage, thus distinguishing it both from "International Union" and "Foreign Labour" material. Several other features of foreign coverage in *Prensa Obrera* justify this new category. One is the heavy dependence on foreign – particularly British Trotskyist – documents. Another is the space devoted to attacking other Leninist vanguard parties. A third is a certain proletarian revolutionary apocalypticism: Two items in one issue (No.166) were entitled "Towards Civil War" (Bolivia) and "Towards the General Strike of 1985" (Britain). These qualifications made, it would seem that *Prensa Obrera* stood at this time closest to the tradition represented by Mariategui's *Labor*.

5. "La Jornada": I had available a list of the 168 daily programs by "La Jornada" from November 23, 1985, to June 10, 1986, including a list of subjects handled by each program: a total of some one thousand items, around six per daily program. Only 29 per cent of the broadcasts had foreign items, amounting to a total of fifty-six, just 5.6 per cent of the items broadcast. If the quantity of foreign coverage was disappointing for a new labour media experiment, the nature of the coverage looked quite promising. Of the fifty-six foreign items, thirty-one, or 55 per cent, were on labour. The foreign coverage of "La Jornada" falls into the by now familiar categories: Foreign Labour, National-Democratic. Unlike the other labour-oriented media in Peru, "La Jornada" does not seem to have used the one-hundredth anniversary of May Day to deal with contemporary internationalism.

6. Occasional publications on international issues: I intended to examine simply the materials commemorating the one-hundredth anniversary of May Day but these, as we are beginning to see, revealed so little internationalism that I felt required to collect whatever other materials I could find (including materials from organizations and publications already mentioned) that might suggest some further interest or new developments.

A handbook on trade-union terminology with a preface by the CGTP president (Oblitas, 1986), provided a definition of proletarian internationalism: "One of the principles of Marxist-Leninist ideology. Consists of the practice of solidarity with the struggles of the workers of the whole world, for their rights, for peace, for democracy, for national independence, for the destruction of the reign of capitalism, for the construction of socialism and communism." Notable about this definition is not so much its content, which merely repeats familiar doctrine, as its brevity. Taking but five lines, it is shorter than the following handbook definitions beginning (in Spanish) with "I": Ideology (twelve lines), Equality (twelve), Imperialism (twenty), National Independence (eight), Inflation (seventeen), Inquisition (nine), Class Instinct (eleven), Second International (thirteen), Communist International (eleven), Intervention (eight).

This material reinforces earlier impressions of the CGTP attitude towards international questions, in addition indicating an interest in internationalism as an abstract doctrine or article of faith. While the editor of *Cuadernos Laborales* was somewhat apologetic about its failure to handle international labour, it had actually made an original contribution to communication on that subject. The magazine produced a sixteen-page pamphlet for May 1, 1986, with sections on the origins of May Day, on the working day in contemporary Peru, on the unregulated working hours of women and – finally and summarily – on the history of the international movement (*Cuadernos Laborales*, 1986). A bibliography listed Spanish-language and other books and resources on labour internationally. Folded into the brochure, however, there was also an attractive, illustrated, two-colour poster, divided into historical periods horizontally and with columns headed "Latin America," "Other Countries," and "International Scene." Since this poster was the most internationalist of all the products examined, it is worth listing what was covered in the last two columns for at least the most recent period:

> Other Countries: Poland, 1970, strikes; Germany, 1973, wildcat strikes; Tripoli, 1973, Organization of African Trade Union Unity; Brussels, 1973, European Trade Union Confederation; United States, 1974, Employee Stock Ownership Plan; Spain, 1978, first post-Franco union elections; Soviet Union, 1978, repression of organizers of "free trade unions"; 1979, South African Allied Workers Union; United States, 1979, attacks on government anti-union activities; Poland, 1980, strikes, the twenty-one trade-union demands, appearance of Solidarnosc, Sczecin and Gdansk agreements; United States, 1980, Chrysler workers accept give-back; Poland 1981, state of emergency; South Africa, May 1981, first national solidarity strike; United States, 1981, strike of air-traffic controllers.

> International Scene: 1972, conference of Nestlé workers, international collective bargaining; 1973, International Trade Union Conference Against Apartheid

(ILO), Trilateral Commission, ICFTU Working Group on Multinationals; 1976, United States withdraws from ILO, Victory in Vietnam; 1981, encyclical "Laborem Excercems" on human labour; ILO Conventions [five listed over the years].

What is offered by this poster, albeit in summary form, is a rich and complex image of labour in foreign countries and of international labour developments. It would be reasonable to characterize this material as being "International Union" in nature since it largely confines itself to the union movement. It also does this in a truly international and non-partisan manner. Unfortunately, I do not recall having once seen this poster pinned up in any of the union offices I visited. It is also difficult to imagine what it might actually communicate to workers and union activists.

It is worthwhile to consider the case of the Mineworkers Federation since it was to be the most internationally conscious and active of the unions I contacted. The Federation hosted, in May 1984, the first co-ordination meeting of mining and metal workers of Bolivia, Chile, and Peru. I looked at two documents relating to this event: first a background paper by Joseph Giguere, a Québécois union educator working in Peru for several years, and Denis Sumont, a leading Peruvian labour specialist of French origin, a prominent academic, and a leading figure in ATC-ADEC; second a brochure published after the meeting.

The background document (Giguere and Sumont, 1984, 1987) was entitled "Build International Trade-Union Solidarity" and had three main parts, the first of which was structured as follows:

> Why International Trade-Union Solidarity? Capitalism is international; Capitalism creates competition between workers internationally; Imperialism, a project of domination based on the systematic division of workers and peoples; Yankee imperialism in Latin America; International working-class solidarity confronts capitalism and imperialism; Ideal conditions for the development of international solidarity cannot be expected; International solidarity develops through international organization.

The brochure of the three-country miners' meeting (FNTMMP, 1984) repeated a few of the above elements, while largely consisting of statements on their national situations by the three unions concerned. I will here concentrate on the proposals of the Commission on Latin America and International Union Unity, which proposed unity on the following principles, among others:

> Anti-imperialist and non-aligned solidarity, open to the different existing international union organizations, establishing multilateral relations, favouring relations of union solidarity at the level of Latin America and the Third World, combating the superpower policy of the blocs and playing an active role in the process of international trade-union unification. Also developing relations for mutual knowledge and solidarity with the workers and peoples of North America and Europe, against international capitalism and imperialist aggression in Latin America.

The resolution and others on wages and conditions or mining policy do not limit themselves to such general principles but go into some detail on fighting the International Monetary Fund, developing national and popular mining policies, mutual support for improving wages and conditions, and proposals for further coordination and meetings.

What we have here, in sum, is the first serious effort I came across at producing and communicating internationalist ideas, as well, of course, as developing internationalist political activity. The materials bear comparison with an educational brochure on the international trade-union movement produced in South Africa (ILRIG, 1984) and, indeed, make an interesting contrast with the South African product. Here I am thinking particularly of the stress in the Peruvian materials on Latin American and Third World interests and identities, an element not echoed in the South African brochure. We could characterize these materials as International Union ones, because they deal with internationalism only in its union form. But we could perhaps also use here the term "International Socialist," because for the first time we have an explicit and specific criticism of capitalism as a world system as well as a discussion of the role of working-class internationalism in the struggle against it.

7. **Labor:** Intended, by Mariategui, to be a biweekly publication of information and ideas for the labour movement, *Labor* produced just ten issues and a supplement before financial difficulties and political repression brought it to an end within one year (1928-29). Of the 132 items listed in the index to the facsimile edition (*Labor*, 1974), 41, or 31 per cent, are foreign or international items. Of the 80 pages published in its regular issues, 29, or 36 per cent, were of this nature. Of the 41 foreign items, 12-13, or about one-third, are specifically on labour, workers, unions, or the labour movement. This suggests that possibly 10 per cent of *Labor*'s space was devoted to foreign labour alone. I have even excluded from my calculations here the special supplement attached to Number 9, which was an anti-war "special" considering almost solely international items. I have also excluded from my calculations the space devoted to reproductions, mostly woodcuts of Mexican origin. Among the subjects covered in *Labor* we find: a conference on proletarian literature; a review of John Reed's book on the Russian Revolution, *Ten Days That Shook the World*; Britain (co-operatives, the textile crisis); organizing the unorganized workers in Latin America; worker struggles in Colombia; nationalization of Bolivian mines; an extract from the Soviet novel *Cement*; the Latin American Trade Union Congress and its opposition to the Chaco War between Bolivia and Paraguay.

There is no obvious logic in the selection of items, but one notices the extensive coverage of Mexico – the most advanced country in Latin America at that time. For a communist labour paper, even of that period, there also seems to be rather limited coverage of Marxism-Leninism and the Soviet Union. Only the last issue carries the long extract from the Soviet novel, plus an item by the Russian Marxist Plekhanov on socialism. Whether the wide range of thematic and geographical coverage was due to deliberate choice or not, the readers of *Labor* were being presented with a rich and stimulating view of the outside world. Which of the categories so far developed would seem to be represented in *Labor*? The National-Democratic, Foreign Labour, International Union? Not, significantly, the Socialist State category, or what I have called the International Socialist. Such elements could, perhaps, be discovered on closer analysis, or in the approach or purpose of the writing, but not as dominant elements. Nor does *Labor* contain obvious new types of foreign material. The limited coverage of the Soviet Union and the absence of International Socialist material may, of course, have been due to the delicate political conditions under which *Labor* was operating. But what we see here is a periodical with a clear but limited mandate, nationally and internationally, clearly expressed in its declared purpose and title.

8. **Tentative conclusions:** In this analysis I have identified five groups by the dominant or specific characteristic of their international coverage: 1) the National-Democratic (*Amauta, Cambio*); 2) Socialist State (*Unidad*); 3) International Party (*Prensa Obrera*); 4) International Union (materials of *Cuadernos Laborales, Labor*); 5) International Socialist (materials of the Mineworkers Federation). We need to relate these orientations with quantities, thus remembering that while *Unidad* and *Prensa Obrera* had high percentages of foreign coverage, this was of a statist or partisan nature. On the other hand, we must equally recognize that in the cases of *Cuadernos Laborales* and the Mineworkers Federation, we are talking about only one or two items. Even if we characterize the coverage of *Labor* as "merely" International Union in nature, we still have to recognize the significance of its 36 per cent foreign and 10 per cent foreign-labour coverage.

In relating these findings to the initial interviews, I am obliged to limit myself to the two major traditions there recognized: communist and *clasista*. The communist tradition was represented in the interviews by the CGTP leaders and in the analyses by *Unidad* and the CGTP. The *clasista* tradition was represented in the interviews by *Cuadernos Laborales*, "La Jornada," and the Mineworkers Federation, and in the analyses by the same. The state-dependence of the CGTP, it appears, is confirmed by the Socialist State nature of its international coverage. And the tradition of *clasista* unionism receives both confirmation and significant extension in the analyses, with the first evidence of international communication activities, including evidence that these activities are of a seriously internationalist nature. One last point: We should avoid too hastily giving out marks for internationalism, with top marks going to the International Socialist category. This is not only because of the caution with which I have applied this last term. It is also because I wish to suggest that the further development of international labour communications and solidarity depends more on the self-activity of labour than on my categories, however helpful these may prove to be.

Conclusion

Now I want to consider the various theoretical and strategic implications of the findings and then return to the opening quotation from Mariategui. The problem is that there exists little or no modern writing on the concept of internationalism, or international labour communication, or even on the democratization of international communication more generally (but see Waterman, 1987, 1988, 1990a,b). So here I simply attempt to develop certain concepts. Naming, of course, is not taming. So let us briefly consider these concepts and see what kind of value can be argued for them.

Conceptualizing the Transmission of International Labour Information
In dealing with Peruvian labour media in terms of information transmission, I have developed the following set of categories: .
- National-Democratic
- Marxist
- Social State
- Foreign Labour
- International Party
- International Union
- International Socialist

Although these terms are value-loaded (are given a particular value by historical usage, by the contemporary context, or by my own implicit and explicit views), they do address themselves more to the content of the materials than to the attitudes of those who produced them, or to a presumed purpose, or to any known effect. I have, moreover, carefully avoided the term "internationalist." This is because I am concerned precisely about avoiding a too early or too facile use of a term that, for me, 1) carries a very high and very positive charge, but 2) has been emptied of meaning and force over the last several decades. My breakdown of the purely descriptive category of "Foreign" or "Foreign Labour" draws attention not only to the variety of elements that constitutes the information, but to the differential weight the elements are given by the various information transmitters. I would here also like to make explicit another implication of the findings: that high or exclusive attention by such transmitters to one such category implies a certain understanding of relations between the labour, popular, or socialist movement locally and those abroad. By the same token, it can be assumed that this attention creates, if it is effective locally, a certain understanding of internationalism and stimulates or blocks certain types of internationally oriented political activity.

Let us discuss what has so far been argued in relation to the first and last categories, the National-Democratic and the International Socialist. National-Democratic coverage means, in the Peruvian context, coverage that is anti-imperialist and anti-conservative-authoritarian (since much of it may favour nationalist or socialist authoritarianism). While it is evident to me that any internationalist information strategy must include coverage of anti-imperialist and anti-conservative-authoritarian struggles, I evidently would not consider exclusive or high concentration on such to represent "internationalism." I have presented very positively the International Socialist category: the critique of capitalism as a world system, the presentation of international working-class action as necessary for its transformation. I feel that this comes close to "internationalism." But whether it actually does would depend on the extent to which this kind of information is articulated with others. A modern Socialist Internationalism could be simply an updated version of the abstract internationalism I have already criticized. It could be apocalyptical ("Towards the European Socialist Revolution of 1992"). It could be sectarian (excluding or alienating non-socialist Catholics and Muslims, democrats, feminists, ecologists). It could be reformist (seeking interstate agreement on a New This That and the Other Order). It could, finally, remain at the level of information, failing as communication, or failing as the alternative communication model that a new kind of internationalism would seem to require (Waterman, 1990a; Jusocan, 1986; Stangelaar 1986).

Based on the interview and analyses, I have argued that there was a relationship between the state-dependence of the CGTP and the Socialist State predominance in its foreign information materials, between the *clasista* line of the *Cuadernos/*"Jornada"/Mineworkers Federation and their International Union or Socialist materials. While I did not interview anyone from Izquierda Unida or from a Trotskyist party, the relationship between the IU and National-Democratic foreign information, between the Trotskyists and an International Party coverage, is clear. It may be thought that I have operated with loaded theoretical dice, drawing conclusions that were written into my premises. But while I might have predicted the international orientation of the CGTP and the PCP, I could not have predicted the impressive extent of foreign coverage in the communist or Trotskyist publications. Nor was I in any way aware, before the investigation, either of the limited amount or the limited nature of the IU-oriented media. And while I might have predicted that the *clasista* tendency would be actively internationalist, I could not have known the limitations of its international information activity or the nature of its coverage. I do not wish, further, to set up the last-mentioned labour movement tendency as some kind of ideological vanguard in this area. Nor do I wish to rule out contributions to the development of a new international labour communication strategy in Peru from other groups or tendencies not considered here, such as social democrats, the church, or feminists. A new model of international labour communications would in any case be pluralistic, allowing for and requiring a variety of forms, contents, and emphases.

Towards a New Model of International Labour Communication
Secondly, on the information/communication distinction, I have, in the title of this piece, employed the word "information" quite deliberately. I use the word to apply to the creation of data about events and ideas. Such an act of creation – with all its implications for selection, exclusion, order, form of presentation, interpretation – is a far from natural or neutral process. "Information" here also means a one-way process – literally from a transmitter to a receiver. "Communication," for me, implies a whole number of additional elements, with the most important being reciprocity and interaction. Since, in this case, I have no evidence of interaction, I

would rather not use this word. I have no evidence of reciprocity between my transmitters and receivers, far less between those about whom the information is being transmitted and those who are receiving it. I am inclined, furthermore, to give "communication" a positive value. I wish to see it and use it in terms not only of interaction but also of dialogue or dialectic, as well as of mutual sympathy and support, or solidarity. In so far as we see international solidarity as a relationship of mutual support between significant collective interests among the peoples concerned (workers, women, citizens faced with militarism, pollution, etc.), then what we need is not simply "information" – and not simply "communication" – but a new model of international communication that by its form, content, organization, and dissemination allows for and encourages maximum participation and control by the relevant collective interests (Waterman, 1987, 1990b).

In the case of workers this means that they would increasingly define, produce locally, disseminate, and internationally exchange information for and about themselves. This is not a matter of either a "popular communication" defined and produced by intellectuals and professionals or some simple notion of "horizontal communication" among and between the popular sectors. A democratic model for international communication would be one that allowed for "vertical communication" also, meaning communication between the popular sectors and those intellectuals/professionals either involved in or with access to the dominant media. This is what Stangelaar (1986) calls a "spiral model" of communication. While I reject the notion that an elite – "revolutionary" or "organic" – will bring enlightenment to the masses, I wish also to reject the notion that the masses – simply because they are exploited and oppressed – are the source of all virtue and progress. "Specific intellectuals" (Poster, 1984:Ch.6) and professionals have particular skills, attitudes, and interests that, when brought together with those of ordinary working people, can contribute to the creation of a new kind of internationalism. Internationalism at present, indeed, is more meaningfully developed amongst middle-class people in the human-rights, women's, environmental, and other such movements than it is in the workers' movement. (See Mies, 1986:205-209 on the role of the middle-class women's movement internationally.) What is necessary is that the different interests are recognized for what they are, that the relationship is open and explicit, that the dialogue is carried out without the traditional divisive and destructive terminology of the old 19th-century labour and socialist movements.

Back to Mariategui: Forward from Mariategui

Let us, finally, return to where we began, with Mariategui on internationalism and on communication as its nervous system. Mariategui is a remarkable figure. One would rather see his profile on a banner, his face on a mural, than that of some maximum and infallible revolutionary leader. But one would also rather see him as one of us and enter into dialogue with him. Much as one is impressed by Mariategui's remarkable insights, it is difficult to accept his formulations on internationalism as in any way adequate to the task today.

If Mariategui had been right on working-class internationalism, then we would have seen either a steady growth or cumulative waves of internationalism amongst workers since his day. This has evidently not been the case, not in Peru or Portugal or Poland. Traditional Marxists will answer this by assuring us either 1) that such internationalism is represented by their particular party, or 2) that the failure is due to the temporary domination of some "labour aristocracy," the passing phenomenon of some "semi-proletarianized peasantry," or both simultaneously, and 3) that international capitalist development is inevitably and inexorably producing its international and internationalist proletarian gravedigger. Where Mariategui, his forerunners, his contemporaries, and his successors were wrong was in understanding the wage-labour relationship as the sole source of internationalism. To say wage-labour is to say "market" and to say "market" is to say "capitalism." In so far as either the spontaneous development of the world market or the conscious efforts of capitalists and capitalist states lead to a surpassing of frontiers or a subjugating of political restrictions, it is to create new frontiers or restrictions to suit the needs of the markets, the interests of the capitalists. In the half-century since the death of Mariategui we have seen the triumph of both the big factory system and the small-workshop system, as well as the repeated restructuring of national and international economies in ways that – by the same tokens and at the same levels – imply new divisions among working people. Even if the textile workers of the United States or Vitarte do interest themselves in a fall of wages in the British textile industry, this may mean nothing more than a consciousness of themselves as commodities in a capitalist market, in other words of a literally capitalist consciousness. That this consciousness is the collective possession of living labourers gives it a special potential. But historically and contemporaneously we see limited outcomes of this potential (see Haworth and Ramsay, 1984, on the limits of multinational worker internationalism). The threat posed by cheap foreign labour can – and does – lead to national labour movements and individual workers throwing themselves into the hands of their capitalist employers, depending ever more on their respective nation states, even becoming more reactionary than the state (the AFL-CIO in the United States over many years).

Capitalism, of course, is much more than the market, much more than an economy. It is a total social system that tends to engulf and incorporate all others, whether earlier (slave, feudal) or later (socialist). It is a political system, based on the nation-state form, that creates a world of nation states and interstate organs (among them the "bad" World Bank and the "good" ILO) and establishes a certain practice and understanding of international relations. Capitalism is also a culture and, indeed, its most powerful and flexible bearers are phenomena like Donald Duck (Dorfman and Mattelart, 1975) and "Dallasty," spreading a cosmopolitan set of bourgeois, racist, and sexist values, invading the mind, occupying the imagination and simultaneously isolating and serializing individuals, classes, social categories, and national communities (Mattelart, Delcourt and Mattelart, 1984).

Capitalism is also, of course, a contradictory phenomenon, repeatedly revealing and creating new opportunities and possibilities that it cannot itself fully develop. One of these is in the area of communications – whether in the sense of transportation or information channels – an area becoming increasingly central to human development (de la Haye, 1980; Williams, 1983; Poster, 1984). Mariategui, as a journalist and an international traveller, a product of the European centre as well as the Latin American periphery, was a privileged witness of the significance of communication in creating a worldwide civilization in place of locally limited cultures. But, again, there is no economic or technical necessity operating here. Neither the dominant nor the opposition media, in Peru, Poland, or Portugal, are required to recognize this international nature of our world. And, if and where they do so, they may do so in quite other ways than Mariategui might have predicted or hoped. Like Marx, Engels, and Lenin, Mariategui was also a prisoner of his insights. Capitalism, imperialism, patriarchy, and the nation state were in his time far from fully developed. Their current interlinked crises may not necessarily prove more than a hiccup in the deadly progress of capitalist civilization. The crisis merely provides an opening, which socialists and labour movements may or may not widen to their own advantage.

Very well then. Here I have presented some ideas that could (given that I am British and that Britain is one major intellectual source of the new internationalism) be considered "British ideas." The ideas are now printed. They will be "launched into space" in English and Spanish. Do they express some "universal truth"? If so, will they be "instantaneously transformed into an internationalist idea"? This depends on two processes with their own dynamics.

The first is that of the relationship between intellectuals and workers – a matter that I have already alluded to. In the development of a new labour internationalism, pro-labour intellectuals make their appearance as communication specialists, as union advisors, as researchers ... and as those most interested in internationalism! Let us – more modestly – present intellectuals as professionals, technicians, academics, and administrators. Then we can, for example, recognize that the international solidarity received by the Mineworkers Federation in Peru comes both from and via such people: "from" in the sense of European union and development agency officers and solidarity committees; "through" in the sense of *centros*. Awareness of the key role of such people enables a positive interpretation and strategy. What we are faced with here can be best interpreted in the terms used by Mark Poster. We are dealing not with the "general intellectual" offering, as Marx and Mariategui did, a total vision of society and identifying the necessary role and consciousness of the masses in overthrowing it. We are dealing with "specific" intellectuals who by "speaking only for themselves and their local situation" (Poster, 1984:155) raise effective arms against domination in particular areas of social life. In so far as the different kinds of "specific intellectual" I have mentioned (and remember that these include labour movement officers) make explicit to themselves and the workers what their own interests, motives, and roles are, and in so far as they increasingly facilitate direct communication and solidarity action between ordinary workers internationally, then we may yet see a new labour internationalism making its long-missing and much-needed addition to the internationalism of the women's, human-rights, peace, environmental, and other such movements.

The second process is that of the uneven development of the international labour and socialist movement. The industrialized capitalist countries may be (because of their level of industrialization, de-industrialization, post-industrialization) sources of new social thinking and even new labour strategies, but these tend to develop outside or on the fringes of the organized labour movement, which – a victim of its own past successes – is in a largely defensive posture. While organized labour in the industrialized countries is engaged in many activities of interest to other labour movements, it does not in general show a capacity to either understand or effectively fight back against the aggressive new capitalist order. Countries on the periphery of capitalism (and we must here include countries such as Poland and South Africa alongside Peru) have thrown up organized labour movements of a "social-movement" kind – inspired by a vision of social transformation, open to or intimately linked with other classes and social interests. These movements become – but in very diverse ways, at different moments and for different periods – open to a new kind of labour internationalism. If the ideas presented here have been launched into space from the capitalist core, it may be at the periphery that they are brought down to earth and converted into a force that will return to grip the minds of labour internationally.

Note

***This paper is based on Waterman and Arellano (1986). Appreciation is expressed to Nebiur Arellano for her assistance with that original study.

References

Ames, Rolando (1986). "Encuentro Nacional: Voluntad de Poder" (National Assembly: Desire for Power), interview, *Amauta*, August 1:8-9.

Angotti, Thomas (1986). "The Contributions of Jose Carlos Mariategui to Revolutionary Theory," *Latin American Perspectives*, 49:33-57.

Arellano, Nebiur (1986a). "Izquierda y Sindicatos en el Peru" (The Left and the Unions in Peru). Lima: Universidad Federico Villareal.

Arellano, Nebiur (1986b). "El Apra y los Sindicatos: Accortando Distancias" (Apra and the Unions: Shortening Distances), *Cuadernos Laborales*, 36:1-3.

Carillo, Roxana (1986). "Women's Centres: Spaces for Women," *Isis International Women's Journal* (Special Issue: The Latin American Women's Movement), 5:40-44.

Cuadernos Laborales (1986). "1o Mayo 1886-1986" (First of May 1886-1986). Lima: Cuadernos Laborales.

Dorfman, Ariel and Armand Mattelart (1975). *How to Read Donald Duck: Imperialist Ideology in the Disney Comic*. New York: International General.

FNTMMP (1984). "1o Encuentro de Coordinacion Minero Metalurgico: Bolivia, Chile, Peru" (First Coordination Meeting of Mining and Metallurgical Workers: Bolivia, Chile, Peru). Lima: FNTMMP.

Giguere, Joseph and Denis Sulmont (1984). "Construir la Solidaridad Sindical

Internacional: Documento de Trabajo para el Primero Encuentro de Coordinacion Minero Metalurgico de Bolivia, Chile y Peru" (Build International Trade Union Solidarity: Working Document for the First Co-ordination Meeting of Mining and Metal Workers of Bolivia, Chile and Peru). Lima.

Giguere, Joseph and Denis Sulmont (1987). "Building International Trade Union Solidarity: An Independent View from Latin America," *Newsletter of International Labour Studies*.

Haworth, Nigel and Harvie Ramsay. (1984). "Grasping the Nettle: Problems in the Theory of International Labour Solidarity." In Peter Waterman, ed., *For a New Labour Internationalism*. The Hague: International Labour Education Research and Information Foundation.

Haye, Yves de la (1980). *Marx and Engels on the Means of Communication*. New York: International General.

ILRIG (1984). *Solidarity of Labour: The Story of International Worker Organisations*. Cape Town: International Labour Research and Information Group.

Jusocan (1986). "Information and the Construction of Socialism." In Peter Waterman, ed., *The Comintercomdoc Papers*. The Hague: International Labour Education Research and Information Foundation.

Kapsoli, Wilfredo (1980). *Mariategui y los Congresos Obreros* (Mariategui and the Workers' Congresses). Lima: Amauta.

Labor. Nos.1-10. Reproduccion in facsimile (facsimile reproduction). Lima: Amauta.

Mariategui, Jose Carlos (1986). "Internationalism and Nationalism," *Newsletter of International Labour Studies*, 30-31. Translated from "Conferencia: Interacionalismo y Nacionalismo" (Lecture: Nationalism and Internationalism), in *Historia de la Crisis Mundial: Conferencias Anos 1923 y 1924*. Lima: Amauta.

Marx, Karl (1935). *Karl Marx: Selected Works*. Vol.1. Moscow: Cooperative Publishing Society of Foreign Workers in the USSR.

Mattelart, Armand, Zavier Delcourt and Michele Mattelart (1984). *International Image Markets – In Search of an Alternative Perspective*. London: Comedia.

Mies, Maria (1986). *Patriarchy and Accumulation on a World Scale: Women in the International Division of Labour*. London: Zed Books.

NACLA (1980). "Peru Today: The Roots of Labour Militancy," *NACLA Report* (Special Issue), 14, 6:2-35.

NACLA (1986). "Garcia's Peru: One Last Chance," *NACLA Report* (Special Issue), 20, 3:13-47.

Oblitas, Alfonso (1986). *Terminologia de Sindicalismo Clasista* (Terminology of Class Unionism). Lima: Ediciones Unidad.

Poster, Mark (1984). *Foucault, Marxism, and History: Mode of Production Versus Mode of Information*. London: Polity Press.

Quijano, Anibal. (1981). *Reencuentro y Debate: Una Introduccion a Mariategui* (Rediscovery and Debate: An Introduction to Mariategui). Lima: Mosca Azul Editores.

Reid, Mike (1985). *Peru: Paths to Poverty*. London: Latin American Bureau.

Salinas, Raquel and Jorge Gomez (1987). "La Experiencia de Chasquihuasi: El Mundo Cabe en una Radio de Aldea," *IFDA Dossier*, 61:3-14.

Southall, Roger, ed. (1987). *Trade Unions and the New Industrialization of the Third World*. London: Zed Books.

Stangelaar, Fred (1986). "Outline of Basic Principles of Alternative Communication." In Peter Waterman, ed. *The Comintercomdoc Papers*. The Hague: International Labour Education Research and Information Foundation.

Sulmont, Denis (1981). "La Historia de la Prensa Obrera y Popular en el Peru" (History of the Working-Class and Popular Press in Peru). In *Manual de Prensa Obrera y Popular*. Lima: Association Trabajo y Cultura/Tarea.

Vanden, Harry (1986). *National Marxism in Latin America: Jose Carlos Mariategui's Thought and Politics*. Boulder, Col.: Rienner.

Wad, Peter, Irene Norlund and Viggo Brun (1986). "Industrialization and Labour in South-East Asia," *Newsletter of International Labour Studies*, 28-29:6-16.

Waterman, Peter (1986). "Proposal for Action-Research Project: Democratising International Communication: The NGOs, the Third World, Labour." The Hague: Institute of Social Studies.

Waterman, Peter (1987). "Needed: A New Communication Model for a New Labour Internationalism." In Southall (1987).

Waterman, Peter (1988). "The New Internationalism: A More Real Thing than Big Big Coke," *Review*, 11,3:289-328.

Waterman, Peter (1990a). "Communicating Labour Internationalism: A Review of Relevant Literature and Resources," *Communications*, 15,1-2:85-103.

Waterman, Peter (1990b). "Reconceptualising the Democratisation of International Communication," *International Social Science Journal*, 123:78-91.

Waterman, Peter and Nebiur Arellano (1986). "The Nervous System of Internationalism and Solidarity: Transmission and Reception of International Labour Information in Peru," *Working Paper*, No.32. The Hague: Institute of Social Studies.

Waterman, Peter and Nebiur Arellano (1987). "Los Trabajadores y la Solidaridad Internacional: Transmission y Recepcion de la Informacion Laboral Internacional en el Peru." Lima: ADEC/ATC.

Williams, Raymond (1983). *Towards 2000*. London: Chatto and Windus.

Contributors

Mashoed Bailie. Ph.D. student and Graduate Teaching Fellow, Telecommunications and Film Department, University of Oregon.

Peter A. Bruck. Associate Professor of Mass Communication, School of Journalism and Mass Communications, Carleton University, Ottawa. Currently Visiting Professor of Communication and head of the internationally comparative research program "Economy and the Future of the Print Media" at the University of Salzburg, Austria. Author and editor of a number of articles and books on news formats, media culture, and democratic politics, including *Das Oesterreichische Format* and *Die Mozart Krone*.

Sean Cassidy. Assistant Professor, Incarnate Word College, San Antonio, Texas. Currently investigating the relationship between the media and the environmental movement and the history and development of wildlife cinematography.

Giovanni Cesareo. Former Director, Archives and Research Branch of *Teleconfronto* (International TV Festival, Chianciano, Italy). Author of *Anatomia del potere televisivo, La televisione sprecata, Fa notizia,* and *Towards an Electronic Democracy?*

Sara U. Douglas. Associate Professor, School of Human Resources and Family Studies, Division of Consumer Sciences, University of Illinois at Urbana-Champaign. Author of *Labor's New Voice: Unions and the Mass Media*.

Stephen A. Douglas. Associate Professor, Department of Political Science, University of Illinois at Urbana-Champaign. Author of *Political Socialization and Student Activism in Indonesia; Blood, Believer, and Brother: The Development of Voluntary Associations in Malaysia;* "Women in Politics: The Myth of Functional Interest in Indonesia," in Chipp and Green, eds., *Women of Asia;* along with numerous other articles on Southeast Asian society.

David A. Frank. Associate Professor of Rhetoric and Communication, Department of Speech, University of Oregon.

Ingunn Hagen. Ph.D. student in mass communication at University of Bergen, Norway. Fulbright scholar at Department of Political Science, University of California, Santa Barbara. Currently working on a study of audience response to Norwegian TV news.

Douglas Kellner. Professor of Philosophy, University of Austin at Texas. Co-author of *Camera Politica: The Politics and Ideology of Contemporary Hollywood Film* and author of *Television and the Crisis of Democracy.*

Fred Lonidier. Associate Professor, Visual Arts Department, University of California at San Diego.

Vincent Mosco. Professor, Department of Journalism and Mass Communications, Carleton University, Ottawa. Author of several books on communications policy, including *Pushbutton Fantasies* and *The Pay-Per Society.*

Deanna Campbell Robinson. Associate Professor, Department of Speech, University of Oregon. Director of the International Consortium for the Study of Youth and Culture. Author of *Music at the Margins: Popular Music and Global Cultural Diversity.*

Marc Raboy. Associate Professor, Department of Information and Communication, Laval University, Quebec City. As a journalist and social activist in Quebec during the past twenty years, he was close to many of the situations and events described in his article. Author of *Movements and Messages: Media and Radical Politics in Quebec* and *Missed Opportunities: The Story of Canada's Broadcasting Policy.*

Mark Schulman. Chairperson of the Department of Communication, New School for Social Research, New York, NY. His action-research experience in overseeing the initiation of WHCR-FM, Harlem Community Radio, as a community communication project is the basis for a manuscript in preparation: "A Station Grows in Harlem: How Community Radio Came to the World's Best Known Neighborhood."

Kusum Singh. Professor of Communications, Saint Mary's College of California, Moraga. Author of "Mass Line Communication: Liberation Movements in China and India" and "The MacBride Report: The Results and Response," both in George Gerbner and Marsha Siefert, eds., *World Communications: A Handbook.*

Janet Wasko. Associate Professor of Communications, Department of Speech, University of Oregon. Author of *Movies & Money: Financing the American Film Industry.*

Peter Waterman. Lecturer, The Institute of Social Studies, The Hague, Netherlands, on social movements, alternative international relations, and communications. Author of numerous articles on these topics. Currently completing a book: *From Labour Internationalism to Global Solidarity.*

Dwayne Winseck. Ph.D. student, Telecommunications and Film Department, University of Oregon.